Java Networking and Communications

Todd Courtois

To join a Prentice Hall PTR internet mailing list, point to
http://www.prenhall.com/mail_lists/

Prentice Hall PTR
Upper Saddle River, New Jersey 07458
http://www.prenhall.com

Library of Congress Cataloging in Publication Data

Courtois, Todd
    Java Networking and Communications / Todd Courtois.
        p.   cm
    Includes index.
    ISBN 0-13-850454-7 (alk. paper)
    1. Java (Computer program language).   2. Internet programming.   3. Computer
networks.   I. Title.
QA76.73.J38C69   1997
005.7'11—dc21   97-22731
                                                 CIP

Editorial/Production Supervision: *Kathleen M. Caren*
Acquisitions Editor: *Gregory G. Doench*
Cover Design Director: *Jerry Votta*
Cover Design: *Scott G. Weiss/Anthony Gemmellaro*
Cover Art: *Karen Streleck*
Manufacturing Manager: *Alexis R. Heydt*
Marketing Manager: *Stephen Solomon*
Editorial Assistant: *Mary Treacy*

 © 1998 Prentice Hall PTR
Prentice-Hall, Inc.
A Simon & Schuster Company
Upper Saddle River, New Jersey 07458

Prentice Hall books are widely used by corporations and government agencies
for training, marketing, and resale.
The publisher offers discounts on this book when ordered in bulk quantities.
For more information, contact: Corporate Sales Department, Phone: 800-382-3419;
FAX: 201-236-7141; E-mail: corpsales@prenhall.com
Or write: Corp. Sales Dept., Prentice Hall PTR, 1 Lake Street, Upper Saddle River, NJ   07458

Printed in the United States of America
10 9 8 7 6 5 4 3 2 1

ISBN 0-13-850454-7

Prentice-Hall International (UK) Limited, *London*
Prentice-Hall of Australia Pty. Limited, *Sydney*
Prentice-Hall Canada Inc., *Toronto*
Prentice-Hall Hispanoamericana, S.A., *Mexico*
Prentice-Hall of India Private Limited, *New Delhi*
Prentice-Hall of Japan, Inc., *Tokyo*
Simon & Schuster Asia Pte. Ltd., *Singapore*
Editora Prentice-Hall do Brasil, Ltda., *Rio de Janeiro*

Contents

Chapter 8
Linking with the Natives, 211

List of Examples

List of Tables

List of Figures

CHAPTER
1

- What This Book Covers...and Doesn't Cover

- What You Will Learn...and Won't Learn

- Who Might Use This Book...and Who Might Not

- What You Should Know Already...But Might Not

- Why Learn Java Networking/Communications Programming?

Introduction

Welcome! This chapter will provide an introduction to the book. Let's talk about what this book is.

What This Book Covers

This book is focused on using the Java language and APIs to creating networking and communications applications.

This book is not an introduction to the Java language nor to networking and communications. However, while it does assume some familiarity with the Java language and APIs, it doesn't assume that you're an expert communications or networking programmer.

What You Need to Know Already

You need to be familiar with object-oriented concepts such as inheritance, methods, polymorphism, and the like. You also need to be familiar with the basics of structured programming, with a language such as C or Pascal.

Ideally, you should be familiar with the Java language and APIs, though perhaps not with the networking , communications, and native library linking APIs. However, if you're already familiar with networking and communications programming in another environment (such as sockets programming under Unix), then you can probably pick up the Java you'll need along the way.

What You Will Learn

You will learn how to interface to a number of communicating devices using the Java language and APIs. After reading this book and working through the various examples, you should be able to interface to a number of unique devices from your Java applications.

You will not learn how to make your web page "come alive" with fancy applets that play animations, sounds, etcetera. If, however, you're interested in building full-fledged communicating applications with Java, this is the book for you.

Who Might Use This Book and Who Might Not

This book is targeted at individuals who have already explored the basic Java language and runtime APIs and are now interested in strengthening their skills with the networking and communications APIs.

This book is also appropriate for folks who wish to understand Java runtime linking to platform-specific native libraries. For instance, if you wish to interface to Macintosh-native libraries from Java, this might be the appropriate book for you.

Platforms Tested and Covered

We've endeavored in this book to cover a good range of the mainstream computing platforms. We provide examples that should be functional under the Win32, Macintosh, and Solaris platforms. We also provide platform-specific native library linking examples for these three platforms. In theory, the generic Java examples should work on any platform that supports the Java runtime APIs; however, we have not tested these on additional platforms, so we won't make any guarantees.

Why Would I Want to Use Java for Networking and Communications?

This is a reasonable question. Many programmers who are not networking or communications gurus have heard or been told that all "serious" communications code is written in C or perhaps C++. Thus, these people are skeptical that any "real" communications code can be written in an interpreted, dynamic language such as Java.

The fact is that the Java runtime implementations currently available link very tightly with platform-native communications libraries that do most of the difficult, speed-and-memory-intensive work of communication. The Java APIs provide a convenient, consistent wrapper for these various platforms so that if you write a networking application in Java, it instantly works on any platform that supports the required Java APIs.

There are some additional solid benefits to writing communicating applications using Java. Because Java is such a nice dynamic, interpreted language, rapid prototyping of your application is potentially easier than with a C or C++ . Instead of lengthy compile cycles, you can usually speed development.

In addition, Java provides some specific language features such as exceptions, which can make communications programming easier.

Finally, the broader Java APIs provide a fairly consistent set of libraries for user interface, filesystem, and so forth that work across platforms, and it's fairly easy to quickly wrap your communications code in a GUI-based testbed.

All in all, Java provides a solid platform for developing communicating applications. This book will attempt to cover the vast majority of material that you as an application developer will need to know to write the communicating portion of a Java application.

Acknowledgments

There are so many people who have helped with the production of this book, and I'd like to thank them here.

Rachel Borden for helping me transform the book idea into a reality. Lori Matsumoto for convincing me to do the book in the first place, and for helping me talk to the right people. Laurel Gaddie for expert help with grammar, sentence construction, and Frame wrangling. Payam Mirrashidi not only for his assistance in building the Solaris dynamic libraries that appear in this book, but for his overall support. Douglas Jones for his AWT and tools suggestions. Jeff Frederick for his assistance with the Borland C++ and Java tools for Win32. Andy Axelrod for consulting on some Win32 DLL issues. Kathleen Caren, Greg Doench, Lisa Iarkowski, Diane Spina, Mary Treacy, and the rest of the team at PTR for helping to transform the raw manuscript into the finished product. Paul Mooser for his feedback on some of the raw chapters. Peter Gadjokov for providing his input on Java tools and the book content. Cay S. Horstmann for his very useful critique of the original book proposal. The book reviewers for their terrific ideas and brutally honest reviews. Thanks especially to Rob Gordon for allowing me to reference his forthcoming JNI book. The folks at AllPen for allowing me the workplace flexibility I needed to get the book done while keeping my day job. Finally, thanks to my family for their support and understanding.

CHAPTER
2

- Overview of Streams

- Using Streams to Filter Communications Data

- Parsing Global Positioning Satellite Data Using Streams

- Using Streams to Parse Communications Data

- Analysis of Stream Usage

- New for JDK 1.1: Character Streams

- New for JDK 1.1: Object Streams / Object Serialization

Streams of Fury

S treams are a key piece of the communications and networking libraries provided by the Java runtime. Streams are the main paradigm used for moving data between client and server hosts, between different threads, between files, and so on. Clearly this emphasis on streams as the means for moving data between varying chunks of code was inherited from a rich combination of C, C++, and the Unix operating system at Sun. As you learn more about the design and implementation of the various Java stream classes, you can see more and more of the correspondence between Java streams and C streams, C++ iostreams, and Unix pipes.

In this chapter we'll cover streams thoroughly, with emphasis on the application of streams to solving communications problems. In the chapters that follow, streams will be the glue that holds together our other code examples.

What is a stream?

A stream is a pipeline for moving data between objects. A stream can be used as a link between a source and a sink of data. Streams themselves do not typically generate data: They act as carriers of data. Whenever you need to move large amounts of data (more than 500 bytes of information), or unknown amounts of data, you might consider using a stream instead of passing Strings around.

The diagram below (Figure 2–1) demonstrates the role that a stream plays:

Figure 2–1 A stream carries data from a data source to a data sink.

In addition to carrying data, a stream can help buffer data. Buffering is important because your source of data might be sending data faster than you can process it, or your output stream might not be able to deal with the data as quickly as you want to push onto it. Buffering, like the clutch in a car, allows the source and sink of data to operate at slightly different speeds, and avoids messy synchronization issues. Because buffering allows each end of a stream to operate at its own speed, buffering helps increase efficiency.

Some Java stream classes also provide the ability to filter data. Filtering can make your job a lot easier by simplifying an incoming or outgoing data stream and reducing the amount of postprocessing you have to do. Later in this chapter we'll examine an example where a stream filters incoming data to make it 7-bit clean.

The Java stream classes can also assist in parsing data into useful tokens. When you reach the end of your chain of streams and you're ready to sink your stream into some other data structure, Java provides some toolbox streams for doing just that— the DataInputStream class, the StreamTokenizer, and so on.

Streams allow you to modularize your code so that each piece modifies a stream of data in some small way. You can later mix and match your stream filters to achieve a different effect.

Stream Basics: InputStreams and OutputStreams

There are two main stream classes, InputStream and OutputStream. Let's look at both of these classes in detail.

The InputStream is the class that allows you to read data from a data source.

Table 2-1 Central InputStream Class Methods

Method	Description
read	This method, which comes in three different flavors, allows you to read data from the input stream.
skip	This method allows you to skip a specified number of bytes on the input stream before reading again.
available	This method should return the number of bytes that are immediately available for reading on the input stream.
markSupported	This method allows you to find out whether an instance or subclass of InputStream supports the mark and reset methods.
mark	Allows you to place a marker on the input stream. You can then use the reset method to subsequently reset the input stream "cursor" to that marker.
reset	Allows you to reset the input stream to the most recent mark. See the mark method.
close	Allows you to close the input stream and free any associated system resources. You cannot read from the input stream once this method has been called.

The InputStream's complement is the OutputStream, which is solely concerned with allowing you to send data to a data sink.

Table 2-2 Central OutputStream Class Methods

Method	Description
write	This method, which comes in three different flavors, allows you to send data out on the output stream. Note that when this method returns there's no guarantee that all of the data you write has been sent to the data sink. The stream may buffer the data before actually sending it to the data sink.
flush	This method allows you to force any data buffered by the output stream to be sent to the data sink. This method does not return until all of the buffered data has been flushed, which could take some time.
close	This method closes the output stream, so you can no longer write out data on it. This action implicitly notifies the data sink that no more data will be provided: Once the data sink has absorbed all buffered data, any additional reads from the stream will fail.

Using InputStream and OutputStream

Here's a simple example of code that uses InputStream and OutputStream to copy an input file to an output file. For this example we're going to use subclasses of InputStream and OutputStream: FileInputStream and FileOutputStream, respectively. These subclasses simply wrap the InputStream and OutputStream interface around standard files.

In this example, we simply read byte-by-byte from the input stream, and write byte-by-byte to the output stream. We detect the end of the input stream by looking at the count of actual bytes read, as returned from read. If this value is – 1, there is no more data to read on the input stream.

We also handle other possible exceptions, for instance, we might not be able to create the output file; we may not be able to open the input file; and the stream might throw an IOException on any read.

Note that FileOutputStream will automatically create a new output file if the file does not already exist. Also note that FileOutputStream will not append to an existing output file— it simply replaces the contents of the existing file.

The sample code for copying data from an input stream to an output stream is shown below.

Example 2-1 Copying Data from an InputStream to an OutputStream

```java
import java.io.*;

/**
 * A simple class for demonstrating the use of
 * FileInputStream and FileOutputStream
 */
class FileStreamCopy
{

/**
 * this is where we kick off the copy
 */
public static void main(String[] args)
{
    //set up some default filenames
    String inputFileName = "streamCopyInput.dat";
    String outputFileName = "streamCopyOutput.dat";

    //if the user passed in filenames, use those instead
    if (args.length == 2) {
        inputFileName = args[0];
        outputFileName = args[1];
    }

    try {
```

```
            FileInputStream inStream =
                new FileInputStream(inputFileName);
            FileOutputStream outStream =
                new FileOutputStream(outputFileName);
            copySrcToSink((InputStream)inStream,
                          (OutputStream)outStream);
            inStream.close();
            outStream.close();
        }
        catch (IOException ioEx) {
            System.err.println("copy threw: " + ioEx);
        }
    }


    /**
     * Take a source data input stream and a sink data ouput stream
     * copy input to output
     */
    public static void copySrcToSink(InputStream src, OutputStream sink)
    {
        byte[] tempBuf = new byte[1024];
        int bytesRead = 1;

        try {
            do {
                bytesRead = src.read(tempBuf,0,1024);

                if (bytesRead > 0) {
                    System.out.println("bytesRead: " + bytesRead);
                    sink.write(tempBuf,0,bytesRead);
                    sink.flush();
                }
            } while (bytesRead >= 0);
        }
        catch (IOException ioEx) {
            System.err.println("copySrcToSink failed with: " + ioEx);
        }

    } /* copySrcToSink */


}//FileStreamCopy
```

When you run this application, the input file will be copied to the output file. To verify this, open the output file and compare its contents with the input file. Note that this application will also print bytesRead: to your standard output window (System.out). Because the default input file (*streamCopyInput.dat*) is very short, only one read operation is necessary to read the entire contents of the file.

A Peek at Marking

The InputStream (or specifically, an InputStream subclass) can implement another set of handy methods: the marking methods. You can check to see whether an input stream subclass supports marking by calling the input stream's markSupported method.

The way marking works is that a client can set a marker at a certain point on the input stream by calling mark(index). This allows a client to "remember" certain points in the input stream. For instance, you might want to mark a point in the stream where a packet header begins or ends. The input stream can later be reset to the last marked point by calling the stream's reset method. As an examples, this can be useful for eliminating header information from a packet and simply handing off the main packet data to a client.

Note that implementing marking usually requires that the input stream buffer as many bytes as the mark index provides. Because of this, only a few input streams support marking.

We'll demonstrate some applications of marking later in this chapter.

Filtering Data with Streams

The java.io package provides two base classes for filtering streams: FilterInputStream and FilterOutputStream. By default the FilterInputStream class just reads data directly from the InputStream you pass to its constructor: It doesn't perform any actual filtering. The FilterOutputStream behaves similarly. In a sense, these classes really just define the interface for streams that filter. You must subclass FilterInputStream or FilterOutputStream and override several of the class methods in order to implement filtering. The most common way to subclass FilterInputStream is to override its read, mark, and available methods.

Fortunately, the `java.io` package also provides several handy
`FilterInputStream` and `FilterOutputStream` subclasses that can be
applied to specific problems. Below is a table showing which methods the built-in
Java `FilterInputStream` subclasses override, and why.

Table 2-3 FilterInputStream Subclasses and the Methods They Override

Subclass	Overrides
`PushbackInputStream`	`markSupported` (returns false)
	`available` (returns `in.available()`, or `avail.` +1 if pushback char is buffered)
	`read` (modified to deal with single-byte pushback buffer)
`DataInputStream`	Overrides two flavors of `read`, but neither override behaves differently than the corresponding `FilterInputStream.read`
`BufferedInputStream`	`available` (returns amount in buffer plus amount in input stream immediately available)
	`mark`, (deals with marking the buffer), `markSupported` (returns true)
	`read` (reads from buffer first, deals with marking), `reset` (deals with resetting into buffer)
	`skip` (skips in buffer first)
`LineNumberInputStream`	`available` (returns amount in buffer plus amount in input stream immediately available)
	`mark` (marks the current line number)
	`read` (deals with counting lines based on `'\r'` or `'\n'`)
	`reset` (deals with resetting to the correct line number) `skip` (deals with updating the line number as bytes are skipped)

It should be noted that the `FilterInputStream` has three different flavors of
`read`. One of these flavors uses another to do the actual reading (the version of
read that accepts just a buffer to read into). So if you're overriding
`FilterInputStream`, you only need to reimplement two of the `read`
methods— the single-byte `read`, and the block `read` with offset and length.

There are also a few FilterOutputStream subclasses in the java.io package. Below is a table showing which methods the built-in Java FilterOutputStream subclasses override, and why.

Table 2-4 FilterOutputStream Subclasses and the Methods They Override

Subclass	Overrides
DataOutputStream	flush (behaves the same as FilterInputStream.flush)
	write (two flavors, both of which track the number of bytes written)
BufferedOutputStream	flush (flushes entire buffer)
	write (two flavors, both of which are buffered until they exceed the buffer size, at which time the output is flushed)

It's interesting to note that neither of these subclasses performs what you might normally consider "filtering". After all, no bytes are replaced or eliminated from the output stream. However, when you think about it, buffering and counting bytes written can be considered filtering operations.

Example: Filtering Garbage Bits

Let's look at an example of a stream that filters out garbage data. In this section we'll look at the SevenBitFilterInputStream, a subclass of FilterInputStream. (This puts SevenBitFilterInputStream in the same family as DataInputStream and such.)

This class takes an input stream and eliminates the high bit from every byte of input. This is useful in communications situations where you might be receiving spuriously set high bits. This is common in situations where information is being carried over a wide variety of networks speaking various protocols, and one or more of the transports or interfaces isn't guaranteed to be "eight-bit clean." In this situation what you want to do is strip the high bit from each byte so that you don't receive spurious values.

Now, you could deal with this problem by removing the high bits by hand in your code, but let's say you wanted to pull in 32-bit, 64-bit, or string values from an input stream. It becomes incrementally more difficult to filter these large-valued data types (especially in the case of a string where you need to strip an arbitrary number of bits). A better solution is to insert a subclass of FilterInputStream somewhere between your main data input stream and your data-processing code, and have the input stream automatically strip the high bits for you, so your code never sees the spurious high bits.

7-Bit Filtering Code

Our solution is a subclass of `FilterInputStream` that overrides two of
`FilterInputStream`'s read methods. (The third `read` method in
`FilterInputStream` relies on one of the two we're overriding, so we don't
need to override that one.)

The implementation of `SevenBitFilterInputStream` is shown below.
Example 2-2 Implementation of **SevenBitFilterInputStream**

```
package JNC;

import java.io.*;

/**
 * A class to allow stripping of spurious high bit
 *
 * We override the various read() methods of FilterInputStream
 */
public class SevenBitFilterInputStream extends FilterInputStream
{


public SevenBitFilterInputStream(InputStream srcStream)
{
    super(srcStream);
}


/**
 * Reads a byte. Will block if no input is available.
 * @return the byte read, or -1 if the end of the stream is reached.
 * @exception IOException If an I/O error has occurred.
 */
public int read() throws IOException {
    int srcByte = in.read(); //get a byte from input stream
    return (srcByte & 127) ;//strip the high bit, whatever it may be
}


/**
 * Reads into an array of bytes.
 * Blocks until some input is available.
 * This method should be overridden in a subclass for
 * efficiency (the default implementation reads 1 byte
 * at a time).
 * @param bufthe buffer into which the data is read
 * @param offset the start offset of the data
 * @param maxCount the maximum number of bytes to read
 * @return  the actual number of bytes read, -1 is returned
 * when the end of the stream is reached.
```

```
 * @exception IOException If an I/O error has occurred.
 */
public int read(byte[] buf, int offset, int maxCount) throws IOException {

    //first, go get some bytes from the source stream
    int numBytesRead = in.read(buf, offset, maxCount);

    //now, walk the buffer and eliminate the high bit of each byte

    for (int byteIdx = 0; byteIdx < numBytesRead; byteIdx++) {
        buf[byteIdx] &= 127; //blow away the high bit of this byte
    }

    return numBytesRead;
}

/*
The FilterInputStream.read(byte[] buf) method uses
read(byte[] buf, int offset, int maxCount) to do its reading,
so we don't need to override it!
*/

}//SevenBitFilterInputStream
```

Note that SevenBitFilterInputStream takes advantage of the fact that FilterInputStream provides a protected instance variable, in, which contains the raw InputStream. It also takes advantage of the fact that, by default, the FilterInputStream class simply forwards calls to methods such as mark and skip to the raw input stream, in. This means that we don't need to override methods that are irrelevant to our filtering process.

To test the SevenBitFilterInputStream class, we've provided two files: StreamCleanerTest.java and the data file highbit.dat. The data file contains a set of mixed 8-bit and 7-bit characters that emulate data you might receive over a pipe that was not "eight-bit clean." (In the real world, you're unlikely to receive a sequence of bytes as corrupt as the sequence contained in the data file, but this file does provide a good stress test.) The StreamCleanerTest class implements a stand-alone application class (with a main method) which creates a new FileInputStream from the highbit.dat data file, and pulls the test data through a SevenBitFilterInputStream, then prints the results to System.out for your viewing pleasure.

To use StreamCleanerTest, run it as follows:

```
% java StreamCleanerTest highbit.dat
```

You might need to move the `highbit.dat` file into the directory where your Java environment system expects it to be; typically, it's the directory where `StreamCleanerTest.class` resides.

When this test executes, you should see something like the following in your standard output window:

```
∞±♢¥µ∂∑∏π0123456789∞±♢¥µ∂∑∏π0123456789∞±♢¥µ∂∑∏π0123456789∞±♢¥µ∂∑∏π0123
456789
the end

01234567890123456789012345678901234567890123456789012345678901234567890123456789012345678901234
56789
the end
```

In this case there are two sets of output. The first couple of lines are a direct dump of the input file (`highbit.dat`) contents. The last couple of lines are a filtered version of the input data with the high bit of each byte removed. The input file contains a series of 8-bit characters, and when these are filtered, they form the simple 7-bit character sequence.

As you can see, it is fairly easy to subclass `FilterInputStream` to achieve the filtering you want, and filtering your input can make the difference between dealing with a string of incomprehensible garbage and processing a pleasing pattern of perfection.

Using Streams for Parsing

Streams are especially suited to parsing incoming data streams. It is fairly easy to glue some code on top of a stream to process incoming data. In this section we'll discuss how to use a stream to parse communications data.

Example: Using Streams to Parse GPS Data

In this section we'll look at how to process Global Positioning Satellite (GPS) receiver data using streams and stream utilities. For the time being we'll just assume that data arrives from a GPS receiver on a stream and we'll worry about how to physically connect a stream to a GPS receiver via a serial connection in later chapters. One nice thing about streams, as we'll see, is that the input data could be coming from a file as well as a GPS receiver— the parser doesn't have to worry about that. This makes it easy to prototype parsing code with data arriving from a "fake" input stream.

GPS Technology Overview

GPS is a sophisticated navigation network comprised mainly of 24 NAVSTAR satellites in orbit around the Earth. These satellites each continuously broadcast a very faint, atomically-precise time-code signal toward the earth at a low data rate. This might not seem very useful— weak signals sent at a low data rate?

It turns out that even with relatively weak signals and slow refresh rates, a GPS receiver on the ground, in the air, or at sea can tie together signals from several satellites and use the differences between them to calculate its own position to an extreme degree of accuracy.

The theory behind GPS goes something like this— A GPS receiver tries to lock in a signal from as many satellites as possible. Once it has locked in one signal, it has an atomically-precise time signal. When it locks in a second signal, it can determine latitude or longitude. When the receiver locks in a third satellite, it can determine both latitude and longitude. Finally, when the receiver locks in four signals, it can determine altitude as well.

Now, in practice, it's difficult to obtain accurate positioning with fewer than four satellite signals. This is because each additional satellite time signal adds accuracy. When the GPS receiver obtains more than four solidly locked signals, it can proceed to calculate other variables such as the exact uncertainty in each of the measurements— latitude, longitude, or altitude.

It's important to note that the GPS signals broadcast from the NAVSTAR satellites are made imprecise intentionally by the U.S. Department of Defense (DOD). Each time-code signal is injected with some amount of error, and this error can only be eliminated through the use of special military GPS receivers that have the correct security "keys" to unlock the full accuracy of the GPS signal. This technique of blocking complete accuracy to civilian receivers while making it available to special "trusted" receivers is termed "selective availability."

As GPS use has grown in popularity among civilians, many have asked the DOD to turn off selective availability. As a result, the DOD and the U.S. Department of Transportation are currently negotiating a date to turn off selective availability.

Differential GPS Service

Because the standard GPS receivers available to civilians have a pseudo-random error imposed upon them, various means to partially overcome the error signal have been devised.

The most common technique for overcoming the error signal is referred to as "Differential Correction." In this scenario a ground station with a well-known physical location sets up its own GPS receiver. It then systematically compares its known latitude, longitude, and altitude with the raw GPS signal it receives. It then broadcasts out the "difference" between its known location and the location GPS is providing.

Typically, this broadcast takes the form of a message sent out via a pager network. Then, subscribers to this service have a pager attached to their GPS receivers that is able to receive the differential correction signal and incorporate it into the GPS location calculations. This typically results in a GPS location fix that is accurate on the order of 10 meters rather than 100 meters.

GPS Data Formats

Different geographic positioning devices provide different data formats. For instance, LORAN devices are unlikely to produce the same format as a GPS device would, simply because both devices use different methods for positioning; however, two GPS devices are quite likely to be able to generate the same format. The National Marine Electronics Association (NMEA) has developed a set of standards for encoding positioning data. This format allows these different devices to export their positioning data in a consistent set of formats. This makes it easier for multiple manufacturers to produce positioning hardware, and for the same software to process expeditiously data provided by various hardware.

A good reference for the NMEA formats is:

NMEA 0183 Standard for Interfacing Marine Electronic Devices, version 2.00, January 1, 1992. Published by the National Marine Electronics Association.

Updates are periodically published in:

Marine Electronics— The Official Journal of the NMEA

330 W. Canton Avenue

Winter Park, FL 32789, USA

You can also contact:

Robert Sassaman

NMEA Executive Director

P.O. Box 50040

Mobile, AL 36605, USA

The various NMEA data encoding formats are referred to as "sentences," and in this example we're going to focus on the "Global Positioning System fix" or "GGA" sentence. Its general format is shown below.

```
$GPGGA,210230,3855.4487,N,09446.0071,W,1,07,1.1,370.5,M,-29.5,M,,*7A
$GPGGA,210231,3855.4483,N,09446.0066,W,1,07,1.1,369.8,M,-29.5,M,,*7C
```

```
$GPGGA,210331,3855.4507,N,09446.0157,W,1,07,1.1,344.2,M,-29.5,M,,*76
```

This sentence format can be broken down into a series of comma-delimited fields:

Table 2-5 Fields in an NMEA GPS Fix Sentence

Field Name	Type	Description
type	String	The type of NMEA sentence this is.
UTC	int	UTC timeStamp Hours:Minutes:Seconds
latitude	double	Latitude in DDDMM.mmm format
latitudeCompass	char	North (N) or South (S), indicating whether the latitude field represents North or South latitude
longitude	double	Longitude in DDDMM.mmm format
longitudeCompass	Char	East (E) or West (W), indicating whether the longitude field represents East or West longitude
signalQuality	short	GPS Signal Quality. Values from zero to two. Zero represents no fix, one represents GPS fix, two represents differential GPS
satelliteUseCount	short	The number of satellites used to calculate the position coordinates
horDilPre	float	Horizontal Dilution of Precision. Briefly, a measure of the inherent uncertainty in the latitude and longitude fields.
altitude		Altitude above mean sea level.
"altitude units"	String	Units of altitude. Since this is typically "M" for meters, we will not store this value explicitly.
geoidalSeparation	float	Geoidal Separation. Briefly, a measure of the current displacement from an imaginary perfect geoid that surrounds the Earth.
"Geoidal Separation Units"	String	Units for geoidal separation. Since this field is typically "M" for meters, we will not explicitly store its value.
diffDataAge	float	Differential Data Age. Optional. Age of last-received differential correction signal, if applicable (can be empty).
diffStationID	String	Differential Station ID. Optional. A unique identifier for the differential station that generated the last-received correction signal, if applicable (can be empty).
CRC	String	"*" + 1-byte CRC in hexadecimal format. We will not explicitly store this value after processing a sentence.

The fields listed in italics above are optional: if the `signalQuality` field value is less than two, they will be missing from the GGA sentence. Notice that in the examples given, the `signalQuality` value is 1, so these optional fields are missing.

All of the fields in a GGA sentence are separated by commas, and NMEA sentences are terminated by a carriage return. This makes it easy to detect new sentences and to detect individual tokens within a sentence. Note that each NMEA sentence format uses a different identifier after the initial dollar sign ($). For GGA it is "`$GGA`", but it's not the same for different NMEA sentence formats. We can use this fact to filter out the GGA sentences only from an incoming data stream. In the real world you often need to filter because most GPS devices will spew a series of different NMEA sentence formats in their default mode, unless you configure the device to generate a single format.

Let's say you wanted to pull GPS positioning to your Java application: How would you do it? Assume for a moment you have an incoming data stream that shows up in the form of a InputStream. In a moment we'll look at two different ways you could deal with parsing that information into something useful.

A Class for Storing Position Information

Before we start, let's define a simple class to hold the position information we parse from an NMEA sentence. The `NMEAPositionStatus` class is shown below.

Example 2-3 The NMEAPositionStatus Class

```
package JNC;
import java.util.Date;

/**
*
* Meant to contain positioning information received from
* a GPS or other NMEA-compliant device
*/
public class NMEAPositionStatus
{

public long UTC = 0;
//the current time coordinate if available (0 otherwise)
//( will be parsed from "hhmmss.ss" where ".ss" is of
//variable length)

public double longitude = 0;
//degrees latitude parsed from: "DDMM.ddd'" where "ddd" is of
//variable length

public boolean longitudeCompass = true;
// true for East, false for West
```

```java
public double latitude = 0;
//degrees latitude parsed from: "DDMM.ddd'" where "ddd" is of
//variable length

public boolean latitudeCompass = true;
// true for North, false for South

public double altitude = 0;
//height above mean seal level in Meters

public float geoidalSeparation = 0;
//height of mean sea level above WGS-84 earth ellipsoid, in meters

public float horDilPre = 0;
//horizontal dilution of precision??? It's a long story:
//"same as GDOP except elevation is ignored" "all geometric
//factors that degrade the accuracy of a position fix"

public byte signalQuality = 0;
//how good is the data we're receiving? (GPS only)
//(0: fix not availible,
//1: GPS fix,
//2: Differential GPS fix)

public byte satelliteUseCount = 0;
//how many satellites are we using? (GPS only) (range 0...12)
public int diffDataAge = 0;
//time since last differential GPS correction, in seconds
//(diff GPS only)

public String diffStationID = "void";
//uniqueID of differential reference station, range 0000 to 1023
//(diff GPS only)


/**
 * Overrides Object.toString
 * Generates a string representation of the object
 */
public String toString()
{

    String UTCstr = "TIME: " + (new Date(UTC)).toString();
    String lonStr = "LON: " + longitude +
                    (longitudeCompass ? " E " : " W ");
    String latStr = "LAT: " + latitude +
                    (latitudeCompass ? " N " : " S ");
    String altStr = "ALT: " + altitude + " M " +
                    " Geoidal Separation: " + geoidalSeparation;
    String qualStr = "Signal Quality: " + signalQuality +
            " Satellites in Use: " +  satelliteUseCount +
            " horDilPre: " + horDilPre +
```

```
                        " Diff. Data Age: " + diffDataAge +
                        " diffStationID: " + diffStationID;

         return"\n" +
             UTCstr + "\n" +
             lonStr + "\n" +
             latStr + "\n" +
             altStr + "\n" +
             qualStr + "\n";

}//toString

}//NMEAPositionStatus
```

Note that this class overrides the `Object.toString` method to generate an
appropriately formatted `String` representation of the position information it
contains.

Meet the StringTokenizer Class

The `java.util.StringTokenizer` class chops a `String` into token `Strings`
separated by a given delimiter character or characters. By default, the
`StringTokenizer` uses whitespace (space, tab, carriage return, and linefeed)
characters as delimiters. That is, if you do not specify a delimiter,
`StringTokenizer` is typically constructed as follows:

```
StringTokenizer(String, " \t\n\r", false);
```

If you wish to use a token delimiter other than whitespace, use one of the two
`StringTokenizer` constructors that take a delimiter:

```
StringTokenizer(String targetString, String delimiterString, boolean
returnDelimiters);
StringTokenizer(String targetString, String delimiterString);
```

The `returnDelimiters` parameter to the first method above specifies whether
you wish to receive the delimiters as tokens. Typically you'll want to turn this
feature off; however, as we'll see in a moment, this feature can be useful in certain
situations.

Note that the `delimiterString` parameter need not be a single character—
typically, it's a String containing the set of characters you wish to use as
delimiters.

Once you've created a `StringTokenizer` instance, you can obtain a series of
tokens by calling the `StringTokenizer.nextToken` method.

Parsing GPS Data Using DataInputStream and String Tokenizer

Let's apply the `StringTokenizer` to the problem of parsing an NMEA data stream. First, we can use a `DataInputStream.readLine` to pull a carriage-return-delimited sentence `String` from an `InputStream`. Then we can use `StringTokenizer` to chop the sentence into its component fields. In this way we'll be using the DataInputStream to chop the `Stream` into sentences, and the `StringTokenizer` to chop the sentences into fields.

In order to set up the `StringTokenizer` correctly, we're going to use commas as the field token delimiters, and we're going to ask the `StringTokenizer` to return the commas as tokens. We want to track the number of commas we receive because in certain cases where differential GPS is not active, some fields will be completely empty (that is, the string will contain two commas in a row: ", , "). The order of the fields in an NMEA sentence is fixed, so counting the commas allows us to detect which fields are empty.

We will instantiate a `StringTokenizer` as follows:

```
new StringTokenizer(targetString, ",", true");
```

Because the `NMEAStringParser` sample code is a bit long, we will divide it into several parts. Below is the code that initially deals with pulling tokens out of an NMEA GGA sentence.

Example 2-4 Chopping an NMEA String Using StringTokenizer

```
/**
*    This code block will process an NMEA string from a GPS device.
*    It looks for the GGA, or Global Positioning System Fix Data, string.
*    The string is broken up into the component fields and stored in an
*    array.  A frame is returned.  The frame contains these slots:
*    Any slot value that isn't contained in the NMEA string is returned
*    as null.
*    If the NMEA string doesn't exist, or it isn't a GGA-type string,
*    null is returned.
*
*    @param nmeaStr A String containing a NMEA "sentence."
*/
public NMEAPositionStatus parseNMEAGGAString(String nmeaStr)
{
    //assume nmeaStr is an EOL-terminated string
    NMEAPositionStatus result = new NMEAPositionStatus();
    StringTokenizer strParser = new StringTokenizer(nmeaStr, ",", true);
    int realTokenCount = 0;
    //assume diff GPS isn't active (until something tells us it is)
    boolean dGPSactive = false;

    int checkSum =  0;
    String lastTok = "";
```

```
   String curTok = "";
   boolean continueParsing = true;


try {
    while ((curTok = strParser.nextToken()) != null) {

       if ((realTokenCount == 0) && curTok.startsWith("$")) {
       //we need to strip the '$' from the first token
       //before we checksum it
       curTok = curTok.substring(1);//strip the first character
       }

       if (!curTok.startsWith("*")) checkSum =
           addToChecksum(checkSum, curTok); //keep adding to checksum

       if ( curTok.equalsIgnoreCase(",") ) {
       if (lastTok.equalsIgnoreCase(",") ) curTok = "";//empty token
          else {
          lastTok = curTok;
          continue; //start back at the top of the while-loop,
          //because we don't want to process a comma by itself
          }
       }

       realTokenCount++;//notice this is only incremented once we've
                   //verified it's a non-comma token
                   //(or forced it to be, anyway)
       lastTok = curTok;//keep track for comma-skipping code above
       if (fDebugOn)
           System.out.println("token\t" + realTokenCount +"\t:" + curTok);

           continueParsing = processToken(curTok, result);
           if (!continueParsing) return null;//break out
       }//while curTok

}
catch (NoSuchElementException noSuchEltEx) {
//This is an EXPECTED exception once we reach the EOL: do nothing
}
catch (Exception tokenizeEx) {
//Unexpected exception-- Give up
if (fDebugOn) System.err.println("tokenize threw: " + tokenizeEx);
   return null;
}

return result;

}/* parseNMEAGGAString */
```

The remainder of the NMEAStringParser boils down to processing the individual tokens. If you're interested in the implementation details, see the source code on the CD. For brevity we'll simply describe the methods here:

- The processToken method tracks the number of tokens processed and decides how to process each token based on which field in the field sequence the token represents. This method also detects whether differential GPS is active and acts appropriately.

- The addToChecksum method adds the checksum of each field to the overall sentence checksum.

- The convertPositionStringToDegrees method converts a position String into a double degrees value. Many of the fields in the GGA sentence must be converted in this manner.

- The parseGGAChecksum method parses the special checksum field at the end of a GGA sentence and checks it against the calculated checksum of the sentence. Notice in the parseGGAChecksum method we take advantage of another utility class provided with this book: the HexConverter class. This class provides several useful methods for converting between hexadecimal strings of different lengths and integer data types.

Meet the StreamTokenizer Class

The StreamTokenizer can be used to quickly parse an incoming stream of data. StreamTokenizer is similar to StringTokenizer in some respect; generally, you simply set up StreamTokenizer and then repeatedly call its nextToken method to obtain a series of tokens. However, StreamTokenizer is a bit more flexible and powerful. For instance, the StreamTokenizer has a built-in number parser so it can return numeric-value tokens as well as String tokens. StreamTokenizer can also deal with comments, quote characters, and can treat end-of-line (EOL) as a special token. StreamTokenizer can also be configured to return all String tokens in lowercase.

StreamTokenizer does not return tokens from nextToken. Instead, after each call to nextToken, the StreamTokenizer's public variables sval, nval, and ttype will contain various aspects of the token's value. The sval variable will contain any String tokens. The nval variable will contain any numeric tokens. The ttype variable will contain an int value indicating the type of the token contained in either sval or nval.

Configuring a `StreamTokenizer` can be a bit tricky. The table below lists the configuration methods and their effects.

Table 2-6 StreamTokenizer Configuration Methods

Method	Description
`commentChar(int ch)`	Allows you to set a comment character. All characters between a comment character and EOL will be ignored.
`eolIsSignificant(boolean)`	Allows you to set whether EOL should be treated differently than other whitespace. If this is set with true, then EOL will be returned in `ttype` as `TT_EOL`.
`lowerCaseMode(boolean)`	Allows you to force all String tokens returned in `sval` to be coerced to lowercase
`ordinaryChar(int ch),` `ordinaryChars(int from, int to)`	Allows you to set aside a certain character or set of characters as being neither word (token) characters nor delimiter characters. All of these characters will be returned as is. For these characters, `ttype` will be 0.
`parseNumbers()`	Turns on number parsing. All numbers will be returned with `ttype` of `TT_NUMBER` and their value will be stored in `nval` as a double-precision floating-point number. Curiously, once number parsing has been turned on, it cannot be turned off.
`quoteChar(int ch)`	Specifies a quote character to be used to delimit word tokens. All characters between quote characters will be treated as part of one `String` token. The token is returned in `sval` and the `ttype` is set to the value of the quote character. (This can be used to determine which kind of quote character was encountered.)
`resetSyntax()`	Completely clears the `StreamTokenizer`'s configuration: effectively makes all 255 character values "ordinary" values.
`slashSlashComments(boolean)`	Toggles "//" comments (comments that start with "//" and run to EOL). All characters between "//" and EOL are ignored if this is turned on.

Table 2-6 StreamTokenizer Configuration Methods (Continued)

Method	Description
slashStarComments(boolean)	Toggles "/*...*/" comments. All characters between "/*" and "*/" are ignored if this is turned on.
whitespaceChars(int from, int to);	Sets a range of characters that delimit token (word) strings. These characters are never returned as tokens.
wordChars(int from, int to)	Sets a range of characters that are to be considered part of word tokens. These tokens will be returned in sval and ttype will be TT_WORD.

For your reference, a StreamTokenizer is set up by default as follows:

```
//basic word chars
    wordChars('a', 'z');
    wordChars('A', 'Z');
//extended ASCII chars are word chars
    wordChars(128 + 32, 255);
//from null to space is whitespace
    whitespaceChars(0, ' ');
//slash is a comment char
    commentChar('/');
//a double quote is a quote char
    quoteChar('"');
//a single quote is a quote char
    quoteChar('\'');
//turn on parsing of numbers
    parseNumbers();
```

Not surprisingly, this configuration is similar to the configuration you would need to parse a stream containing Java code.

Note that the StreamTokenizer supports "pushback" of the current token: that is, it allows you to buffer the current token so that the next call to nextToken will return the current token. This is useful in cases where you want to peek at the next token on the stream and decide how to change your parsing strategy on the fly. To push back the current token, simply call StreamTokenizer.pushBack, and the next call to StreamTokenizer.nextToken will return the same token.

Parsing GPS Data Using StreamTokenizer

Now let's look at a more advanced way of parsing an incoming data stream, using a StreamTokenizer to parse the stream directly.

This solution is more general than the StringTokenizer-based solution because it can be easily adapted to other situations where your packets may vary in format, end-of-packet condition, and so on. Since you don't have to read in an entire packet before parsing, you can switch parsing strategies midpacket.

Since this example is rather long, we'll break it up into its critical components and analyze them individually.

First we need to set up a StreamTokenizer to chop up a stream into individual sentences and fields. The NMEStreamParser constructor does this as shown below:

Example 2-5 The NMEAStreamParser Constructor Initializes a StreamTokenizer

```
/**
 * This method initializes the parser on the given stream.
 */
public NMEAStreamParser(InputStream sourceStream)
{
    fStreamChopper = new StreamTokenizer(sourceStream);
    //clear the default parsing tables
    fStreamChopper.resetSyntax();

    //set whitespace range to be: from null to space (" ")...
    fStreamChopper.whitespaceChars(0,32);
    //set word range to be: exclamation point ("!") to plus ("+")...
    fStreamChopper.wordChars(33,43);
    //set word range to be: from dash ("-") to tilde("~")...
    //(we'll parse the number tokens ourselves, thanks)
    fStreamChopper.wordChars(45,126);
     //forces comma to be returned as a special token type
     //(type == value == 44 )
    fStreamChopper.ordinaryChar(44 /*comma*/);

     //forces StreamTokenizer to return special token when we get EOL
    fStreamChopper.eolIsSignificant(true);
} /* NMEAStreamParser */
```

The two main points to notice here are that we set up the StreamTokenizer to recognize EOL and commas. EOL is significant to us in this case because it separates NMEA sentences. Commas are significant to us because they separate fields within a sentence.

Now that we've initialized the StreamTokenizer, we can go about the business of pulling a series of NMEAPositionStatus records out of the stream.

The getNextPosition method should be called repeatedly to return a series of NMEAPositionStatus records, one for each valid GGA sentence that arrives on the stream.

The source for `getNextPosition` is shown below.

Example 2-6 **Implementation of NMEAStreamParser.getNextPosition**

```
/**
 * This method continues parsing the InputStream and returns
 * the next _valid_ position status.
 * @returns The next position status from the input stream.
 */
public NMEAPositionStatus getNextPosition() throws Exception
{
    int realTokenCount, commaCount, checkSum;
    String curTok;
    boolean dGPSactive;

    //start off with an EOL, which is ignored
    fCurTokenClass = StreamTokenizer.TT_EOL;

parseStream: //use a label for clear break/continue
    while (fCurTokenClass != StreamTokenizer.TT_EOF)
    try {
        //prepare to parse a new sentence
        fCurPosStatus = null;//clear it
        realTokenCount = 0;
        commaCount = 0;
        curTok = null;
        checkSum = 0;
        dGPSactive = false;

        fCurPosStatus = parseOneLine();
        if (fCurPosStatus) break parseStream;
    }
    catch (NumberFormatException ex) {
        if (fDebugOn) System.err.println("parseStream threw: " + ex);
        skipPastEOL();//skip to the next sentence...
        continue parseStream; //start over again
    }

    return fCurPosStatus;

} /* getNextPosition */
```

This method consists mainly of a `while` loop that repeatedly pulls NMEA sentences from the stream, passes the sentences off to `parseOneLine`, and continues doing so until `parseOneLine` is able to parse a valid GGA sentence.

The parseOneLine method itself is based upon the
NMEAStringParser.processToken method. However, parseOneLine is
structured a little differently. At the top it has some code to analyze the sentence
header and to automatically add the appropriate token checksums to the
checksum. This code is shown below.

Example 2-7   NMEAStreamParser.parseOneLine

```
parseLine: //use a label so we can break/continue easily
do  {
if (fDebugOn) System.out.println("parseLine");
//process the current sentence, if any
switch (fCurTokenClass) {

case (StreamTokenizer.TT_WORD):
    realTokenCount++;
    curTok = fStreamChopper.sval;//current token string value
    if ( curTok.startsWith("$") ){

        if  (!curTok.endsWith("GGA"))  {
            skipPastEOL();
            return null;
        }
        //we need to strip the '$' from the first
        //token before we checksum it
        curTok = curTok.substring(1);//strip the first character
    }

    if (!curTok.startsWith("*"))
        checkSum = addToChecksum(checkSum, curTok); //keep adding to checksum
    break;

case (44): //got a comma!
    commaCount++;
    curTok = ",";
    checkSum = addToChecksum(checkSum, curTok); //keep adding to checksum
    continue parseLine; //jump back to start of do..while loop, ignore comma

case (StreamTokenizer.TT_EOL):
    continue parseLine;//just ignore it, skip to next sentence

default:
    //we set up the StreamTokenizer so that we shouldn't receive
    //anything but TT_WORD and comma tokens.
    // except when we force TT_EOL to be received:
    //otherwise, something's horribly wrong.
    fCurPosStatus = null;
    if (fDebugOn) System.err.println(
        "bogus token class: " + fCurTokenClass + " sval: " +
fStreamChopper.sval);
    skipPastEOL();
```

```
       return null;

    } //switch fCurTokenClass
```

The rest of `parseOneLine` is basically the same as
`NMEAStringParser.processToken`. The remainder of the utility methods in
the `NMEAStreamParser` are also similar to those in the NMEAStringParser;
however, the `skipPastEOL` method is new and interesting. The point of this
method is to allow us to skip ahead in the stream as soon as we realize that the
rest of the current NMEA sentence is useless. For instance, if we start receiving an
NMEA sentence that is not a GGA sentence, we can immediately skip the rest of
the sentence without bothering to parse it. The source for the `skipPastEOL`
method is shown below.

Example 2-8 Implementation of **NMEAStreamParser.skipPastEOL**

```
/**
 * This utility method allows us to skip ahead in the stream past an EOL
 */
public void skipPastEOL()
{
    fCurTokenClass = 0;
    if (fDebugOn) System.out.println("skipPastEOL!");

    try {
        while ((fCurTokenClass = fStreamChopper.nextToken()) !=
                    StreamTokenizer.TT_EOF) {

                if (fCurTokenClass == StreamTokenizer.TT_EOL)
                    return;//we've found the EOL: we're done!
        }
    }
    catch (Exception e) {
        if (fDebugOn) System.err.println("skipPastEOL threw: "+ e);
    }

}/* skipPastEOL */
```

Notice that in this example we've repeatedly taken advantage of Java's labeled `break` and `continue` statements to skip fruitless parsing and resume parsing at an appropriate place in the stream. This allows us to skip NMEA sentences that are not GGA sentences, and to skip parsing the current sentence if we encounter an error.

Using Pushback and Mark/Reset to Aid Parsing

In some situations parsing a data stream would be easier if you could just peek at the input stream, do some preprocessing, then hand off the stream data, untouched, to the appropriate processing code. Fortunately, the `java.io` package provides two kinds of input stream interfaces for achieving this effect: the pushback interface (as implemented by the `PushbackInputStream`) and the `mark/reset` interface (as implemented in `InputStream` subclasses such as `BufferedInputStream`).

The PushbackInputStream

The pushback interface allows you to push a byte back onto the input stream after you've already read the byte. For instance:

```
int theByte = inStream.read();
System.out.println("theByte: "+ theByte);
inStream.unread(theByte);
theByte = inStream.read();
System.out.println("theByte: "+ theByte);
```

In this example, the value displayed for `theByte` will be the same both times it's printed.

The `PushbackInputStream` implements a single-byte pushback buffer. It doesn't really push any data back onto the input stream; it simply holds the byte pushed back and returns it the next time you call `read`.

There are a couple things to note about the `PushbackInputStream` implementation in the current Java runtime. First, once you pushback a byte, the next time you call any of the `read` methods, you'll always just get a single byte returned. This isn't exactly the most efficient way to read data, but it is the way that implementation works.

The second thing to note is that the `unread` method accepts the byte to push back. This means that you don't have to be happy just pushing back the byte that was actually read off the input stream: you can push back any arbitrary byte. This might be useful for filtering or converting stream data.

Using Mark/Reset with BufferedInputStream

A perhaps more useful pushback mechanism can be achieved with the mark and
reset methods of InputStream subclasses that support marking. (To find out
at runtime whether an InputStream subclass supports marking, call the
markSupported method.)

The mark method places a marker at the current location in the stream. The mark
method takes a single parameter: the number of bytes the stream should buffer
after the mark so that a reset can be achieved. For instance, if you expect to read
500 bytes after calling mark and before calling reset, then you should call mark
with something like 512. It's best to allocate too big a buffer rather than too small
a buffer since, if the number of bytes read exceeds the buffer size, reset will fail
or give unpredictable results.

To achieve "pushback" with marking, you simply do something like the
following:

```
stream:mark(maxChars);
//reading something like maxChars - 10
stream:reset(); //resets to most recent mark
```

Note that when using this interface you cannot push back arbitrary bytes onto the
input stream (unlike with PushbackInputStream). Also, you need to have
some idea of how many bytes you think need to be buffered between mark and
reset.

Coupling OutputStreams to InputStreams using Pipes

The java.io package also provides a set of classes for obtaining a streams
interface between different threads. These "Pipe" classes can be thought of as
thread-safe input and output streams. Because we haven't covered Threads in
great detail yet, we'll just provide a brief introduction to Pipes here.

Let's say you had two classes: StreamEater and StreamProducer.The
StreamProducer class takes an OutputStream and writes out data on it. The
StreamEater class takes an InputStream and reads data from it. Now, how do
you tie these two streams together so that the OutputStream the
StreamProducer produces can provide the InputStream for the
StreamEater?

The PipedInputStream and PipedOutputStream allow you to transform an
InputStream into an OutputStream and vice versa, in a thread-safe manner.
(Briefly, the thread-safe issue arises because of the basic question: "What happens
when the OutputStream is trying to write at the same time the InputStream

is trying to read?" This is only an issue in a multithreaded environment.) Below is an example of how to transform an OutputStream to an InputStream using PipedInputStream and PipedOutputStream.

Example 2-9 Coupling an OutputStream to an InputStream using Pipes

```
PipedOutputStream producerOut = new PipedOutputStream();
PipedInputStream eaterIn = new PipedInputStream(producerOut);

StreamProducer myProducer =
    new StreamProducer((OutputStream)producerOut);
StreamEater myEater =
    new StreamEater((InputStream)eaterIn);
```

After this initial setup, the StreamProducer can write data on the producerOut PipedOutputStream. The StreamEater can read data from the eaterIn PipedInputStream. As the StreamProducer writes data on the producerOut stream, the StreamEater will be able to read that same data from the eaterIn stream. We've effectively transformed an OutputStream into an InputStream.

New for JDK 1.1: Character Streams

The JDK 1.0 stream classes we've covered in detail so far are based on the concept of a "byte stream"— you can write and read data to and from these streams one byte at a time. However, this provides no easy way to switch to different character encodings, such as between ASCII, Unicode, and Shift-JIS (commonly used in Japan). JDK 1.1 introduced some facilities for more easily internationalizing applications that use streams, based on the concept of a "character stream."

A character stream allows you to write and read characters to and from streams without worrying about the underlying character-to-byte mapping. This also allows the mapping to be changed without affecting your code.

JDK 1.1 provides a set of facilities for converting between raw bytes and various character encodings. These facilities are wrapped in convenient stream like interfaces called "readers" and "writers." Most of these facilities are only useful if you plan on internationalizing your application by transmitting or storing data in some encoded character format.

For every stream class and stream utility class provided by the `java.io` package, there is generally a corresponding class for working with character streams in JDK 1.1. The new classes are listed below along with their corresponding byte stream class.

Table 2-7 Character stream classes and their corresponding byte stream classes

Byte Stream Class	Character Stream Class
InputStream	Reader
OutputStream	Writer
BufferedInputStream	BufferedReader
BufferedOutputStream	BufferedWriter
ByteArrayInputStream	CharArrayReader
ByteArrayOutputStream	CharArrayWriter
FileInputStream	FileReader
FileOutputStream	FileWriter
FilterInputStream	FilterReader
FilterOutputStream	FilterWriter
LineNumberInputStream	LineNumberReader
PipedInputStream	PipedReader
PipedOutputStream	PipedWriter
PrintStream	PrintWriter
PushbackInputStream	PushbackReader
StringBufferInputStream	StringReader

In addition, a `StringWriter` character stream class has been added, which allows you to stream characters into a buffer, then use `StringWriter.toString` to obtain a new `String` that contains the characters you wrote. You can also use the `StringWriter.getBuffer` method to obtain the actual `StringBuffer` used to hold the characters. Notice that there is no equivalent class among the JDK 1.0 byte streams.

JDK 1.1 also provides two "bridge" classes that help convert between character streams and byte streams. The `OutputStreamWriter` class writes characters to an `OutputStream`. The `InputStreamReader` reads characters from an `InputStream`.

Starting with JDK 1.1, JavaSoft is encouraging developers to use character streams instead of byte streams whenever possible. Some classes, such as `StreamTokenizer`, which previously worked only with byte streams have now been modified to support character streams. In fact, JavaSoft has officially deprecated the use of byte streams with these utility classes in favor of using character streams.

New for JDK 1.1: Object Streams / Object Serialization

Under JDK 1.0 there was no easy way to ship entire objects over a stream. To do so involved breaking down an object into its component primitives (`String`, `Integer`, `Double`, etc.) and sending those over a stream one at a time using perhaps a `DataOutputStream`. At the receiving end, objects would have to be reconstructed one primitive at a time using perhaps a `DataInputStream`. This was a very tedious process, and to make matters worse there was essentially no easy way to ship arbitrary classes around.

JDK 1.1 solved these problems with Object Serialization. Object Serialization allows you to take an instantiated object and condense it into a "frozen," byte-encoded format that can then be stored or written onto a stream. The byte-encoded format can subsequently be read from a stream and "thawed" back into a live object.

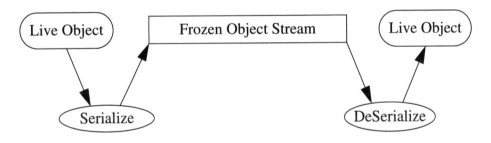

Figure 2–2 The Object Serialization and Deserialization Process.

This section will provide a brief introduction to Object Serialization as you might use it for a communicating application. We will not get into great detail about how to create your own object serialization methods or the object serialization format. We will treat serialization as a black box to be used with what we already know.

Sending Objects with an ObjectOutputStream

To stream objects, you'll use an `ObjectOutputStream`. An `ObjectOutputStream` takes Java objects, serializes them in a byte-encoded format, and writes them onto an `OutputStream`.

In order to send an object on an `ObjectOutputStream`, you must first make certain that it's `Serializable`. The `Serializable` interface has no methods, but requires that you mark nonpersistent fields with the `transient` keyword. By doing so, you insure that the values of those fields will not be transmitted across the stream. Thus `transient` fields are made class-instance-specific.

The example below shows how to write whole objects to a stream using `ObjectOutputStream`. This example writes objects that are already `Serializable` (such as `String`) via a new `Serializable` class (`ObjSerTest`).

Example 2-10 Writing Out Objects on an ObjectOutputStream

```
public class ObjSerTest implements Serializable
{
public int fMyID = 5;
public String fMyStr = " hello whirled!";
public Vector fList;
public static final String FILENAME = "test.out";

public static void main(String args[])
{
    serializeSelf();
}//main

//write a serialized version of this object to a file
public void serializeSelf()
{
    fMyID = (new Random()).nextInt();
    fMyStr += fMyID;
    fList = new Vector(23);

    System.out.println("serializing object " + fMyID + "...");
    try {
        FileOutputStream fout = new FileOutputStream(FILENAME);
        ObjectOutputStream objOut = new ObjectOutputStream(fout);
        objOut.writeObject(this);//serialize this object
    }
    catch (Exception ex) {
        System.out.println("serializeSelf threw: " + ex);
    }
    System.out.println("done serializing object "+ fMyID);
}//serializeSelf


}/* class ObjSerTest */
```

Notice here that the object we serialize, `ObjSerTest`, implements the `Serializable` interface. Many of the standard Java library classes such as `java.lang.String` and `java.util.Vector` implement `Serializable` under JDK 1.1; however, not all of the standard classes do. When you create your own classes, you need to make certain they implement the `Serializable` interface if you wish to ship them over an `ObjectOutputStream`.

Receiving Objects from an ObjectInputStream

An ObjectInputStream is responsible for reading the byte-encoded serialized object format from an InputStream and translating that encoded format into a set of objects.

You should understand that an `ObjectInputStream` is similar to a `StreamTokenizer` in that it needs to keep a great deal of context. Every time you ask the `ObjectInputStream` to read a single object, it may need to read in many objects and keep references to those objects lying around. Thus, if you're reading in numerous objects or a complex object, the memory overhead can be tremendous.

The example below shows how to read objects from an `ObjectInputStream`.

Example 2-11 **Reading Objects from an ObjectInputStream**

```
public class ObjSerTest implements Serializable
{
public int fMyID = 5;
public String fMyStr = "hello whirled!";
public Vector fList;
public static final String FILENAME = "test.out";

public static void main(String args[])
{
    serializeSelf();
    deserializeSelf();
}//main

//write a serialized version of this object to a file
public void serializeSelf()
{
//...same as described previously
}//serializeSelf

//read a new ObjSerTest instance from a file
public void deserializeSelf()
{
    try {
        FileInputStream fin = new FileInputStream(FILENAME);
        ObjectInputStream objIn = new ObjectInputStream(fin);
        ObjSerTest thatOtherGuy = (ObjSerTest)objIn.readObject();
```

```
        System.out.println("got new object: " + thatOtherGuy.fID);
    }
    catch (Exception ex) {
        System.out.println("deserializeSelf threw: " + ex);
    }

}//deserializeSelf


}/* class ObjSerTest */
```

Note that in this example the class of the object being transferred was known ahead of time: the `serializeSelf` method will always serialize an `ObjSerTest` object, and the `deserializeSelf` method will always deserialize an `ObjSerTest` object. However, it is possible to transfer objects whose class is not known until runtime. The object shows up at the receiving end as an `Object` with class information intact. You can use `Object.getClass` to obtain a `Class` for the object, then decide what to do with the object based on this class information. This is a tremendous improvement over JDK 1.0, where there was essentially no easy way to transfer class information over a stream.

A Note on Object Serialization Efficiency

If you have an existing JDK 1.0 object serialization scheme of your own, or if you are just a do-it-yourselfer, you might ask, Just how efficient is the JDK 1.1 object serialization implementation?

Without getting into too much implementation detail, it appears that the implementation is very efficient for objects of reasonable complexity. For simple objects (such as single strings) you would probably not have a difficult time coming up with a more efficient way to send the object. However, for objects that contain references to several other objects, perhaps even circular references, you would probably have a hard time developing a much more efficient transmission scheme.

The diagram below shows a simplistic representation of the JDK 1.1 object serialization format.

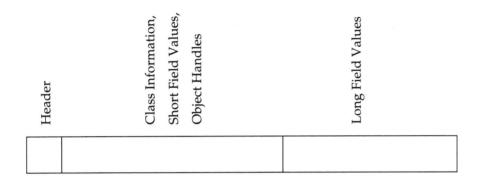

Figure 2-3 A sketch of the JDK 1.1 object serialization format.

What this diagram shows, roughly, is the ordering of information in the serialized encoding. There is a short header followed by information about the class itself, the fields within the class, and short field values (or forward references to data to be sent in the long field values data block). If this object contains references to other objects, the stream will also contain "object handles" that forward- or back-reference these other objects on the serialized stream. Object handles are simply integer values that uniquely identify objects on a given stream. These handles make it possible to send a specific object only once on the stream, even if the object is referenced multiple times. Object handles are the key to this implementation's efficiency.

Now, if you're still not satisfied that this implementation is the most efficient format for your particular application, you have an alternative. You can use the `Externalizable` interface for your objects instead of the `Serializable` interface. The `Externalizable` interface allows you to essentially encode your own objects in your own way.

To create an `Externalizable` object, you only need to implement two methods:

```
public void readExternal(ObjectInput in) throws IOException;
public void writeExternal(ObjectOutput out) throws IOException;
```

You implement the `writeExternal` method to encode your object, and the `readExternal` method to decode it. The `ObjectOutput` and `ObjectInput` parameters to these methods provide you with a way to read and write either a byte at a time or use the default object serialization encoding. For instance, if you wanted to simply replicate the default behavior of object serialization, your `writeExternal` and `readExternal` methods would look like this:

```
public void writeExternal(ObjectOutput out) throws IOException
{
out.writeObject(this);
}

public void readExternal(ObjectInput in) throws IOException
{
    this = (thisClass) in.readObject();//essentially, not literally
}
```

However, you would typically add some way to efficiently encode one or more of your own object's fields instead of relying on the default behavior.

Summary: Picking the Right Stream for the Job

When choosing a particular stream for your project, you should compare stream classes on a number of points: speed, memory footprint, and programming convenience. Depending on your priorities, different streams might be right for your application.

Speed/Performance versus Programming Convenience

This is one of the main trade-offs. You can daisy-chain numerous streams together for convenience, but this does affect the runtime performance of your code. You might also use this as a quick hack when you're just trying to develop a prototype and you're not worried about high performance.

As an example, we'll see later that using `DataOutputStream` to dump a string to `stdout` can be extremely slow. While `DataOutputStream` and some other streams provide methods for manipulating strings, it seems that only the `StringBufferInputStream` is really designed for pulling large amounts of data from a `String` quickly.

Also, it's silly to use streams to perform very simple operations (such as moving a short string between objects), unless you're more concerned about modularity and flexibility than you are about performance.

Filtering

Some streams are designed to allow you to strip or replace incoming characters. This is convenient if you don't want to go through the hassle of parsing everything by hand; you just want to filter out the garbage. We've seen already how easy it is to extend FilterInputStream to filter out unwanted data. The PushbackInputStream's unread method can also be used to achieve some level of filtering.

Parsing

Some streams are specifically designed to allow convenient parsing of incoming data. For instance, the BufferedInputStream and the FilterInputStream provide interfaces that make parsing easier. The StreamTokenizer class can also assist in the parsing of input streams.

Buffering

Some streams, such as the BufferedInputStream and the BufferedOutputStream, are designed to speed up communications by buffering, so that the underlying input or output stream doesn't need to perform a read or write on the physical device every time you call read or write on the input or output stream. While this clearly has a speed impact when you're performing numerous small reads or writes, it also has a significant memory impact since the stream needs to buffer the data somewhere.

Memory Footprint

Some streams use more memory than others. Typically you can determine how much memory a stream uses based on the buffers you explicitly or implicitly ask it to allocate. For instance, when you call the BufferedInputStream's mark method, you explicitly provide a buffer size. However, depending on the BufferedInputStream constructor that you use, you either explicitly allocate a buffer or implicitly have one allocated for you. If you know precisely how many bytes you're likely to read from the BufferedInputStream, and how many are likely to be provided on each read on the underlying InputStream, then it's a good idea to set the buffer size explicitly.

CHAPTER
3

- Overview of the URL Class

- Retrieving Web Content

- Overview of the `URLConnection` Class

- Loading Multiple URLs at Timed Intervals

- New for 1.1: The `HttpURLConnection`

Making the URL Connection

T he powerful Internet access library provided with Java is one of the most compelling reasons to use it for Internet networking. This chapter will introduce the possibilities of creating networking applications using classes contained in the `java.net` package. These classes are intended for applications that utilize existing Internet protocols such as HTTP and FTP. This chapter will provide some ideas for network applications that use these specific classes.

The Possibilities

There are two main classes provided by the `java.net` package for exchanging Web data: the `java.net.URL` class and the `java.net.URLConnection` class.

The `java.net.URL` class provides a very high-level interface to Web transactions. This class tries to hide as many of the details of obtaining Web content as possible.

The `java.net.URLConnection` provides more comprehensive control over Web transactions. This class allows you finer control over when the connection to the remote Web host is made, what the request made of the host consists of, and better access to the host's response.

Both of these classes assume that the underlying infrastructure for making an Internet connection is in place: that is, before using these classes, you'll need to have an Internet connection set up on the computer executing your Java code.

Meet the URL Class

This class allows you to make high-level Web document transaction requests. The URL class represents a Uniform Reference Locator — a reference to a content object (such as an HTML document, a GIF image, a sound file, or an MPEG movie) stored somewhere specific on an Internet server.

Generally you create a URL instance from a String that contains a URL (e.g., "http://www.rawthought.com/"). Once the URL instance has been created, you can connect to the Internet site where the content given by the URL is stored using one of the appropriate URL class methods and retrieve the content.

Here's a list of the most useful URL class methods

Table 3-1 Commonly-Used `java.net.URL` Class Methods

Method	Description
URL	This method comes in four (4!) different flavors. You can create a new URL from a String, from a relative string and a base URL, from a protocol String, a host String, and a filename String, or from a protocol, host, filename String and a port number. One of these methods should fit your needs.
openConnection	This method opens a connection to the remote Web server and returns a URLConnection object. Invokes the appropriate protocol Handler.
openStream	This method opens a connection to the remote Web server and returns an InputStream object.
getContent	Get an Object that represents the retrieved content. This method isn't really useful unless you're downloading something that can be represented as an Image or as a String object. Also useful if you're writing a Web browser such as HotJava and you want to create "handlers" for various content types (such as HTML).
getFile	Get the filename String embedded in the URL.
getHost	Get the host name String embedded in the URL (might be in dotted-decimal format "165.227.67.1" if there is no DNS-associated domain name such as "www.allpen.com").
getPort	Get the port number embedded in the URL. Note that if there is no explicitly specified port number (if the URL is using the default port for the given protocol), this may return -1. This does not indicate that the protocol is using the port -1, which is a bogus port number.
getProtocol	Get the protocol String embedded in the URL. This will typically be something like "HTTP" or "FTP".

Table 3-1 Commonly-Used `java.net.URL` **Class Methods (Continued)**

Method	Description
`getRef`	If the URL contains a "ref" such as `"#gohere"`, then this String will be returned. Refs are commonly used to reference specific sections of an HTML page, and allow you to jump between sections easily.
`hashCode`	This method provides a unique ID hash code for this URL. This value can be used to store a URL in a `Hashtable`, or to store a document reference in a cache.
`sameFile`	This method can be used to test two URLs for equality. This can be useful for document caching: you can determine whether you've already loaded the content given by the URL.
`toExternalForm`	Generates a URL String that can be displayed to the user, typed into a Web browser, et cetera. This method complements the URL constructor.

Note that once you create a URL instance, you cannot change the object's fields: they are read-only. Also, as of this writing the URL class only supports a limited set of Internet protocols. The supported protocols are listed below:

Table 3-2 Internet Protocols Supported by the `java.net.URL` **Class**

Protocol	Description
HTTP	The HyperText Transfer Protocol, the key data exchange protocol of the World Wide Web. This is what Web browsers use to communicate with Web servers.
FTP	File Transfer Protocol. This protocol is used to exchange files between Internet hosts. Some Web browsers can retrieve files from FTP servers using this protocol. More typically, this protocol is used to move files between computers using an FTP client such as Fetch under MacOS.
Gopher	This is a protocol similar to HTTP that allows "browsing" of Internet sites in order to find and retrieve information. Some Web browsers will allow you to browse Gopher servers. There also exist applications such as TurboGopher under MacOS and Archie under Unix that are stand-alone Gopher clients.
mailto	This protocol can be used to submit (post) mail messages to an SMTP mail server. Note that when you try to use this protocol programmatically, the URL class returns some HTML data with an embedded applet. The applet links to `sun.hotjava.applets.MailDocumentApplet` in order to provide the user interface and SMTP protocol support for sending a mail message. This may not be what you expect or desire, since it requires that you open an applet, and that the user fill in a form.

Warning: The protocols supported by the URL and URLConnection classes depends entirely on the underlying Java runtime environment. The runtime environment must have a protocol handler installed for each protocol you want to use. At the time of this writing, the MacOS Java runtime from JavaSoft for JDK 1.0 supported all of the above listed protocols; however, the Win32 runtime from JavaSoft only supported HTTP.

Of all these protocols, HTTP, FTP, and Gopher are the most useful. The mailto protocol is probably only useful to you if you are writing a HotJava-like Web browser or Web-enabled application. Note that if you attempt to open a URL which contains the mailto protocol, you receive some HTML data containing an embedded applet. This applet object contains the user interface and code necessary to enter and send a mail message via SMTP. If your application doesn't know how to run an applet, this isn't a particularly useful interface.

In general, when trying to understand the operation of the URL and URLConnection classes, it helps to remember that these classes were designed specifically to work within the HotJava web browser. Thus these classes have some quirks which don't make much sense outside of a web browser environment.

URL Class Limitations

There are some limitations to what you can do with the URL class. For instance, you cannot use the URL class to send data to a Web server. Since this class uses the default protocol "mode" for transactions (such as GET for HTTP), this class can only be used to retrieve information. Of the protocols the URL class currently supports, only mailto defaults to being a "send" protocol: You use it to send a mail message. The other supported protocols all default to retrieve mode. This means that, for instance, you cannot submit HTML form data if the form uses the HTTP POST method instead of the default HTTP GET method. (This is an exceptional case because there's essentially no difference between the URL used for a normal HTTP GET and the URL data submitted during an HTML form submission that uses the HTTP GET method).

The States of a URL

In understanding the operation of the URL class, it's important to know that a URL instance passes through several states as it's used:

Initialized

In this state, no connection exists from the local computer to any remote server. In this state, URLs can be compared, have their various parts extracted, be converted back to URL strings, and so on. No data can be downloaded in this state.

Connecting

As soon as the URL client calls `openStream`, `getContent`, or `openConnection`, a connection is opened to the remote Internet server. This includes dialing a modem, opening an Ethernet driver, or whatever else is necessary to connect to the Internet, and finally opening a TCP connection to the Internet host given in the URL.

Connected

If the connection opens correctly, the client will be able to retrieve content data.

Downloading Web Content Using the URL Class

In order to access the content stored at a certain URL directly, you can use the `URL.openStream` method as follows:

```
//first, create a URL instance from a URL string
URL aURL = new URL("http://www.rawthought.com/");
//next, get an input stream that returns the content data
InputStream inStream = aURL.openStream();
```

Once you've opened an input stream in this manner, you can read the content data from the input stream just as you would for any other `InputStream`.

Note that the URL constructor we used here, which accepts just a single URL String parameter, isn't very robust. If, for instance, you provided the string "`www.rawthought.com/index.html`" to this constructor, the constructor would throw the following exception:

```
java.net.MalformedURLException:
no protocol: www.rawthought.com/index.html
```

This particular constructor takes the URL string at face value, and makes no assumptions about protocol, host, or filename. If the URL String you provide doesn't include a protocol, this constructor doesn't assume that it should use HTTP— it throws a "no protocol provided" exception.

This lack of robustness has certain implications. If you're going to be loading URLs based purely on a URL string that the user types, you should probably set up more robust default behavior. For instance, you could use another of the URL constructors to provide some default context as follows:

```
//first, build a base URL
try {
```

```
    URL fDefaultURL = new URL("http://www.rawthought.com/");
}
catch (MalformedURLException ex) {
    System.err.println("build of fDefaultURL failed: " + ex);
}
//(user types in a URL: userURLString = "/newt/";)
URL newURL := newURL(fDefaultURL,userURLString);
//newURL is now equivalent to "http://www.rawthought.com/newt/"
```

By wrapping the user's URL string in a base URL context, you insure that the user can take shortcuts such as not typing in the `http://` every time. Incidentally, this is also the way you deal with base versus relative URLs. (Base URLs are completely specified URLs such as `http://www.rawthought.com/index.html`, which contain a protocol, a hostname, a directory path, and a filename. Relative URLs are specified relative to a base URL and thus do not have to be completely specified; they can be missing protocol or hostname information, and their directory path can overlap with the base directory path or be missing entirely). You can pass the base URL as the first parameter to `URL(URL, String)`, and the relative string URL as the second parameter.

Handling Web Content with getContent

You can also download web content via the URL class by using the `URL.getContent` method. This method behaves differently from `openStream` in that, instead of providing you with direct access to the stream of content data, the data stream is parsed and an appropriate "content handler" `Object` is instantiated based on this data. Typically, a content handler is subclassed from something like `java.awt.Frame`, and can be displayed to the user.

This method is out of the scope of this book because it does too much for you. It receives all the content data for you, parses it, and creates a content handler `Object` for displaying the given content. This makes this method useful only to something like a HotJava Web browser that comes with relevant content handler classes and knows how to display various content handlers.

Example: A Simple URL Loader Class

In this section we'll construct a simple application that uses the URL class to take a single typed-in URL string and load the content given by the URL into a file.

This example consists of two main parts. The first part is mostly user interface; we open a simple text input window, then wait for the user to type in a URL string, and click on a "Go!" button. The second part of this example contains the main URL construction and content download code. All of this code is encapsulated in the `loadURL` method.

The URL_Loader class implementation is shown below.
Example 3-1 **Downloading Web Content Given a URL String**

```java
import java.awt.*;
import java.io.*;
import java.net.*;

/**
 * A class to demonstrate simple programmatic access of
 * Web content using the URL class.
 */
public class URL_Loader extends Frame
{
    public boolean fDebugOn = true; //toggles debugging

    protected TextField fInputField;//user input field
    protected URLfDefaultURL = null;//used as default URL

    /**
     * Build the appropriate UI elements for punching in a URL.
     */
    public URL_Loader() {
        //create the main window
        setTitle("Load a URL");
        Panel p = new Panel();
        p.setLayout(new FlowLayout());

        //create an input field for typing in the URL
        fInputField = new TextField(40);
        p.add(fInputField);

        //add a button so the user can tell us to go
        p.add(new Button("Go!"));

        add("North", p);

        //build the default base URL
        try { fDefaultURL = new URL("http://www.rawthought.com/");}
        catch (MalformedURLException ex) {
            System.err.println("build of fDefaultURL failed: " + ex);
        }

    }//URL_Loader()

    /**
     * Handle the WINDOW_DESTROY event as an app closure.
     */
    public boolean handleEvent(Event evt)
    {
        if (evt.id == Event.WINDOW_DESTROY) System.exit(0);
        return super.handleEvent(evt);
    }//handleEvent
```

```
/**
* Handle the user clicking on the "Go!" button
*/
 public boolean action(Event evt, Object arg)
 {
  if (arg.equals("Go!")) {
     //slurp the string from the input field
    String urlString = fInputField.getText();
    loadURL(urlString);
    return true;//we handled this event
  }
  else
     //allow our superclass to handle the event
     return super.action(evt, arg);

 }//action


/**
* Load a document given a URL string
* @param specStr A String containing the URL to
* load: i.e. "http://www.rawthought.com/"
*/
public void loadURL(String specStr)
{
    URL tempURL;//the URL to be loaded
    InputStream tempInputStream;//stream from which to read data
    int curByte; //used for copying from input stream to a file

     try {
        //create new URL using fDefaultURL as the base or default URL
        tempURL = new URL(fDefaultURL, specStr);

        if (fDebugOn) {
            System.out.println("protocol: " + tempURL.getProtocol());
            System.out.println("host: " + tempURL.getHost());
            System.out.println("port: " + tempURL.getPort());
            System.out.println("filename: " + tempURL.getFile());
        }

     try {
        if (fDebugOn) System.out.println("Opening input stream...");
        //open the connection, get InputStream from which to read
        //content data
        tempInputStream = tempURL.openStream();

        //if we get to this point without an exception being thrown,
        //then we've connected to a valid Web server,
        // requested a valid URL, and there's content
        //data waiting for us on the InputStream
        try {
```

```
                //use URL.hashCode() to generate a unique filename
                String newFileName =
                    String.valueOf(tempURL.hashCode()) + ".htm";

                if (fDebugOn) System.out.println(
                    "Opening output file: " + newFileName);
                    //open output file
                    FileOutputStream outstream =
                        new FileOutputStream(newFileName);

                if (fDebugOn)
                    System.out.println("Copying Data...");
                    try {
                        while ( (curByte = tempInputStream.read()) != -1 ) {
                            //simple byte-for-byte copy...could be improved!
                            outstream.write(curByte);
                        }
                        if (fDebugOn)
                            System.out.println("Done Downloading Content!");
                        //we're done writing to the local file, so close it
                        outstream.close();
                    }
                    catch(IOException copyEx) {
                        System.err.println("copyEx: " + copyEx);
                    }
            }
        catch (Exception fileOpenEx) {
                System.err.println("fileOpenEx: " + fileOpenEx);
        }
    }
    catch (IOException retrieveEx) {
            System.err.println("retrievEx: " + retrieveEx);
    }
    }
    catch (MalformedURLException murlEx) {
        System.err.println("new URL threw ex: " + murlEx);
    }
} // loadURL


} //class  URL_Loader
```

Here are a few important things to note about the URL_Loader class:

- We wrap the URL input string that the user types in a default URL context in our call to the URL constructor. As we talked about a bit earlier, this provides some default protocol and host context in case the user doesn't want to bother typing those details, or the code that calls this method doesn't want to provide complete absolute URL strings.

- The connection to the remote host isn't actually opened until we call `URL.openStream`. Before then, the URL instance is in the Initialized state described previously. The easiest way to watch this is to run this example on a computer that uses a dial-in (modem-based SLIP or PPP) Internet connection. Before `openStream` is called, the dial-in connection need not be established; however, as soon as we call `openStream`, the OS will attempt to open an dial-in Internet connection.

- We use the `URL.hashCode` method to generate a unique filename for the downloaded data. This method generates a mostly-unique integer hashcode from a `URL`. This is generally useful for storing Web documents in hash tables or databases based on their URL. In our example, we're simply using this method to generate a relatively short, relatively unique filename for each Web document downloaded.

- The code that copies data from the `InputStream` to the file `OutputStream` is very inefficient. It makes two function calls per byte copied: one call to read a byte from the input stream, and one call to write the byte to the file output stream. A faster and more efficient method would read data in reasonably-sized blocks and write data in the same reasonably-sized blocks. This is left as an exercise for the reader.

- All of the major method calls that are likely to fail are wrapped in their own exception handlers. Although the `loadURL` method doesn't provide for any real error recovery after an exception is thrown, you can imagine adding handler code for the `MalformedURLException` (for instance), which notifies the user of the error and perhaps asks for a new URL. Wrapping your code with exception handlers in this manner allows you to pinpoint very quickly which portion of the code is failing, and notify the user appropriately.

As you can see, it is easy to create a URL downloader application using the `java.net.URL` class; however, there are some major limitations to URL's capabilities. In the next section we'll look at the `URLConnection` class, which provides more extensive control over Web content download.

Meet the URLConnection Class

The `URLConnection` class allows more fine-grained control over Web transactions. The `URLConnection` class is used to represent the active connection to the Web content object represented by a URL object.

With a `URLConnection` instance you can connect to any Internet host that supports one of the supported URL protocols (such as HTTP or FTP), and download content.

The only way to obtain a URLConnection instance is to first create a URL instance, then call the URL.openConnection method. The name of this method is inappropriate since it doesn't actually force a connection to the remote Internet server to be opened, but it does return a URLConnection instance that can open that connection. A list of the more commonly used URLConnection methods is shown below:

Table 3-3 Commonly Used URLConnection Methods

Method	Description.
connect	Forces a connection to the host provided in the URL object. This method is implicitly called by other methods that require a connection, such as getInputStream, getOutputStream, getContentLength, getContent, and so forth.
getAllowUserInteraction setAllowUserInteraction getDefaultAllowUserInteraction setDefaultAllowUserInteraction	Allows you to toggle whether the user should be allowed to interact with the transaction (such as by entering a username/password for HTTP or FTP authentication).
setDoInput	This is true by default. Toggles whether this URLConnection can be used to receive data.
setDoOutput	This is false by default. Toggles whether this URLConnection can be used to send data to the remote host.
setIfModifiedSince	By default this field isn't used. However, if you call setIfModifiedSince() with a date, this field is set. In the case of HTTP this tells the remote host that you only want to receive content if it has changed since the given date.
getURL	This returns the core URL object.
setUseCaches getUseCaches	This can be used to toggle whether the document content can be obtained from local cache, or whether the content should be loaded "live" from the remote host every time.
getRequestProperty setRequestProperty	This can be used to set/get a request property such as HTTP header fields (e.g. "Accept", "If-Modified-Since", "User-Agent", etc.). The property named by key is set to the value string. The protocol handler used in the request determines which of these request properties are utilized, if any. For instance, the FTP protocol handler ignores most of these properties. Note: these methods only work in JDK 1.1 and above; they are broken under JDK 1.0.

Table 3-3 Commonly Used URLConnection Methods (Continued)

Method	Description.
`setDefaultRequestProperty` `getDefaultRequestProperty`	Sets/gets the default value of a general request property. When a `URLConnection` is created, it is initialized with these properties. Typically, you won't need to use these methods.
`getHeaderField` `getHeaderFieldInt` `setHeaderField`	These methods allow you to get and set attributes of the request header, and are mainly applicable to HTTP. Note: these methods only work in JDK 1.1 and above; they are broken under JDK 1.0.
`getDate`	Returns the last modified date of the content. Note: This method only works in JDK 1.1 and above: it is broken under JDK 1.0.
`getContentLength`	Returns the content length. Note that this method is broken under JDK 1.0 but JavaSoft claims to have fixed it in JDK 1.1.
`guessContentTypeFromName`	This is a very useful utility function that guesses what MIME content type you're dealing with based only on the filename extension (".html", ".txt", ".exe", and so on). This static method returns a String such as "application/octet-stream" or null if it has no ideas. Unfortunately, this method is protected, so you can only access it from subclasses. More on this later.
`guessContentTypeFromStream`	This method peers into the innards of a byte stream and guesses as to what MIME type that data is. This is a very handy utility function for anyone who is receiving data in an unknown format. This function allows you to get an idea of what kind of data a stream is carrying and act accordingly. This static method returns a String such as "image/gif" or null if it has no ideas. Note that this method currently only returns one of a few basic types: "image/gif", "image/x-bitmap", "image/x-pixmap" or "text/html". You might want to use this method in conjunction with guessContentTypeFromName to get a more accurate guess.

The States of a URLConnection

URLConnection has a loosely-defined set of states, during which certain methods of a URLConnection instance can be executed. There are three basic states: Initialized, Connected, and Idle. Let's look at each of these states in detail.

Initialized

After a URLConnection object has been constructed by a call to URL.openConnection, but before a connection to the remote host given in the URL has been formed, the URLConnection is in the Initialized state. In this state no connection exists with the remote host. (Because of this, openConnection is badly named.) In this state you can set up the document transaction by configuring various attributes. This is the only state in which it's legal to call all of the setFoo methods. This is also the only state in which you can set up output parameters used for sending data with this URLConnection.

Connected

Whenever you call any URLConnection method that requires a connection to the host given in the URL, the URLConnection fires off its connect method. This forms a connection to the remote server or fails. Since the connect method is synchronous, there is no "Connecting" state: a URLConnection is either connected or it isn't. Some examples of methods that implicitly kick off the connect method are: getInputStream, getOutputStream, getContentLength, and getContent.

Idle

With some Web protocols such as HTTP, after the URLConnection has connected to the remote host and has downloaded the content data, the remote host disconnects. This means that the URLConnection no longer has a connection to the remote host, and yet you can still call "context" methods such as getContentLength to determine how long the downloaded content is. This is because, especially with HTTP, the URLConnection has already received the important content header information such as the content type (plain text, HTML, JPEG image, etc.) and length, even though the connection is no longer open.

Below is the source of the URLConnectionTest application, which demonstrates the various states of a URLConnection.

Example 3-2 **An Application for Demonstrating the URLConnection States**

```
/**
 * Code snippet from URLConnectionTest.java
 * A method that loads the given URL and
 * demonstrates the various states of a URLConnection.
 * @param specStr The  URL to be loaded.
```

```java
*/
public void loadURL(String specStr)
{
    URL tempURL;
    URLConnection theURLConnection;

    InputStream tempInputStream;
    int curByte;

  try {
    tempURL = new URL(specStr);
    System.out.println("protocol: " + tempURL.getProtocol());
    System.out.println("host: " + tempURL.getHost());
    System.out.println("port: " + tempURL.getPort());
    System.out.println("filename: " + tempURL.getFile());

    try {
        //first, get a URLConnection for the
        //given URL object
        System.out.println("openConnection...");
        theURLConnection = tempURL.openConnection();

        //Check stuff that doesn't require that an actual
        //connection be opened
        System.out.println("getUseCaches: " +
            theURLConnection.getUseCaches());
        System.out.println("getDefaultUseCaches: " +
            theURLConnection.getDefaultUseCaches());

        System.out.println("getDefaultAllowUserInteraction: " +
            theURLConnection.getDefaultAllowUserInteraction());
        System.out.println("getAllowUserInteraction: " +
            theURLConnection.getAllowUserInteraction());

        System.out.println("ifModifiedSince: " +
            theURLConnection.getIfModifiedSince());
        System.out.println("doInput: " +
            theURLConnection.getDoInput());
        System.out.println("doOutput: " +
            theURLConnection.getDoOutput());

        //Now, go ahead and connect
        System.out.println("getInputStream...");
        //open the connection, get data.
        //calls connect implicitly
        tempInputStream = theURLConnection.getInputStream();

        //Check stuff that requires a connection be open
        System.out.println("getContentEncoding: " +
            theURLConnection.getContentEncoding() );
        System.out.println("getContentLength: " +
            theURLConnection.getContentLength() );
        System.out.println("getContentType: " +
```

```
            theURLConnection.getContentType() );
        System.out.println("getLastModified: " +
         theURLConnection.getLastModified() );
        System.out.println("getDate: " +
            theURLConnection.getDate() );
        System.out.println("getExpiration: " +
         theURLConnection.getExpiration() );


        //note that at this point it's too late to
        //call things like setDoOutput. If you do,
        //it throws a java.lang.IllegalAccessError:
        //Already connected.

        try {
            //create a unique output filename
            String newFileName =
                String.valueOf(tempURL.hashCode()) + ".htm";
            System.out.println("Opening outstream..." + newFileName);
            //open output file
            FileOutputStream outstream =
                new FileOutputStream(newFileName );

            System.out.println("Copying Data...");
            try {
                while ( (curByte = tempInputStream.read()) != -1 ) {
                    //simple byte for byte copy
                    outstream.write(curByte);
                }
                System.out.println("Done!");
                outstream.close();//be nice
            }
            catch(IOException copyEx) {
                System.err.println("copyEx: " + copyEx);
            }
        }
        catch (Exception fileOpenEx) {
            System.err.println("fileOpenEx: " + fileOpenEx);
        }
    }
    catch (IOException contentEx) {
        System.err.println("retrieve ex: " + contentEx);
    }
}
catch (MalformedURLException murlEx) {
    System.err.println("loadURL threw ex: " + murlEx);
}
}//loadURL
```

Note that when you run this code snippet, the connection to the remote host isn't initiated until the call to `getInputStream`. The easiest way to note this with a MacOS or Win32 computer is to simply be disconnected from the Internet before you run this code. If your system uses dial-up SLIP or PPP to connect to the Internet via modem, you'll notice that the dial-up connection starts just after the "getInputStream" message prints to stdout.

There are several other important things to notice about this example:

- We look at the URL returned by `URLConnection.getURL()` to obtain the final URL of the data presented on the input stream. This is because, due to HTTP "redirects" and such, the final URL of the data we download might differ from the URL we originally specified.

- We've extended the filename generation code so that it makes a best guess as to what the filename extension should be. It does this by looking for an extension (delimited by a period) in the filename returned by `URL.getFile()`. If it finds an extension, it uses it, otherwise it defaults to `".html"`. Note that this doesn't handle HTML forms URLs such as `"http://www.rawthought.com/cgi-bin/search.exe?word=groovy"`. In this case it would mistake the extension of the CGI script to be executed (`".exe"`) for the extension of the returned content data.

- We extended the `InputStream` to `OutputStream` copy code so that it reads and writes data in much bigger blocks than in the `URL_Loader.loadURL` method. This should result in much faster downloads.

- We have a bunch of `println` statements that display the disposition of the content before we actually start copying the content data to a file. It's important to note here that the `URLConnection` must connect to a Web server and download some header data before it is able to make assessments such as determining the content length for `getContentLength`.

The following table summarizes the various `URLConnection` states and the various methods that can be called from each state.

Table 3-4 URLConnection States versus applicable methods

State	Applicable Methods	Description

Initialized	`connect`
	`setAllowUserInteraction`
	`setContentHandlerFactory`
	`setDefaultUseCaches`
	`setDefaultAllowUserInteraction`
	`setDefaultRequestProperty`
	`setDoInput`
	`setDoOuput`
	`setIfModifiedSince`
	`setRequestProperty`
	`setUseCaches`
	+ all methods applicable in the Connected state
		No connection to the back-end server exists. As soon as a method such as `connect` or `getInputStream` is called, the connection is opened. Only in this state can you configure the `URLConnection` with the various setFoo methods: It is an error to call these methods in the Connected state. Note that in this state you can call all of the methods that are also applicable in the Connected state; however, some of these methods (such as `getContentLength`) will force the `URLConnection` into the Connected state.

Connected	`getAllowUserInteraction`
	`getDefaultRequestProperty`
	`getInputStream`
	`getOutputStream`
	`getUseCaches`
	`getDefaultUseCaches`
	`getDefaultAllowUserInteraction`
	`getIfModifiedSince`
	`getDoInput`
	`getDoOutput`
	`getIfModifiedSince`
		The connection to the back-end server has been opened, so you can download or upload content and find out header information about the content. Note that many of the getFoo methods, such as `getUseCaches` and `getDoInput`, are also useful in the Initialized state because they don't require a connection in order to return useful information.

Idle	All methods applicable in the Connected state	In order to reach this state, the connection to the back-end server must be opened at least once. The connection might have been subsequently closed. Note that you may have problems with methods such as `getOutputStream` if the connection has already been closed.

All of the URLConnection document disposition methods obtain their information from the protocol handler itself (the object that handles the underlying protocol such as HTTP or FTP). In the case of HTTP, the URLConnection obtains its information by parsing the HTTP header. For reference, here's how the various disposition methods correspond to the various HTTP header fields:

Table 3-5 HTTP Header Fields Returned by `java.net.URLConnection` Methods

Method	HTTP Header Field
getContentLength	Content-Length
getContentType	Content-Type
getDate	Date
getExpiration	Expires
getLastModified	Last-Modified
getContentEncoding	Content-Encoding
getHeaderField("label")	arbitrary field "label"

Note that several of these methods only have applicability to the HTTP protocol. For instance, the getContentType method doesn't apply to the FTP protocol. This HTTP-centrism is perhaps unsurprising, since Java itself is Web-centric, and HTTP is the core protocol of the Web.

Implementing an Automatic Web Drone

Let's look at a practical use for the URLConnection class. In this section we'll implement a "Web Drone" that automatically downloads URLs at timed intervals. For instance, you could set up a Web Drone-based application that automatically downloads stock quotes, daily news, and other time-critical information at scheduled times, in batch mode.

Here are the basic requirements for this application:

- Needs to be able to provide a list of your favorite Web sites, and scheduled times at which to download documents.

- Needs to be able to store the downloaded Web content in a local file.

The ScheduledEvent Class

In order to implement the drone, we'll need a way to fire off actions at a scheduled time. In "The ScheduledEvent Class" beginning on page -305, we've detailed the implementation of a `ScheduledEvent` utility class that allows us to schedule transactions. Refer to that section if you want to learn about the implementation of this class in detail.

The SimpleWebDrone Class

The `SimpleWebDrone` will have at its core a method similar to the `loadURL` method we looked at previously. Around this we'll wrap a loop that iterates through a list of `ScheduledEvents` that represent scheduled web transactions, and executes those transactions at the appropriate time.

As part of this example, we're going to use a method of the `Object` class (from which `SimpleWebDrone` is subclassed) called `wait`. We'll explain this method in much greater detail in "Better Living through Threads" beginning on page -67, but briefly, this method provides us with a way to pause the operation of the main loop for a fixed period of time.

The source code for this is shown below.

Example 3-3 Implementation of SimpleWebDrone

```
package JNC;


import java.net.*;
import java.util.*;
import java.io.*;


/**
* a class that takes a list of URLs
* and  a list of ScheduledEvents
* and downloads those URLs at those times
*/
public class SimpleWebDrone
{

//list of URLs to load
protected URL[]    fSourcesList;
////list of times at which to load the URLs
protected ScheduledEvent[]fEventList;

protected boolean fContinueSlurp = true;
protected long fLastCheckupTime = 0;

/**
* Loop forever, downloading documents as appropriate
```

```
*/
public void run()
{
    while (fContinueSlurp) {
        //check scheduled transactions
        checkForExpiredTimers();
        //sleep for awhile
        try {
            //park here for 60 seconds...
            wait(60000);//we'll explain this in Threads chapter
        }
        catch (InterruptedException intEx) {};
    }
}//run


/**
 * Build a SimpleWebDrone
 * @param sourceList A list of URLs to slurp in
 * @param eventList A list of times at which to slurp in the URLs
 */
public  SimpleWebDrone(URL[] sourceList, ScheduledEvent[] eventList)
{
    fSourcesList = sourceList;
    fEventList = eventList;

}// SimpleWebDrone



/**
 * Run through the timer list...see if anything needs attention
 * This method iterates through the list of scheduled events,
 * checks for any transactions that need to be executed, and
 * launches a new URL handler to execute the transaction.
 */
protected void checkForExpiredTimers()
{
    long curTime = (new Date()).getTime();

    //run through the event list
    for (int evtIdx = 0; evtIdx < fEventList.length; evtIdx++)
    {
        ScheduledEvent curEvent = fEventList[evtIdx];
        long nextEventTime =
            curEvent.getNextOccurenceAfterRaw(fLastCheckupTime);

        if ( nextEventTime <= curTime) {
            //handle the transaction
            loadURL(fSourcesList[evtIdx],
                        "file" + evtIdx + ".html");
        }
    }

    fLastCheckupTime = curTime;
```

```
}//checkForExpiredTimers


/**
* The method that downloads the URL and stores it in a file.
* @param theURL The URL to load.
* @param outFileName The name of the file in
*    which to store the content.
*/
public static void loadURL(URL theURL, String outFileName)
{
    URLConnection theURLConnection;

    InputStream tempInputStream;
    int curByte;


    try {

        //first, get ahold of a URLConnection for the given URL object
        theURLConnection = theURL.openConnection();

        //open the connection, get data.
        //calls connect() implicitly
        tempInputStream = theURLConnection.getInputStream();

        try {
            //open output file
            FileOutputStream outstream =
                new FileOutputStream(outFileName );

            int curBytesRead = 0;
            byte[] copyBlock = new byte[1024];//for copying data

            try {
                while ((curBytesRead =
                        tempInputStream.read(copyBlock,0,1024)) != -1) {
                    outstream.write(copyBlock,0,curBytesRead);
                }
                outstream.close();//be nice
            }
            catch(IOException copyEx) {
            System.err.println("copyEx: " + copyEx);
            }
        }
        catch (Exception fileOpenEx) {
        System.err.println("fileOpenEx: " + fileOpenEx);
        }
    }
    catch (IOException retrieveEx) {
    System.err.println("retrieve ex: " + retrieveEx);
    }
}// loadURL
```

```
}// class SimpleWebDrone
```

Note that the `checkForExpiredTimers` method iterates through the list of `ScheduledEvents` and looks for events that need to be serviced. Once an "expired" event is found, the `loadURL` method is called to download the given URL.

New for JDK 1.1: `HttpURLConnection`

JDK 1.1 introduces a subclass of `URLConnection` that overcomes some of the obstacles to using URLConnection for real web work: the `HttpURLConnection` class.

Probably the biggest improvement in `HttpURLConnection` over `URLConnection` is that you can now specify the kind of HTTP transaction to be carried out. You are no longer stuck with just GET— you can use the GET, POST, PUT, HEAD, TRACE, DELETE, and OPTIONS HTTP/1.1 methods.

You can also control whether the `HttpURLConnection` will follow redirects by default. If you enable this feature, you do not have to implement redirection handling yourself. If you disable this feature, you can track exactly when the HTTP server tries to redirect.

The `HttpURLConnection` class provides a set of methods for controlling and monitoring an HTTP transaction. These methods are described below.

Table 3-6 Commonly Used **HttpURLConnection** Methods

Method	Description
`disconnect()`	Explicitly close the connection opened to the server by `connect`.
`boolean getFollowRedirects()`	Indicates whether the HttpURLConnection will follow server redirects (HTTP response code 302) automatically.
`String getRequestMethod()`	Get the request method. Will be one of: "GET", "POST", "HEAD", "PUT", "OPTIONS", "DELETE", "TRACE".
`int getResponseCode()`	Gets HTTP numeric response code, e.g., 200 for "OK".

65

Table 3-6 Commonly Used **HttpURLConnection** Methods (Continued)

Method	Description
String getResponseMessage()	Gets the HTTP response message, if any, returned along with the response code from a server. This is typically a text message that follows the numeric response code from the server (e.g., "OK" from "HTTP/1.0 200 OK")
setFollowRedirects(boolean)	Sets whether HTTP redirects (requests with response code 3xx) should be automatically followed by this class. False by default. Applets cannot change this value.
setRequestMethod(String)	Set the method for the URL request. Method can be one of: "GET", "POST", "HEAD", "PUT", "OPTIONS", "DELETE", "TRACE". See HTTP protocol for details.
boolean usingProxy()	Indicates if the connection is going through an HTTP proxy.

HttpURLConnection class also provides for better handling of HTTP-specific errors and results codes. It provides an extensive list of error constants that can be used to match specific error conditions. After a transaction has been completed, your code can call the getResponseCode method to determine which response code was returned by the server and respond accordingly.

Summary

The URL and URLConnection classes provide a good high-level interface to Internet protocols and content. These classes do not provide a great deal of control over how transactions are carried out, and they are not currently friendly to two-way communications; that is, they currently don't deal well with sending data from the Java client to an Internet server via a protocol handler. However, this seems to be a limitation of the current implementation; the APIs, although not optimal, seem to provide the capability for submitting data to a web server.

The new HttpURLConnection available under JDK 1.1 provides more explicit control over retrieving and sending information via HTTP. Given that Java is designed to be Web centric, this is a tremendous improvement.

CHAPTER
4

- Introduction to Threads

- Multithreaded Web Content Retriever

- Using `object`'s Synchronization Controls

- ThreadGroups

Better Living through Threads

T hreads are one of the biggest advantages Java provides for dealing with communications and networking. If you're already familiar with how Java threads work, you might want to read this chapter to become familiar with how Java threads can be applied to communications and networking. If you've never really used Java threads before, this chapter will serve as an introduction to Java threads.

Threads and Multithreading: The Basic Idea

If you've never used threads or worked with multithreaded systems before, you need to learn just a few concepts in order to start working with Java threads.

All Code Is Part of a Thread

First, you need to grasp the fact that every line of Java code you write is part of a thread of execution. As your code executes, it is bathed in an execution environment that includes things like local and global variables, the stack, and so on. At any given time, the state of your code could be described completely by the execution environment plus the current program counter (the current instruction being executed). This is the basic concept of a thread: It's just the sum of your executing code and the execution environment it carries with it.

Multithreading Means Simultaneous Execution

Now, some operating systems such as Unix provide for multithreading. To the end user this means that several programs can be executed simultaneously. What this really means at the operating system level is that the OS provides a facility for sharing the CPU between several different threads. Each thread is executed on the CPU for a little while; then the thread is paused; all of its relevant execution environment information is saved; and another paused thread is loaded onto to the CPU to execute. To the executing thread, none of this pausing and swapping is apparent: The program simply executes as if it were the only thread running on the CPU. This kind of multithreading (or more accurately "multitasking") is referred to as "preemptive" because threads are preempted by the OS in order to swap other threads onto the CPU.

The Java runtime provides this same thread time-sharing facility for all Java code. Even under operating systems such as MacOS that do not provide true preemptive multitasking, the Java runtime environment provides the capability for several Java threads to be run simultaneously. Each Java thread is given a time-slice in which to run.

A Java Program Can Be Multithreaded

So far we've just talked about single-threaded programs that operate in a multithreaded environment. However, sometimes it'd be nice if you could launch, from inside your current thread, another thread that could carry out a separate but related task in parallel to your current thread. That is, it would be nice if you could create your own threads. For instance, you might want another thread to read data from an `InputStream` while your main thread is busy sending data on an `OutputStream`. Or you might want one thread to draw a "Please Wait" animation on the screen while your main thread calculates Pi to ten billion digits.

Fortunately, the Java thread API provides a way for your main thread to launch additional threads, as we'll see in a bit.

Why Use Threads for Communications?

If you haven't written much communications code before, it might not be immediately clear to you why threads would be useful for communications. To understand the fundamental reason, you need to understand the difference between synchronous and asynchronous communications programming.

Typically when you're communicating with a remote system, there are some time lags between when you start listening for data on an input port and when data starts arriving. This means that there will be a lag between when you activate serial port hardware, input buffers, and the like and when data actually starts arriving via that hardware at the input buffers.

There are two ways to deal with this lag from a software perspective. You can synchronously loop waiting for the data to arrive. That is, the CPU continuously polls the input buffers until the data arrives or some time-out condition occurs. Here's a pseudocode outline of how you could receive data synchronously:

```
byte receiveData()
{
    while (!System.dataAvailable()) {
        //keep checking
    }
    //return the byte so you can do something with it
    return System.readByte();
}
```

The alternative is that you can set up some kind of asynchronous callback mechanism. With this technique, you create some function to be called when data has been received, hand it off to the OS, and wait for it to be called. Here's a pseudocode outline of how you receive data asynchronously. Let's say the OS supports an interface called `ReceiveCallbackable` that implements a single method:

```
public interface ReceiveCallbackable
{
    public abstract receiveCallback(byte recvdByte);
}
```

You would then implement a class with methods such as the following:

```
byte setupReceiveCallback()
{
    //tell the OS we want to be notified as soon as
    //some data is received
    System.setReceiveCallback(this);
}

receiveCallback(byte recvdByte)
{
    //do something with the received byte
}
```

Now, the synchronous method is convenient because you simply make one synchronous call to check the input buffers, and you know that when the call returns, you've received some data or encountered an error condition. However, synchronous methods aren't very efficient. You lock up most of the CPU by sitting in a tight loop, polling the input buffers, while waiting for them to fill up.

The asynchronous method, on the other hand, is much more efficient. Typically, you register with some kind of OS service that monitors the status of the input buffers using interrupts, and once the status changes, your code is notified. Your application needn't sit in a tight polling loop. However, asynchronous callbacks are programmatically inconvenient. For every asynchronous call you make, you need to set up an asynchronous callback function to deal with the callback.

Threads are a great boon to communications code because they combine the convenience of synchronous programming with the efficiency of asynchronous programming. Basically, you can create a separate thread that deals only with communications. Whenever the communications thread blocks in a tight loop waiting for input or output status to change, it's ok; the fact that the synchronous call is wrapped in a thread means that the system will give time to other threads in the system. Just because your communications thread is blocked doesn't mean the entire system comes to a halt.

Here's a quick rundown of some of the additional advantages of using threads with communications:

- In a sophisticated communications application, you might have one thread managing communications, another thread handling screen drawing, another collecting user input, and yet another thread dealing with file I/O.

- Threads make it easier to create multiple simultaneous communications sessions; you simply create a new thread each time you create a new session manager. The multithreaded Java environment will help to guarantee (to some extent) that each session has sufficient resources to execute. Threads also make it safer to synchronize these separate sessions with each other.

- Java threads can potentially execute on separate processors (such as under Solaris or Windows NT running on a multiprocessor platform), potentially resulting in much faster execution. For communications this means your serial communications thread might be handled by one processor, and your screen drawing thread by a completely separate processor. Thus the thread interface allows your code to take advantage of all available resources.

- You can potentially solve certain kinds of problems faster (problems which involve tasks that can be run concurrently) using concurrent threads. Examples of such problems include raytracing (image rendering), digital signal processing (sound filtering), and some scientific simulations.

- By the same token, you can handle certain applications in a manner that *appears* to be faster than if you performed all of the required operations sequentially. For instance, when downloading and parsing an HTML document in a Web browser, you could download data, parse it, and display it as the data arrives. To the user this might appear "faster" than if you downloaded all of the data, parsed it all, then displayed it all in sequence.

- Java threads provide a means to synchronize tasks that may run at different speeds. This helps prevent "race conditions" that are common in time-sensitive communications code.

Let's look at the core Java class used to implement threading— the `java.lang.Thread` class.

The Thread Class

The Java `Thread` class provides an interface to code execution that is similar to the interface of an audiocassette tape or compact disc player. It has a *Play* button, a *Pause* button, and a *Stop* button. But since code can only execute in one "direction," and only one-instruction-at-a-time, the `Thread` class can't provide a *Rewind* button or *Fast-Forward* button. A `Thread` executes a series of instructions in sequence and can be paused, resumed, and stopped at any time.

Start/Run   Suspend/Resume   Stop

Figure 4–1 The Thread Interface.

The Java `Thread` class has a straightforward start/run/suspend/resume/stop interface. In order for a `Thread` to start running, you need call its `start` method. While the `Thread` is running, the code placed inside its `run` method executes. If the code in the `run` method finishes and returns, the `Thread` is finished executing and will wait to be garbage-collected. While the `run` method is executing, you can call the `Thread`'s suspend method to *pause* the `Thread`'s execution. This causes the `Thread` to remember its current state and wait for `resume` to be called. When you call `Thread.resume`, the `Thread` continues executing from exactly the point in the `run` method where it was paused. To completely stop a `Thread` from executing, call the `Thread`'s `stop` method.

Here's a detailed review of each of the `Thread` methods:

start

This method starts the thread executing. Note that there is no guarantee as to when the `run` method will be called after you call the `start` method. That is, you can't count on a minimum or maximum time until the thread is run for the first time after it is started. Generally, however, this delay is at most a few milliseconds after the `start` method returns.

run

This method is where the body of the code to be executed by the `Thread` in a `Thread` subclass or a `Runnable` class is placed. When this method returns, the thread is finished. Thus, you typically place a loop or a lengthy operation within this method. For instance, you might have a `while(true)` loop, or you might call some synchronous communications methods that take a long time to complete.

sleep

Pause the thread for a finite length of time. Note that depending on the platform, this length of time might not be absolutely guaranteed— this is guaranteed to be the minimum time the thread will sleep. It may sleep a bit longer depending on the system overhead of swapping threads, the current load on the system, et cetera.

suspend

Pause execution of the thread. This allows you to pause the thread at the current instruction and later resume it at the same point. This might be useful if you have a thread that needs to block on a certain condition; however, you might find it easier to use the `Object.wait` and `Object.notify` methods we will discuss later in this chapter.

resume

Resume execution after a `suspend`. This allows you to resume `Thread` execution at the same point where the `Thread` was paused. This might be useful if you have a thread that needs to block on a certain condition; however, you might find it easier to use the `Object.wait` and `Object.notify` methods to be delved into later in this chapter.

yield

Allow any other threads of the same priority to execute. This is a nice procedure if you know your thread will be idling for an unspecified length of time. Note that technically this method is guaranteed to give up time to threads of equal or greater priority, not to threads of lesser priority. So, to be kind to threads of all priorities, you might want to use `sleep` instead.

stop

Stops the thread. It doesn't matter where in the `run` method the `Thread` is— it's stopped cold. You could be in the middle of a `while` loop, and it'll stop executing at the current instruction. Note that there is no guarantee as to when the `Thread` will be stopped after this method is first called, nor a guarantee as to where the `Thread` will stop. The only thing guaranteed is that when this method returns, the thread will have been stopped.

join

This method sits around waiting for a `Thread` to die. There are several different versions of this method, but all basically wait synchronously for the `Thread` to become inactive. This is mainly useful in that allows different threads a chance to coordinate their activities. Thread A can call this method in Thread B; this causes Thread A to block until Thread B has completed; Thread A can then continue.

Two Ways to Thread

With the existing Java thread API there are two ways to achieve threaded behavior using the `Thread` class:

- You can subclass `Thread`, and override the `run` method.

- You can create a class that implements the `java.lang.Runnable` interface, and use a `Thread` object to "drive" that class.

Either of these methods will provide the threaded behavior we talked about earlier. Let's look at both of these techniques in detail.

Subclassing Thread

Subclassing `Thread` is fairly straightforward; you simply create a class that extends `Thread` and implements a `run` method, as shown below.

Example 4-1 Creating and Using a Thread Subclass

```
public class SubThread extends Thread
{
    public void run()
    {
        //do something lengthy/complicated
```

```
            //when this method returns, the thread dies
    }
}
SubThread theSubThread = new SubThread();
theSubThread.start();
```

The SubThread class need only implement a single method: run. Inside the run method, the SubThread class should perform whatever lengthy or blocking operation it needs to perform asynchronously. For instance, it might read some data from a stream in its run method. The Java runtime will make sure that even though the code inside the run method might consume a great deal of computing resources, other tasks are given their fair share of time.

Implementing the Runnable Interface

Subclassing Thread is fairly easy and convenient; however, what happens if we really need to create a subclass of some other class (such as Frame or InputStream), and we want that class to have Thread-like behavior? In this case we can't subclass both Frame and Thread, so Java provides a Runnable interface. A class can both subclass Frame and implement the Runnable interface.

Implementing the Runnable interface is almost as easy as subclassing Thread, as shown in the example below.

Example 4-2 Implementing and Using the Runnable Interface

```
public class MyRunnable extends Frame implements Runnable
{
    public void run()
    {
        //do something lengthy/complicated
    }
}
MyRunnable theRunnable = new MyRunnable();
Thread newThread = new Thread(theRunnable);
newThread.start(); //kickstart theRunnable
```

The MyRunnable class implements the Runnable interface simply by implementing the run method. So far, implementing Runnable is as easy as subclassing Thread. However, in order to kickstart and drive the MyRunnable object in a thread-like manner, we need a "driver" Thread that will drive the Runnable's run method.

Thus we create a new Thread instance and pass the Runnable object to that Thread's constructor. This makes the Runnable object the Thread's target, so that the Thread will drive the Runnable's run method.

Using Thread's Static Methods to Operate on Any Code

Now that we know how to create subclasses of `Thread` as well as `Runnable` classes, let's look at some utility methods of `Thread` that can be used from within any code.

The Thread class provides a set of static methods. At first, this doesn't make any sense; why provide static methods for an object that is really only useful instantiated or subclassed? The answer is that the static `Thread` methods operate on the currently running thread.

The currently running thread in Java is, at any time, simply the current set of instructions being executed. Since every chunk of Java code is part of a thread, you don't need to explicitly create a `Thread` subclass or a `Runnable` object to have your code executed in a `Thread`. The fact is that all of your code executes in a `Thread` that is suspendable, resumable, stoppable, and so on.

Now how useful is it to obtain the current thread? First of all it's useful if you want obtain a reference to the current thread and provide it to other threads. This can allow the current thread to be manipulated by another thread at some future time. You can provide another `Thread` with a reference to your thread by using the static `Thread.currentThread` method.

Obtaining the current thread is also useful if you wish to `sleep` the current thread or yield time to other threads. This can be useful if you simply want to give up time to other threads while you're executing in a tight loop. .

There is obviously some danger to manipulating the current thread. For instance, if you call `Thread.currentThread().suspend()`, your program parks forever. Similarly, if you call `Thread.currentThread().stop()`, your program stops executing altogether. This is generally a bad idea, and the results vary from platform to platform.

Here's a summary of the static `Thread` class methods:

Table 4-1 Handy `java.lang.Thread` **Static Class Methods**

Method	Description
`currentThread`	Returns a `Thread` reference to the currently-executing thread (the thread that calls this method).
`dumpStack`	Debugging method that dumps a list of the current thread's execution stack in Exception-like manner to System.err (stderr).
`sleep`	You can call `sleep` anywhere in your code and the currently executing thread will be paused.
`yield`	You can call `yield` anywhere in your code to give up processor time to other equal or greater priority tasks.
`activeCount`	Get the total number of threads currently active in the Java interpreter.
`int enumerate(Thread[])`	This method stuffs a `Thread` array full of all of the currently active threads. Note that you need to call `activeCount` first to determine what the minimum size of the `Thread` array should be.

Thread Priorities

Java provides a priority scheme for threads. Threads with higher priority are supposed to be run more often or be given a bigger CPU time-slice than lower-priority threads.

Typically, there are only three thread priorities you should be concerned with; `Thread.MAX_PRIORITY` is the absolute maximum priority a Java thread can have. Similarly, `Thread.MIN_PRIORITY` is the minimum priority a thread can have without being a daemon thread. A daemon thread has absolutely the lowest priority and runs only when all other threads are blocked or sleeping. The Java interpreter exits automatically as soon as there are only daemon threads running. Daemon threads are perfect for "watchdog" tasks and other low-priority service tasks.

You can set the priority of a `Thread` using the `setPriority` method. This might be useful if you have several threads and you know which thread should be given priority over another. It might also be useful if your thread needs to run faster or slower under certain conditions. For instance, a thread that polls while waiting for the user to type some input, might idle at a fairly low priority, then increase in priority as the user types in information and that information needs to be processed.

Note that because implementations of the Java thread libraries vary so greatly from platform to platform, you should be careful not to rely upon the behavior exhibited by a single platform. You should be sure to test your thread-dependent code on multiple platforms to make sure it behaves as you expect.

A Multithreaded URLConnection Client

Let's now take our `SimpleWebDrone` example and improve it using threads.

One of the biggest limitations of the original `SimpleWebDrone` is that it downloads only a single document at a time. Let's now pull out the core document download code and place it into a separate helper class called `URLDownloadSlave`. This class is a subclass of `Thread` with only one purpose: to call the `MLoadURL` method.

The next limitation is that the `SimpleWebDrone` class itself runs in the same thread as the application's main thread. On platforms such as MacOS that don't provide preemptive multitasking, this can cause problems for the user. So let's make the `SimpleWebDrone` class itself a subclass of `Thread`.

The source for the improved `WebDrone` class and the `URLDownloadSlave` class is shown below.

Example 4-3 **Multithreaded WebDrone Downloads Several Web Pages Simultaneously**

```
package JNC;


import java.net.*;
import java.util.*;
import java.io.*;


/**
 * a class that takes a list of URLs and a list of ScheduledEvents
 *  and downloads those URLs at those times
 */
public class WebDrone extends Thread
{

protected URL[]    fSourcesList;//list of sources to load
protected ScheduledEvent[]fEventList;//list of times at which to load

protected boolean fContinueSlurp = true;
protected long fLastCheckupTime = 0;
```

```
/**
 * Loop forever, downloading documents as appropriate
 */
public void run()
{
    while (fContinueSlurp) {
        checkForExpiredTimers();
        try {sleep(60000);} catch (InterruptedException intEx) {};
    }
}//run

/**
 * Build a WebDrone
 * @param sourceList List  of URLs to slurp in
 * @param eventList List of times at which to slurp in the URLs
 */
public  WebDrone(URL[] sourceList, ScheduledEvent[] eventList)
{
    fSourcesList = sourceList;
    fEventList = eventList;

}/* WebDrone */


/**
 * Run through the timer list...see if anything needs attention
 */
protected void checkForExpiredTimers()
{
    long curTime = (new Date()).getTime();

    //run through the event list
    for (int evtIdx = 0; evtIdx < fEventList.length; evtIdx++)
    {
        ScheduledEvent curEvent = fEventList[evtIdx];
        long nextEventTime =
            curEvent.getNextOccurenceAfterRaw(fLastCheckupTime);

        if ( nextEventTime <= curTime) {
            handleDocumentTransaction(fSourcesList[evtIdx],
                                        "file" + evtIdx + ".html");
        }


    }

    fLastCheckupTime = curTime;
}//checkForExpiredTimers


/**
 * Handle the Web transaction
```

```
*/
public void handleDocumentTransaction(URL targetURL, String fileName)
{
    //create a new download slave to deal with getting this document
    URLDownloadSlave newSlave =
        new URLDownloadSlave(targetURL, fileName);
    //we should really keep a list of slaves so they don't get
    //gc'd too soon
}//handleDocumentTransaction

}/* class WebDrone */


/**
* Class that implements downloading of a  URL
*/
class URLDownloadSlave extends Thread
{
URL fTargetURL = null;
String fTargetFilename = null;

/**
* @param theURL The URL to download
* @param filename the filename to use to store the result.
*/
public URLDownloadSlave(URL theURL, String filename)
{
    fTargetURL = theURL;
    fTargetFilename = filename;
    this.start();
}//URLDownloadSlave

/**
* our asynchonrous run method
*/
public void run()
{
    loadURL(fTargetURL, fTargetFilename);
}//run

/**
* The main method wihich downloads the URL and stores it in a file.
* @param theURL The URL to load.
* @param outFileName The name of the file in
*    which to store the content.
*/
public static void loadURL(URL theURL, String outFileName)
{
    URLConnection theURLConnection;

    InputStream tempInputStream;
    int curByte;
```

```
try {

    //first, get a URLConnection for the given URL object
    theURLConnection = theURL.openConnection();

    //open the connection, get data.
    //cals connect() implicitly
    tempInputStream = theURLConnection.getInputStream();

    try {
        //open output file
        FileOutputStream outstream =
            new FileOutputStream(outFileName );

        int curBytesRead = 0;
        byte[] copyBlock = new byte[1024];

        try {
            while ((curBytesRead =
                    tempInputStream.read(copyBlock,0,1024)) != -1) {
                outstream.write(copyBlock,0,curBytesRead);
            }
            outstream.close();//be nice
        }
        catch(IOException copyEx) {
        System.err.println("copyEx: " + copyEx);
        }
    }
    catch (Exception fileOpenEx) {
    System.err.println("fileOpenEx: " + fileOpenEx);
    }
}
catch (IOException retrieveEx) {
System.err.println("retrieve ex: " + retrieveEx);
}


}/* loadURL */


} /* class URLDownloadSlave */
```

In this example, a new URLDownloadSlave is created every time one of the ScheduledEvents is reached. Each URLDownloadSlave runs in its own thread. Thus, we could have several URLDownloadSlave running simultaneously.

Now that we've seen how to create multiple simultaneously-executing threads, let's look at how you might tie these threads together.

ThreadGroups

Often in a complicated application you'll want to tie several thread-based operations together and start/pause/resume/stop them based on user actions. For instance, searching a database might involve several threads that read data from a file, sort the data, and display record overviews to the user. If, while your code is searching the database, the user finds the record she needs and hits the application's *Stop* button, your code needs to quickly stop several threads in progress.

Java provides a class for grouping threads in just this manner: the `ThreadGroup` class. It turns out that every `Thread` is actually part of a `ThreadGroup`. Normally any `Threads` you create are simply part of the same `ThreadGroup` as your application's main thread. However, you can explicitly create your own `ThreadGroups` and place new threads inside of them.

`ThreadGroup` provides a single point-of-contact interface to multiple threads. By calling a `ThreadGroup`'s `suspend` and `resume` methods, for instance, you can suspend and resume a bunch of threads at the same time. `ThreadGroup` provides an interface similar to Thread, but it doesn't provide all the same functionality. For instance, there is no `ThreadGroup.start` method. This means you have to start each member `Thread` running either before or after you insert it into the `ThreadGroup`. Also, there is no equivalent of `Thread.sleep`; thus you can't pause an entire `ThreadGroup` for a certain length of time, unless you do some fancy footwork with `suspend` and `resume`. Also, you can't `yield` the entire `ThreadGroup`, `join` it, or set the specific priority of all member threads at the same time. However, you can set the maximum priority that the group as a whole is allowed to have. You can also make the entire group a daemon. This is handy if you want to make a bunch of threads daemons.

Placing a Thread in a ThreadGroup

You can set the `ThreadGroup` of a `Thread` at constructor time only, thus you have to create or obtain a `ThreadGroup` prior to assigning threads to it.

Listing Threads in a ThreadGroup

The `ThreadGroup.list` method can be used to print a list all of the `Thread` members of a given `ThreadGroup` to stdout. This can be useful for debugging. Similarly, `ThreadGroup.activeCount` returns the total number of `Threads` that fall under a `ThreadGroup`'s "umbrella." This includes all `Threads` owned by subgroups under the `ThreadGroup`. However, when you call `ThreadGroup.enumerate`, you get a list of only the immediate `Threads` owned by the `ThreadGroup`, unless you specify the `recursive` parameter as true.

Using ThreadGroups to Control Groups of Threads

Let's look at an example of how you might use ThreadGroups in a communicating application. Let's say you were downloading a bunch of related data using the URLConnection example above, but that you wanted to stop the download immediately. This gets a bit complicated if you have to stop all of the threads one by one. You may also have some complicated timing issues and race conditions if two threads aren't killed at exactly the same time. For instance, there may be a source thread and a sink thread, where the source may push data to the sink, or the sink could pull data from the source. If one of these threads is killed before the other, there could be disastrous results.

Here we'll expand upon the multithreaded client we talked about above by embedding all of the transaction threads into a single ThreadGroup. Then, if the user decides she wishes to stop all of the threads related to a transaction at the same time, then we can simply kill the main ThreadGroup, thus killing all of the embedded threads.

We're going to make a couple of simple changes to the WebDrone class and the URLDownloadSlave class. First, we're going to modify the WebDrone class so that it has methods for pausing, resuming, and stopping all the URLDownloadSlaves from running. The modified WebDroneGroup sources are shown below.

Example 4-4 Placing WebDrones in a ThreadGroup

```
public class WebDroneGroup extends WebDrone
{

protected ThreadGroup fDroneGroup =null;

/**
* stop all of the current URLDownloadSlaves...
*/
public void stopAllDownloads()
{
    fDroneGroup.stop(); //should kill all download slaves
}

/**
* pause all downloads
*/
public void pauseAllDownloads()
{
    fDroneGroup.suspend();
}

/**
```

```
 * resume all downloads
 */
public void resumeAllDownloads()
{
    fDroneGroup.resume();
}


/**
 * Build a WebDrone
 * @param sourceList List of URLs to slurp in
 * @param eventList List of times at which to slurp in the URLs
 */
public  WebDroneGroup(URL[] sourceList, ScheduledEvent[] eventList)
{
    super(sourceList,eventList);
    fDroneGroup = new ThreadGroup("DroneGruppe");

}/* WebDroneGroup */


/**
 * Run through the timer list...see if anything needs attention
 * This method iterates through the list of scheduled events,
 * checks for any transactions that need to be executed, and
 * launches a new URL handler to execute the transaction.
 */
protected void checkForExpiredTimers()
{
    long curTime = (new Date()).getTime();

    //run through the event list
    for (int evtIdx = 0; evtIdx < fEventList.length; evtIdx++)
    {
        ScheduledEvent curEvent = fEventList[evtIdx];
        long nextEventTime =
            curEvent.getNextOccurenceAfterRaw(fLastCheckupTime);

        if ( nextEventTime <= curTime) {
            //build a new URLDownloadSlave to handle the transaction
            URLDownloadSlave newSlave =
                new URLDownloadSlave(fSourcesList[evtIdx],
                                     "file" + evtIdx + ".html",
                                     fDroneGroup);
        //since the slave is ref'd by the group,
        //it won't get gc'd
        }

    }

    fLastCheckupTime = curTime;
}//checkForExpiredTimers

}/* class WebDroneGroup */
```

Notice that we simply add all of the URLDownloadSlaves to the same fDroneGroup ThreadGroup. This allows us to pause, resume, and stop all the URLDownloadSlaves at the same time.

We need now to modify the URLDownloadSlave class so that it can deal with being part of a ThreadGroup. We only need to modify the class constructor so that the class adds itself to the ThreadGroup. The modified constructor is shown below.

Example 4-5 Adding ThreadGroup Support to URLDownloadSlave

```
/**
* @param theURL The URL to load.
* @param filename The name of the file in which to store the downloaded
content.
*/
public URLDownloadSlave(URL theURL, String filename, ThreadGroup
parentGroup)
{
    super(parentGroup);//add ourselves to the correct ThreadGroup
    fTargetURL = theURL;
    fTargetFilename = filename;
    this.start();
}
```

Notice that we added a parameter to the URLDownloadSlave's constructor. This parameter provides the URLDownloadSlave with a parent ThreadGroup with which the URLDownloadSlave thread should associate itself.

See the WebDroneGroupTest.java file on the sample code disk to see an example of how to test the behavior of WebDroneGroup's pauseAllDownloads, resumeAllDownloads, and stopAllDownloads methods.

Synchronizing Threads and Sharing Objects Between Threads

Now that we've explored the basics of threads, there is a critical issue we need to explore: synchronization. This issue arises because there are two things you want to share between threads, code and data, and you want to share these things smoothly. With code, you sometimes want to make sure that only one thread at a time is allowed to execute a given method. With data, you sometimes want to make sure that only one thread at a time is allowed to read/write a given variable. What you really want to do in both cases is *synchronize* access to variables and methods so that only one thread is given access at a time.

Fortunately, the Java language and the base `java.lang.Object` class have some features that make thread synchronization easy. The Java language itself has the `synchronized` keyword, which allows you to mark a given method or a given block of code within a method as being mutually exclusive— only one thread can execute the method or code block at a time. The `java.lang.Object` class has two methods, `wait` and `notify`, which make it easy to share objects between threads. Each class that descends from `Object` inherits these methods.

Calling an object's `wait` method blocks the current thread on that object's state. Basically, calling `wait` on an object sets up a "monitor" in the Java interpreter that monitors the object's state. As soon as the object's state changes (typically as a result of the object's `notify` method being called), the monitor is released and the current thread returns from the `wait` call. Calling an object's `notify` method notifies one monitor blocking on that object (from calling `wait`). Calling an object's `notifyAll` method notifies all monitors blocked on the object. Typically you will not need to use `notifyAll`.

Below is an example that uses `wait`/`notify` and `synchronized` to smoothly swap strings between two objects.

Example 4-6 Two Threads Use Wait and Notify to Communicate

```
/**
 * An example of how wait/notify work.
 */
public class StringSwapper extends Thread
{
public int fID = 0;
protected String fPrivateString = null;
protected StringSwapper fSwapTarget = null;

public StringSwapper(String startString)
{
    fPrivateString = startString;
}

public void setTarget(StringSwapper target)
{
    fSwapTarget = target;
}

public synchronized void setString(String newString)
{
    //set the string as soon as it's null
    while (fPrivateString != null) {
        try {wait();} catch (InterruptedException intEx) {};
    }

    fPrivateString = newString;
```

```
        notify();//let any monitors know we're finished setting
}

public synchronized String getString()
{
    //get the string as soon as it's non-null
    while (fPrivateString == null) {
        try {wait();} catch (InterruptedException intEx) {};
    }

    String tempString = fPrivateString;
    fPrivateString = null;
    notify();//let any monitors know we're finished getting
    return tempString;
}


/**
 * swap strings with our target many times
 */
public void run()
{
    String holder;
    for(int count = 0; count < 100; count++) {
        holder = fSwapTarget.getString();
        System.out.println("object " + fSwapTarget.fID +
                           " had: " + holder);
        this.setString(holder);
    }
}

}/* class StringSwapper */


/**
 * A class that tests the StringSwapper
 */
class StringSwapperTest
{
    public static void main(String[] args)
    {
        StringSwapper a,b;
        a = new StringSwapper("cheezeball");
        b = new StringSwapper("cornpuff");
        a.fID = 1;
        b.fID = 2;
        a.setTarget(b);
        b.setTarget(a);
        a.start();
        b.start();
    }
}//class StringSwapperTest
```

Using Wait to Achieve an Interruptible Delay

We've already learned that you can use the
`Thread.currentThread().sleep(100)` technique to achieve a delay in the
current thread. But let's say your need is more like this: You need to delay for
some length of time, or until another thread wakes you up. Achieving this effect is
simple with the `Object.wait` method. Simply call your object's `wait` method
with the maximum delay that you want, then be prepared to catch the
InterruptedException like so:

```
boolean wasInterrupted = false;
try {
    this.wait(10000);
}
catch (InterruptedException intEx) {
    wasInterrupted = true;
}
System.out.println(wasInterrupted? "interrupted!": "wait completed");
```

Note that this timed `wait` will only throw the `InterruptedException` if
another thread comes along and calls the object's `notify` method.

Below is a summary of the `java.lang.Object` synchronization methods.

Table 4-2 Key `java.lang.Object` **Class Synchronization Methods**

Method	Description
wait()	Block on the current object until someone else calls `notify`.
wait(timeout)	This version of `wait` waits around for a certain period, instead of "forever."
notify	Tell the first monitor waiting on this object to stop waiting.
notifyAll	Tell all monitors waiting on this object to stop waiting.

Using Synchronization to Make Code Thread-Safe

As you might imagine, you need to take precautions to make your code thread-safe. The easiest way to do this is to make sure that you synchronize the code
blocks and objects that could possibly interfere with each other. For instance, if
you have a thread that writes objects into an array, and a method that pulls objects
from the same array, make sure that you use the array's `wait` and `notify`
methods to synchronize access to the array.

Another issue you may need to deal with is method reentry. If you have several
threads accessing the same object's methods, the same method may be called
while it is already executing— that is, one thread might be executing a method,
and then be preempted by another thread that then executes the same method. If

the method can't deal with this case appropriately, then you should make the method `synchronized`. This will prevent two threads from executing the same method simultaneously.

Summary

The Java language and the Java class libraries provide a variety of useful interfaces for creating and managing threads. Java threads can be used to make communications and networking easier since you can place communications code in a thread apart from other application threads. In the chapters that follow we will use threads extensively in our example applications.

CHAPTER
5

Networking with Sockets

The `java.net` class library provides some of the key components of the Java technology. This chapter explores networking with Java using the various Java-provided reliable stream socket classes. The chapter begins with a brief review of Internet standards, then delves into using sockets for TCP networking.

Network Clients versus Network Servers

Before we jump into using Sockets for networking, let's briefly review the basics of networking. Let's start with definitions of the terms Client and Server.

Network Client

A network client actively forms a connection to a computer, printer, and so forth on the network. Clients typically, but not always, have a dynamic network address, connect to and disconnect from the network frequently, and might not have a domain name (i.e., "`www.rawthought.com`") associated with their network address. A client connects to services provided by servers on the network.

Network Server

A network server waits around for a client to connect to it and request services. A server does not actively seek to open a connection to remote network hosts; instead, it waits for connection requests to arrive from clients. A server typically, but not always, has a static network address, is connected to the network continuously, and has a domain name associated with its network address. A server provides services to clients that connect to it over a network.

Internet Networking Review

In order to understand how Java networking behaves, you really have to understand the infrastructure of the Internet. If you already understand Internet concepts such as TCP, UDP, DNS, and IP addresses, you could probably skip this section. Otherwise, this section should provide a good review of how the Internet works.

IP: The Internet Protocol

The Internet Protocol standard consists of a packet format definition and a rough description of how packets are to be routed between hosts on a network. The packet format definition includes things such as source and destination address, time-to-live, et cetera.

IP also provides a specification of network addresses.

Internet Addressing

IP defines a network host address as a unique 32-bit number, known as an "IP Address." Various bits within the 32-bit number have certain specific meanings, and not all IP networks directly connected to the Internet. Suffice it to say, however, that if your computer is attached directly to the Internet, it has a unique 32-bit address associated with it that other computers can use to communicate with it.

On Solaris you can view your IP address by issuing the `ifconfig -a` command. On a Mac using MacTCP you can view the IP address info by going into the MacTCP control panel (or the "TCP/IP" control panel in case of OpenTransport). With Windows/95, you can look in your "Network" control panel.

A typical IP address is listed as four "octets" of eight bits using "dotted decimal notation"— as an example: `165.227.67.1`. Each dot-separated number represents eight bits of the machine's address.

Addresses versus Ports

IP also includes the concept of a host port. A port is a 16-bit number associated with a given IP address. This number is used to label a specific entity on the host specified by the 32-bit IP address. Thus, to completely specify where an IP packet should be sent, you need to specify not only the 32-bit IP address but also the 16-bit port number.

Typically, port numbers below 100 are reserved for "well-known services" such as DNS, FTP, HTTP, SMTP, POP, TFTP, and so on. These services have well-defined default port numbers associated with them, though some can deal with having the default changed to some other port number. For instance, HTTP defaults to port 80, but an arbitrary port number can be included in an HTTP URL.

UDP: The Unreliable Datagram Protocol

UDP is a simple connectionless datagram protocol layered immediately above IP. This protocol is used by Internet infrastructure protocols such as DNS, BootP, and SNMP. We will be discussing UDP in much greater detail in "Datagrams A-Go-Go" beginning on page 157.

TCP: The Transmission Control Protocol

TCP is a reliable, connection-oriented stream protocol that utilizes IP to carry packets of data. TCP sets up a connection, exchanges IP packets, and disconnects. TCP guarantees that packets are sent as a reliable stream; that is, packet delivery is guaranteed and the order in which the packets are sent is guaranteed to be the order in which they are delivered. TCP provides error handling and retransmission facilities in order to enforce these guarantees.

DNS: Domain Name Service

DNS provides for the translation of network host names (i.e., "www.rawthought.com") into IP addresses (165.227.67.1). We'll discuss DNS in much greater detail in "Datagrams A-Go-Go".

The Effect of Firewalls

Not every computer that utilizes IP is in fact directly connected to the Internet. Many IP subnets are isolated from the main Internet by a firewall. What this typically means is that, while the firewall host can see the entire Internet and the entire subnet, the subnet and the Internet cannot see each other. They are essentially on separate networks, and the firewall host controls how much access each has to the other. You can't, for instance, place your Web server behind a firewall, because no host outside your subnet will be able to connect to it. The Web server would have no interface to the external network in order to accept incoming connections. However, you can typically carry out all network client activities from inside the firewall, since the firewall will route connections from the inside to the external network correctly.

Internet Summary

So here's the quick summary of how the Internet works: Certain network hosts known as servers listen on their IP address and a certain port for other network hosts known as clients to send them IP packets. Network clients generally find the

IP address of network servers using DNS. IP packets are generally sent via either the UDP or TCP protocols. When a connection is formed using TCP, the client and server can exchange packets in a reliable, streamed manner.

Domain Name Service and Sockets (Meet InetAddress!)

When you're forming a TCP connection to a server, you need to know what the server's IP address is. DNS provides a means to discover a server's IP address given the server's domain name (i.e., "`www.rawthought.com`").

When you're using the `Socket` class, you have two ways of specifying the remote server to connect to— either provide the server's domain name or provide the server's IP address directly. If you know the server's name, just jump straight into that interface. If you want to be a bit more adventuresome, you can use one of the static method provided by the `InetAddress` class to obtain the IP address, `InetAddress.getByName`.

Another reason to use the `InetAddress` methods to find the IP address for a host is that a given host might be "multihomed": that is, there might be multiple IP addresses associated with a given host name. This is especially common for large, heavily trafficked domain names such as "`microsoft.com`". When you look up the IP address for "`www.microsoft.com`" (using a tool such as `nslookup` under Unix) you find that there are about 12 IP addresses representing the single domain name.

Because of this fact, you may sometimes want to provide a way for your code to access more than just the first IP address in the list. This allows your code to be more robust. To do this, use the static `InetAddress` method `getAllByName`:

```
InetAddress[] addrs = InetAddress.getAllByName("www.microsoft.com");
```

This provides an array of `InetAddresses` to which you can try to connect. You can iterate through this array until you find a good connection.

Meet the Socket Class

Sockets are a software abstraction for a network connection. They provide a means for your software to communicate with other hosts over a communications network. Sockets don't care about the kind of information carried over them, they simply act as dumb carriers of that information.

The socket interface has a long history in the Unix community, and so it's not surprising that Sun chose sockets to be the backbone of Java's networking architecture. For the two main types of network entities, Java provides the socket to meet their needs. The `Socket` class is used by network clients: The `ServerSocket` class is used by network servers.

Note: This chapter covers the streaming sockets but leaves out the `DatagramSocket`, which is covered in "Datagrams A-Go-Go".

The `Socket` class provides a good interface to the TCP protocol. It provides a streams interface and an easy way to open and close TCP connections.

The most commonly-used `Socket` methods are listed below.

Table 5-1 Commonly-Used `java.net.Socket` Methods

Method	Description
`Socket`	This method comes in four (4!) different flavors. Each requires that you specify the host and port to which you wish to connect. As discussed in the text, you can provide either the host's domain name or IP address in the form of an InetAddress. (Two of the constructors allow you specify a non-stream-based protocol. This will be covered in detail in "How to Create a Datagram "Connection" Using the Socket Class, and Why You Shouldn't" beginning on page 160.)
`getInputStream`	Get an input stream for the connection.
`getOutputStream`	Get an output stream for the connection.
`close`	Disconnect from the remote server.
`getLocalPort`	Returns the local port this Socket is using.
`getPort`	Returns the remote port to which this Socket is connected.
`getInetAddress`	Returns the InetAddress to which this Socket is connected.

When you create a new `Socket` instance, a TCP connection is opened to the `InetAddress` or hostname you specify in the constructor. As soon as the constructor completes, a connection has been opened to the remote host.

After a connection has been opened, you can obtain input and output streams for communicating with the remote host. These streams rely on the error-correcting, reliable aspects of TCP to provide a reliable pipe to the remote host. At this time you can call the `getLocalPort`, `getPort`, and `getInetAddress` methods to obtain information about the connection.

When you're finished communicating with the remote host, call `close` to close the socket. This in turn disconnects the underlying TCP connection.

A Simple Socket Client

In this section we'll look at implementing a simple `Socket`-based client class that performs all of the basic client operations.

Here's what a client typically needs to do:

1. Connect to a remote server

2. Send/receive some data

3. Shut down the connection.

To understand the client life cycle a bit better, let's walk through each of these steps quickly.

- To create a connection to the remote server, we're going to create a new instance of `Socket` with the name of the server and port to which we wish to connect. This will automatically form a new connection or throw an exception if the connection cannot be made.

- To send and receive data, we're going to obtain input and output streams from the connected `Socket` instance. These streams will provide us a way to send data to and receive data from the remote server: to send data we simply write to the output stream— to receive data we simply read from the input stream.

- To shut down the connection we're going to call the `Socket.close` method. This forces an active close of the TCP connection.

SimpleSocketClient Implementation

The implementation of `SimpleSocketClient` consists of a few methods:

- The constructor takes a hostname and a port to connect to, and tucks away that information into instance variables.

- `MOpenConnection` performs the actual connection to the remote server, given the host and port info in the instance variables. This method creates a new Socket, then grabs the input and output streams from the Socket once it's connected.

- `MHandleSession` is the core method for handling a session. The default method in this class doesn't do much (it dumps the contents of the input stream to stdout), but we'll write subclasses later that do useful work in this method.

- `MCloseConnection` shuts down the connection to the remote server by calling `Socket.close` and cleans up.

- run calls the above methods in sequence. This method is only executed if the code using the `SimpleSocketClient` calls the `start` method. This starts `SimpleSocketClient`'s thread running. In this asynchronous mode, the `SimpleSocketClient` connects, handles a transaction session, and then closes the connection. The reason we call everything from `run` in this mode is that it allows us to avoid completely blocking our main thread on potentially time-consuming operations such as connecting the Socket. Note, however, that all of the methods of `SimpleSocketClient` are public, so that the code using `SimpleSocketClient` can decide to use it in a synchronous mode simply by avoiding the call to `SimpleSocketClient.start`.

The implementation of `SimpleSocketClient` is shown below.

Example 5-1 **Implementation of a Simple Socket Client**

```
package JNC;

import java.net.*;
import java.io.*;


/**
 * A class that implements simple client to a remote service using
 * a Socket
 */
public class SimpleSocketClient extends Thread
{
public static final int
    PORTNUM_ECHO = 7, //RFC 862
    PORTNUM_DAYTIME = 13,//RFC 867
    PORTNUM_CHARGEN = 19;//RFC 864


public boolean fDebugOn = true;

protected DataInputStream fRemoteInputStream;
protected DataOutputStream fRemoteOutputStream;

protected SocketfRemoteHostSocket;
protected String fHostName;
protected int fPortNum;



/**
 * Default constructor
 */
public SimpleSocketClient()
{
    fHostName = "netcom.com";
    fPortNum = PORTNUM_DAYTIME;
```

```
    }

    /**
     * Give a host name and a port to connect to
     *
     * @param hostName The name of the host to connect to--
     *    i.e. "www.rawthought.com"
     * @param portNum  The port to connect to-- i.e., 80 for
     *    HTTP, 79 for Finger, etc.
     */
    public SimpleSocketClient(String hostName, int portNum)
    {
        //tuck away our instance variables
        fHostName = hostName;
        fPortNum = portNum;

        //note that somebody, someplace else decides whether to
        //kickstart our thread-- we don't do it here!
    }//SimpleSocketClient


    /**
     * We use this method as an "autopilot."  Given the initial
     * setup info, proceeds to execute a single session in
     * a separate thread. It opens a connection, handles the session,
     * then closes the connection when done
     */
    public void run()
    {
        if (fDebugOn)
            System.out.println("Running SimpleSocketClient...");
        if (MOpenConnection() ) {
            //if we opened the connection successfully
            MHandleSession(); //handle the session...
            MCloseConnection();//close the connection
        }
    }//run

    /**
     * Actually connect to the remote host.
     * When this fails, it's typically because we can't get a connection,
     * either because our local host is having Inet access problems,
     * or because the remote host isn't there
     * (or was incorrectly specified),
     * or because the remote host doesn't provide a service on
     * the given port.
     * @return True if connection was opened successfully.
     */
    public boolean MOpenConnection()
    {
        boolean success = true; //start off assuming we'll be successful

        if (fDebugOn) System.out.println("Opening Connection...");
```

```
    try {
        //create and open a socket to the given host and port
        fRemoteHostSocket = new Socket(fHostName, fPortNum);

        try {
            //get the output stream that we can use to send data
            fRemoteOutputStream =
                new DataOutputStream(
                    fRemoteHostSocket.getOutputStream());
            //get the input stream that we can use to receive data
            fRemoteInputStream =
                new DataInputStream(
                    fRemoteHostSocket.getInputStream());
        }
        catch (IOException streamEx) {
            success = false;
            if (fDebugOn) System.err.println(
                "building streams failed: " + streamEx);
            //need to shut down the socket we've already opened!
            MCloseConnection();
        }
    }
    catch (IOException sockEx) {
        success = false;
        if (fDebugOn)
            System.err.println("open socket failed: " + sockEx);
    }

    return success;
} /* MOpenConnection */


/**
 * Handle a single session with the remote host.
 * This default method reads input until it's done, then gives up
 */
public void MHandleSession()
{

    String curLine = "";

    if (fDebugOn) System.out.println("Handling Session...");

    do {
        //dump the current line to stdout
        if (fDebugOn) System.out.println(curLine);

        try {
            //get the next line
            curLine = fRemoteInputStream.readLine();
        }
        catch (IOException readEx) {
```

```
                //we expect this throw when we reach EOF on the stream
                curLine = null;
            }
        } while (curLine != null);

        //dump a finished note to stdout
        if (fDebugOn) System.out.println("<EOF>");

    } /* MHandleSession */



    /**
     * Close the open connection.
     */
    public void MCloseConnection()
    {
        if (fDebugOn) System.out.println("Closing Connection...");

        try {
            //only attempt to close if we've got a valid socket
            if (fRemoteHostSocket != null)  fRemoteHostSocket.close();

            fRemoteOutputStream = null;
            fRemoteInputStream = null;
        }
        catch (IOException closeEx){
            if (fDebugOn)
                System.err.println("socket close threw: " + closeEx);
        };
    }


}/* class SimpleSocketClient */
```

To test the `SimpleSocketClient` implementation, we've provided a `SimpleSocketClientTest` class that simply causes the `SimpleSocketClient` to connect to the "daytime" protocol well-known port on a host and pull down the result. The `daytime` protocol (as specified in Internet RFC 867) can be used to obtain the current day and time.

In our tests we invoked "`SimpleSocketClientTest netcom.com`" and got the following result in `System.out`:

```
Sat Aug 31 12:01:07 1996
```

On servers that support it, the `daytime` server simply returns the date and time in standard Unix string date format, as shown above. The client doesn't need to send any "request" string to activate the `daytime` server: as soon as the client connects to the proper port, the `daytime` server immediately spews the date string and closes the connection.

Now let's look at a slightly more sophisticated subclass of `SimpleSocketClient`.

A Finger Client

In this section we'll implement a `SimpleSocketClient` subclass that performs a simple Internet protocol: the Finger protocol.

The Finger protocol is traditionally used to discover information about a user on a given network host. Typically, this information includes things such as full name, office telephone number, home telephone number, and so on. On some platforms the Finger server would also provide info from a user's "plan file," a plain text file, so that the user could provide a brief description of herself and her interests.

Before the advent of the Web, a user's plan file was the closest thing many users had to a "home page." Some users created long and detailed plan files filled with their favorite quotes, favorite song lyrics, their own writing, and so forth. The obvious advantage of HTML pages over a plan file is that the user can include hypertext links in the HTML page (instead of trying to cram everything into a single document), and the user can include images and layout/formatting information.

While Finger was at the peak of its popularity, some very creative people realized that you could hook up devices such as vending machines to an Internet host and, using the Finger protocol, provide information about the status of these devices to the rest of the world. As the Web has come into vogue, these machines are rapidly being converted to a Web interface, but there are still a few vending machines connected to the Internet that provide a Finger interface.

The Finger Protocol

There are two entities involved in a Finger transaction. There's the Finger server, which waits on port 79 for Finger clients to connect and there's the Finger client. The latter connects to a given Finger server on port 79, makes a request about a particular user, and waits for a (potentially lengthy) text response.

The Finger request itself consists of a username or an empty string followed by a carriage return. If the username is empty, the Finger server will generally provide a list of all users currently logged onto the host in its response.

We can simulate a Finger session using Telnet. To do this, we'll use a Telnet client to perform the same actions that our Finger client needs to. First, we'll Telnet to port 79 (this is the well-known port for Finger) on the host slumbering.lungfish.com. Next we'll type the username we're looking up: carolee. We'll then type a carriage return to complete the request.

The server responds with some basic user information for the user carolee followed by the contents of carolee's plan file.

Figure 5–1 shows a screen capture of the simulated Finger session:

```
▤□▤▤▤▤▤▤▤▤▤▤▤▤▤▤▤▤▤ shellн.best.com 2 ▤▤▤▤▤▤▤▤▤▤▤▤▤▤▤▤▤▤▤
shellx 1%
shellx 1%
shellx 1%
shellx 1%
shellx 1% telnet slumbering.lungfish.com 79
Trying 205.179.84.1...
Connected to slumbering.lungfish.com.
Escape character is '^]'.
carolee
Login: carolee                    Name: Great Spangled Fritillary
Directory: /home/carolee          Shell: /bin/tcsh
Last login Thu Aug 22 15:41 (PST) on ttyp3 from kelly.teleport.c
Mail last read Wed Jul 24 23:34 1996 (PST)
Plan:

"At once it struck me what quality went to form a person of achievement,
especially in literature, and which Shakespeare possessed so enormously --
I mean _negative capability_, that is when a person is capable of being
in uncertainties, mysteries, doubts, without any irritable reaching after
fact and reason."
                                  John Keats

Connection closed by foreign host.
shellx 2% ▮
```

Figure 5–1 Fingering with Telnet.

Once the server has finished sending all of the response text, it closes the connection (note the "Connection closed by foreign host" message in the screen shot above). In our Finger client, this is how we'll detect when we're finished receiving data (since there is no length information provided elsewhere).

Implementing the Finger Client

Our finger client will take a username and a hostname, perform a finger request for that username at that hostname, and dump the results into a log file. To do this, we need to implement the following stages:

1. We need to open up a Socket connection to the host given by hostname on the well-known Finger port.

2. We need to send the username and a carriage return to the remote server.

3. We need to wait for the server to respond with a bunch of text of unspecified length.

4. We need to write the result to `System.out`.

Below is the source for the `FingerClient` implementation.

Example 5-2 **Implementation of a Finger Client**

```
package JNC;

import java.net.*;
import java.io.*;


/**
 * A class which extends SimpleSocketClient to
 * implement a Finger client.
 */
public class FingerClient extends SimpleSocketClient
{
public static final int PORTNUM_FINGER = 79;

//by default we just make a blanket finger request
//(no specific username)
protected String fUserName = "";

/**
 * This constructor takes two strings:
 * @param hostName The host on which to perform the Finger
 * @param userName The user on which to perform the Finger
 */
public FingerClient(String hostName, String userName)
{
    //give SimpleSocketClient the required connection info
    super(hostName, PORTNUM_FINGER);

    //tuck away the userName for our MHandleSession method
    fUserName = userName;

    //kickstart the SimpleSocketClient's thread
    this.start();
}//FingerClient

/**
 * This constructor takes one string:
 * @param targetStr A string of the form "username@host"
 */
public FingerClient(String targetStr)
```

```
{
    super(); //call superclass constructor first

    //find the last @
    int atSignIdx = targetStr.lastIndexOf('@');

    if (atSignIdx > 0) { //valid username
        //get the username
        fUserName = targetStr.substring(0,atSignIdx);
        String hostName =
            targetStr.substring(atSignIdx + 1,
                targetStr.length());
        //set the host name in the superclass
        fHostName = hostName;
    }
    else { //just a hostname
        fUserName = "";//empty user name
        //set the host name in the superclass
        fHostName = targetStr;
    }
    //set the port number in the superclass
    fPortNum = PORTNUM_FINGER;

    //kickstart the SimpleSocketClient's thread
    this.start();
}//FingerClient


/**
 * Overrides SimpleSocketClient.MHandleSession
 * Perform a Finger session.
 */
public void MHandleSession()
{
    String curLine = "Reading data...";

    try {
        //Start by sending the requested username
        //Send the requested username plus a
        //terminating carriage return
        fRemoteOutputStream.writeBytes(fUserName + "\n");
    }
    catch (IOException writeEx) {
        if (fDebugOn)
            System.err.println("write failed with: " + writeEx);
        return;//bail out immediately
    }

    do {
        //dump the current line to stdout
        System.out.println(curLine);

        try {
```

```
        //get the next line of input
        curLine = fRemoteInputStream.readLine();
    }
    catch (IOException readEx) {
        //we expect this throw when we reach EOF
        //on the stream
        curLine = null;
    }

} while (curLine != null);

System.out.println("<EOF>");//dump a finished note to stdout

}//MHandleSession

} /* class FingerClient */
```

To test the `FingerClient` class, we've provided a simple stand-alone class that takes parameters from `stdin` and gives them to `FingerClient`. When we tested this class, we invoked

```
%FingerClientTest carolee@lungfish.com
```

and verified that we received results in `System.out` similar to our previous simulated Finger session. You might want to test this class with the target string "`coke@l.gp.cs.cmu.edu`" to see an interesting example of one of the vending machines still attached to the Internet via a Finger server.

Meet the ServerSocket Class

The `ServerSocket` is class complementary to the `Socket` class. It provides listening socket services for a server that complement the connecting socket services for a client. The main difference between the `ServerSocket` interface and the `Socket` interface is that the `ServerSocket` provides a way to wait for an incoming connection. Thus, as its name suggests, the `ServerSocket` allows the creation of servers.

The table below lists the most commonly used `ServerSocket` methods.

Table 5-2 Commonly-Used `java.net.ServerSocket` Methods

Method	Description
`ServerSocket`	This method comes in two flavors: one that accepts just a local port to listen on, and one that accepts both a port and a timeout to listen. If you do not specify the listen time, `ServerSocket` just waits forever on the `accept`.
`accept`	This method listens for an incoming connection and once a client connects, this method returns a `Socket` that is connected to the client. You can then use this `Socket` to communicate with the client and call `accept` again to listen for additional clients.
`close`	This method closes the `ServerSocket` so that it can no longer listen for new connections. It is best to dispose of the `ServerSocket` after calling this method.
`getInetAddress`	Before a client has connected, this method returns the local host address. After a client has connected via `accept`, returns the address of the connecting client.
`getLocalPort`	This method returns the local port used by the `ServerSocket` for listening.

You create a server by creating a new `ServerSocket` on a certain port. You then call the `ServerSocket.accept` method and wait for clients to attempt to connect on that port. If you specified a timeout in the ServerSocket constructor and a connection request isn't received in that amount of time, then the `accept` will throw an exception. Once you receive a connection request from a client, `accept` returns with a `Socket` instance. You then use this `Socket` to communicate with the client. You can also call `accept` again to listen for additional clients. Note that you can repeatedly listen for new clients on the same local server port. This is because TCP connections are uniquely identified by the combination of local server IP address and port, and remote (client) IP address and port. Thus, although clients can only form one connection from a given IP address and port, numerous clients can connect to the same server IP address and port.

The States of a ServerSocket

It helps to understand that a ServerSocket goes through a series of states depending on which methods you call. The basic states are: Instantiated, Accepting, Connected, Closed.

Instantiated

As soon as the `ServerSocket` constructor completes, the `ServerSocket` is in the Instantiated state. In this state you should really only call `ServerSocket.accept` to begin listening for a client to connect. You can call the `getLocalPort` and `getInetAddress` methods in this state, but they return useless values.

Accepting

Once you call the `ServerSocket.accept` method, the `ServerSocket` starts waiting for a client to connect. This method is synchronous: it either waits forever for a connection or waits for the amount of time you specified in the `ServerSocket` constructor.

Connected

As soon as `ServerSocket.accept` completes, you are provided with a `Socket` instance that is connected to the remote client. In this state you can use the `getInetAddress` method to obtain the address of the remote client, and the getLocalPort method to obtain the local port that the new Socket occupies. From this state you can call `ServerSocket.accept` again to obtain additional clients, or you can call close to shutdown the ServerSocket. Note that the Sockets returned by `ServerSocket.accept` need to be shut down independent of the ServerSocket.

To summarize, to create a server using `ServerSocket`, you do something similar to this:

```
ServerSocket servSock = new ServerSocket(portNumber);
Socket newConnection = servSock.accept();
```

That's really all there is to it. Of course, to create a well-behaved server, you need to wrap these calls in the right error handling code and thread environment. In the sections that follow we'll show in detail how to create a sophisticated Web server.

Creating a Simple Synchronous Web Server

In this section we'll look at a simple application of the ServerSocket: a simple blocking (synchronous) HTTP server. You should be able to connect to this server using a Web browser.

This example uses a utility class: the `HttpTransactionHandler`. The implementation of this class is covered in detail in "An HTTP Transaction Handler" beginning on page 291.

This example presents a very simple HTTP daemon (httpd). In this example we just call `ServerSocket.accept` directly from our main thread. This blocks anything else from executing in our task. This presents a problem on platforms that have cooperative multitasking (such as MacOS), but not on platforms (Unix, Win32) which provide preemptive multitasking.

The task that called `ServerSocket.accept` (your code) blocks, but every other task in the system proceeds. On a platform that lacks preemptive multitasking, such as MacOS, this causes the entire system to hang waiting for a client to connect on the port. This is definitely not a well-behaved server and is useful only as an example.

The source code for this simplest Web server is shown below.

Example 5-3 A Simple Web Server Implementation

```
package JNC;

import java.io.*;
import java.net.*;
import java.util.*;


/**
* A class that implements a simple, synchronous HTTP server
*/
public class HttpdSimple
{
public final static int DEFAULT_PORT = 80;

public boolean fDebugOn = true;

protected int fPort;
private ServerSocket fMainListenSocket = null;
private boolean fContinueListening = true;
Socket          fClientSocket = null;
DataInputStream fClientInputStream;
DataOutputStreamfClientOutputStream;

HttpTransactionHandler fTransactionHandler;

/**
*   set the port
*/
public HttpdSimple(int port) {

    if (port == 0) fPort = DEFAULT_PORT;
    else fPort = port;

}//HttpdSimple
```

```
/**
 *   This method waits for an incoming connection,
 *   opens input and output streams on that connection,
 *   then uses HttpTransactionHandler to complete the request.
 *   Once the request has been completed, shuts down the connection
 *   and begins waiting for a new connection.
 */
public void doIt()
{
    //first, bump down our priority a little bit...
    try {
        Thread.currentThread().setPriority(Thread.MIN_PRIORITY + 1);
    }
    catch (IllegalArgumentException badPriorityEx) {
        System.err.println("setPriority ex: " + badPriorityEx);
    }


    //create a new ServerSocket
    try {
        if (fDebugOn) System.out.println(
            "building fMainListenSocket...");
        fMainListenSocket = new  ServerSocket(fPort);
    }
    catch (Exception e) {
        System.err.println(
            "build fMainListenSocket threw: " + e);
        return;
    }
    finally {
        if (fMainListenSocket == null) {
            System.err.println(
                "Couldn't create a new ServerSocket!");
            return;
        }

        if (fDebugOn) System.out.println(
            "fMainListenSocket initialized on port..." + fPort);
    }


    try { while (fContinueListening ) {

        if (fDebugOn) System.out.println("server accepting...");
      fClientSocket = fMainListenSocket.accept( );//this blocks!

      if (fClientSocket != null) {
        //okay, we now have a client!
            if (fDebugOn)
                System.out.println("building iostreams...");
          fClientInputStream =
            new DataInputStream(fClientSocket.getInputStream());
            fClientOutputStream =
```

```
                    new DataOutputStream(fClientSocket.getOutputStream());

                    if ((fClientOutputStream != null ) &&
                            (fClientInputStream != null)){
                        //now, handle the transaction
                        fTransactionHandler = new HttpTransactionHandler(
                            fClientInputStream,fClientOutputStream);
                        try { fTransactionHandler.handleTransaction();}
                        catch (Exception handleTransEx) {
                            System.err.println(
                                "handleTransaction ex: " + handleTransEx);
                        }
                        //we no longer need the transaction handler
                        fTransactionHandler = null;
                        //we no longer need the client input stream!
                        fClientInputStream = null;
                        //we no longer need the client output stream!
                        fClientOutputStream = null;
                    }
                    else {
                        if (fClientOutputStream == null)
                            System.err.println("fClientOutputStream null!");
                        if (fClientInputStream == null)
                            System.err.println("fClientInputStream null!");
                    }

                    if (fDebugOn)
                        System.out.println("closing fClientSocket...");
                    try { fClientSocket.close();   }
                    catch (Exception clientSocketCloseEx) {
                        System.err.println(
                            "fClientSocket.close() threw: " +
                                clientSocketCloseEx);
                    };

                    fClientSocket = null;
                    if (fDebugOn)
                        System.out.println("done with cleanup...");
                }

        } //while fContinueListening
        } //try
        catch (Exception loopEx) {
        System.err.println("main loop ex: " + loopEx);
        }

} /* HttpdSimple.doIt */


} /* class HttpdSimple */
```

Notice that the only way to quit this Web server, once it's started, is to kill the task that launched it (typically by typing ctrl-C at the command line). Of course, if you're running this server under MacOS, your entire machine locks up while this server is running, and the only way to stop the server is to force-quit it, or drop into MacsBug.

An Asynchronous (Background) Web Server

Let's now modify the basic Web server to provide more friendly asynchronous behavior. This should allow it to run on platforms such as MacOS that do not yet provide preemptive multitasking.

We will modify the simple Web server so that it spawns a separate thread that deals with the HTTP connection itself. This separate thread will basically call the doIt method from within the run method of a Thread. Here again we recycle the HttpTransactionHandler class to handle a single http transaction after a client has connected.

While this version of httpd should, in theory, allow a series of clients to connect to a MacOS-based server running MacTCP, the reality is that when we tested this server with the current MacOS JDK, the server would sporadically quit with a fairly low-level monitor error being dumped to stderr. By the time this book is published, a new version of the MacOS Java runtime may be released that fixes this problem.

The source for the asynchronous Web server is shown below.

Example 5-4 An Asynchronous (Background) Web Server Implementation

```
package JNC;

import java.io.*;
import java.net.*;
import java.util.*;

/**
 * Improved version of httpd server:
 * Places main loop into a separate thread,
 * so it doesn't lock up the system.
 */
public class HttpdAsync extends Thread
{
public final static int DEFAULT_PORT = 80;
```

```java
public boolean fDebugOn = true;

protected int fPort;
protected ServerSocket fMainListenSocket = null;
protected boolean fContinueListening = true;
protected Socket fClientSocket = null;
protected DataInputStream fClientInputStream;
protected DataOutputStreamfClientOutputStream;
protected HttpTransactionHandler fTransactionHandler;

/**
*Instantiate and init
*/
public HttpdAsync(int port) {

    if (port == 0) fPort = DEFAULT_PORT;
    else fPort = port;

    if (fDebugOn)
        System.out.println("done instantiating...");

}


/**
*   This method waits for an incoming connection,
*   opens input and output streams on that connection,
*   then uses HttpTransactionHandler to complete the request.
*   Once the request has been completed, shuts down the connection
*   and begins waiting for a new connection.
*/
public void run()
{

    //create a new ServerSocket
    try {
        if (fDebugOn) System.out.println(
            "building fMainListenSocket...");
        fMainListenSocket = new  ServerSocket(fPort);
    }
    catch (Exception e) {
        System.err.println(
            "build fMainListenSocket threw: " + e);
        return;
    }
    finally {
        if (fMainListenSocket == null) {
            System.err.println(
                "Couldn't create a new ServerSocket!");
            return;
        }

        if (fDebugOn) System.out.println(
```

```
            "fMainListenSocket initialized on port..." + fPort);
}


try {
while (fContinueListening ) {

    if (fDebugOn) System.out.println("server accepting...");
 fClientSocket = fMainListenSocket.accept( );//this blocks!

  if (fClientSocket != null) {
    //okay, we now have a client!
        if (fDebugOn) System.out.println(
            "building iostreams...");
     fClientInputStream =
       new DataInputStream(fClientSocket.getInputStream());
       fClientOutputStream =
       new DataOutputStream(fClientSocket.getOutputStream());

       if ((fClientOutputStream != null ) &&
          (fClientInputStream != null)){
           //now, handle the transaction
           fTransactionHandler =
              new HttpTransactionHandler(fClientInputStream,
                     fClientOutputStream);
           try { fTransactionHandler.handleTransaction(); }
           catch (Exception handleTransEx) {
               System.err.println(
                   "handleTransaction ex: " + handleTransEx);
           }
           //we no longer need the transaction handler
           fTransactionHandler = null;
           //we no longer need the client input stream!
           fClientInputStream = null;
           //we no longer need the client output stream!
           fClientOutputStream = null;
        }
        else {
           if (fClientOutputStream == null)
              System.err.println("fClientOutputStream null!");
           if (fClientInputStream == null)
              System.err.println("fClientInputStream null!");
        }

        if (fDebugOn) System.out.println(
            "closing fClientSocket...");
        try { fClientSocket.close();   }
        catch (Exception clientSocketCloseEx) {
            System.err.println(
                "fClientSocket.close() threw: " +
                    clientSocketCloseEx);
        };
```

```
            fClientSocket = null;
            if (fDebugOn)
                System.out.println("done with cleanup...");
        }
    }   //while fContinueListening
    } //try
    catch (Exception loopEx) {
    System.err.println("main loop ex: " + loopEx);
    }

} /* run */
}/* class HttpdAsync */
```

Implementing a Multiclient Web Server

The biggest remaining problem with the Web servers we've presented so far is that they can only handle one client connection at a time. Obviously, this makes for a poor Web server.

In order to support multiple clients, we're going to separate the code that deals with each new Socket returned by `ServerSocket.accept`, and handle that `Socket`'s transaction in a separate thread. We'll place this code in a separate class called a `http_connection_mgr`. This will free up the main server thread to call `ServerSocket.accept` again as soon as possible.

The source for the multiclient Web server is shown below.

Example 5-5 **Implementation of a Web Server which Supports Multiple Clients**

```
package JNC;

import java.io.*;
import java.net.*;
import java.util.*;


/**
 * A class that manages a single HTTP connection
 * We've migrated all the connection-oriented stuff
 * from HttpdAsync into this class.
 */
class HttpConnectionMgr extends Thread
{
public boolean fDebugOn = true;

protected Socket fClientSocket = null;
protected DataInputStream fClientInputStream;
protected DataOutputStreamfClientOutputStream;
protected HttpTransactionHandler fTransactionHandler;
```

```
public HttpConnectionMgr(Socket clientSocket)
{
    fClientSocket = clientSocket;
    this.start();
}//HttpConnectionMgr

/**
 * This method executes the core connection-mgmt stuff
 */
public void run()
{
    try {

        if (fDebugOn) System.out.println("building iostreams...");
        fClientInputStream =
            new DataInputStream(fClientSocket.getInputStream());
        fClientOutputStream =
            new DataOutputStream(fClientSocket.getOutputStream());

        if ((fClientOutputStream != null ) && (fClientInputStream != null)){
            //now, handle the transaction
            fTransactionHandler =
                new
HttpTransactionHandler(fClientInputStream,fClientOutputStream);
            try { fTransactionHandler.handleTransaction(); }
            catch (Exception handleTransEx) {
                System.err.println("handleTransaction ex: " + handleTransEx);
            }
            //we no longer need the transaction handler
            fTransactionHandler = null;
            //we no longer need the client input stream!
            fClientInputStream = null;
            //we no longer need the client output stream!
            fClientOutputStream = null;
        }
        else {
            if (fClientOutputStream == null)
                System.err.println("fClientOutputStream null!");
            if (fClientInputStream == null)
                System.err.println("fClientInputStream null!");
        }

        if (fDebugOn) System.out.println("closing fClientSocket...");
        try { fClientSocket.close();  }
        catch (Exception clientSocketCloseEx) {
            System.err.println("fClientSocket.close() threw: " +
clientSocketCloseEx);
        };

        fClientSocket = null;
        if (fDebugOn) System.out.println("done with cleanup...");
    }
```

```
        catch (IOException ioEx) {
            System.err.println("HttpConnectionMgr run ioEx: " + ioEx);
        }

}//run

} /* class HttpConnectionMgr */


/**
 * Improved version of httpd server:
 * Allows multiple "simultaneous" clients
 */
public class HttpdMulti extends Thread
{
public final static int DEFAULT_PORT = 80;

public boolean fDebugOn = true;

protected int fPort; //which port we actually end up using
protected ServerSocket fMainListenSocket = null; //main server socket
public boolean fContinueListening = true;

/**
 *Instantiate and init
 */
public HttpdMulti(int port) {

    if (port == 0) port = DEFAULT_PORT;
    fPort = port;

    if (fDebugOn) System.out.println("done instantiating...");

}//HttpdMulti


/**
 *    This method waits for an incoming connection,
 *    opens input and output streams on that connection,
 *    then uses HttpTransactionHandler to complete the request.
 *    Once the request has been completed, shuts down the connection
 *    and begins waiting for a new connection.
 */
public void run()
{

    //create a new ServerSocket
    try {
        if (fDebugOn) System.out.println("building fMainListenSocket...");
        fMainListenSocket = new  ServerSocket(fPort);
    }
    catch (Exception e) {
        System.err.println("build fMainListenSocket threw: " + e);
```

```
        return;
    }
    finally {
        if (fMainListenSocket == null) {
            System.err.println("Couldn't create a new ServerSocket!");
            return;
        }

        if (fDebugOn)
            System.out.println("fMainListenSocket initialized on port..." +
fPort);
    }


    try {
    while (fContinueListening ) {

        if (fDebugOn) System.out.println("server accepting...");
      Socket clientSocket = fMainListenSocket.accept( );//this blocks!

      if (clientSocket != null) {
        HttpConnectionMgr mgr = new HttpConnectionMgr(clientSocket);
        }

    } //while fContinueListening
    } //try
    catch (Exception loopEx) {
    System.err.println("main loop ex: " + loopEx);
    }

} // HttpdMulti.run

}/* class HttpdMulti */
```

We now have a fairly complete Web server. You should be able to use this example as the core of other servers you may write. Obviously, there are other improvements we could make to this server. For instance, we could use ThreadGroups to make it easier to shut down all client connections at once (when the server is being shut down, for example).

New for JDK 1.1: New Socket Options

In JDK 1.0 there were several major limitations to what you could do with a Socket or ServerSocket. Specifically, there were major limitations as to how you could create and configure these classes.

JDK 1.1 adds some ways to create these classes, and then adds a few ways to configure them with some popular Unix (BSD) socket options.

Socket and ServerSocket Can Now be Subclassed

Under JDK 1.0 it was not possible to create a subclass of `Socket` or `ServerSocket` because these classes were declared as `final`. However, in JDK 1.1 the `final` keyword has been removed from these class definitions, allowing them to be subclassed.

This is a very important change because it allows you to create classes that behave like sockets but that may implement some sophisticated protocol behind the socket interface. Let's say, for instance, you want to create a Socket subclass that implements the Secure Socket Layer (SSL) protocols. To your clients you could export your class using the Socket interface. However, behind-the-scenes you could implement all of the security measures you need in order to adhere to SSL.

It's important to note that as part of this change, a default constructor was added to the `Socket` and `ServerSocket` classes to allow them to be constructed without actually forming a connection. This allows new subclasses their superclass constructor without forming a connection.

In addition, a new `protected` method was added to `ServerSocket` that allows subclasses of `ServerSocket` to tell `ServerSocket` which Socket to use for a connection. The method is declared as follows:

```
protected final void implAccept(Socket sock)
```

You would typically use this method to inform the `ServerSocket` which `Socket` to return from subsequent `accept` calls.

New Socket Configuration Options

You can now call various configuration methods to configure the precise behavior of Socket and ServerSocket. These methods are shown below.

Table 5-3 New Socket and ServerSocket Configuration Methods

Method	Description
setSoLinger(boolean, integer msec)	Set milliseconds to linger when closing. Only available for Socket.
setSoTimeout(int msec)	Specify milliseconds to wait on blocking socket operations (such as read). If operation doesn't complete within the time period, an exception is thrown but the socket remains useful.
setTCPNoDelay(boolean)	Set whether Nagle's algorithm is used for the TCP connection.
int getSoLinger	Get the milliseconds to linger on close. A value of -1 means option is disabled. Only available for Socket.
int getSoTimeout	Get the number of milliseconds for the timeout. A value of 0 means no timeout.
boolean getTCPNoDelay	Find out whether TCP_NODELAY is set.

Depending on your particular application, you may find that adjusting these options results in higher performance. For instance, for a server application, you may find that by adjusting SO_TIMEOUT via setSoTimeout, you can optimize service for the fastest clients by spending less time waiting for slower clients to send data.

Sockets Can Now Specify Local Address and Port

Under JDK 1.0 there was no way for a Socket or ServerSocket to specify the local IP address to be used. This critical flaw assumed that the machine on which the socket was running would only ever have one IP address. However, as we mentioned previously, some high-traffic servers are linked to several IP addresses.

Under JDK 1.1 this has been fixed by creating overloaded constructors for Socket and ServerSocket that allow you to specify which particular local IP address to use.

Summary

The `Socket` class can be used to easily create a network client. The `ServerSocket` class can be used to quickly create a network server. These two easy-to-use classes are among the main reasons to use Java for network programming.

CHAPTER

6

- Picking the Right Target Environment

- Optimizing Communications under Java

- Prototyping and Debugging Using Java

- A Sample Chat Application

Working Smart with Java

This chapter will cover three main topics: How to pick the basic design for your application, what platform-specific pitfalls to avoid, and integrating what we've learned so far into a network chat application.

Application, Applet, or Class Library?

One of the first decisions you need to make before starting any Java project is: What are you going to build? Should you build a Java application, an applet, or a class library? Let's talk about how you choose between these three particular kinds of projects and what advantages and disadvantages each has for a communications or networking application.

Applets

Applets are subclasses of the `java.applet.Applet` class and are invoked inside a Java-enabled Web browser or "applet viewer." The `Applet` class interface and the runtime context of the browser/applet viewer are designed to isolate the code in the applet from the machine on which the applet is running. That is, they're designed to prevent an applet from wreaking havoc on a user's machine. Because of this, applets have significant security restrictions:

- Applets are client-side only. You can't build a server from an applet.

- Applets have limited access to files, and perhaps none at all depending on how the end user has configured Java support in the browser, the means used to load the applet into the browser, and so forth.

- Applets are limited to making connections to the host from which they arrived. An applet cannot make a connection to an arbitrary host.

- Applets cannot utilize platform-native libraries. This prevents an applet from launching potentially destructive native libraries, or from launching ordinary native libraries in a destructive manner.

Another factor to consider with applets is that they're Internet-centric. They're designed to run inside a Web browser, and thus be loaded over the network. This means that the end user is going to be loading the applet code again and again over the network, which could be very slow depending on the speed of the user's network link. This places some de facto size restrictions on applets.

Applications

A Java application is a full-blown application that runs on any platform with the Java interpreter and runtime environment. Depending on the platform you're using, an application is invoked with the `java` command, Java Runner, or the equivalent.

The biggest advantage of applications is that they obtain full access to all of the public Java APIs without having to worry about the security restrictions that applets face.

Class Libraries

A class library is a Java class or set of Java classes that is not, in itself, runnable. Other classes, applications, or applets link to a class library and utilize its classes at runtime. Class libraries are typically released as Java packages.

Class libraries are a great place to put "toolbox" or utility classes— classes that you know you'll need again and again in various projects. For instance, the `java.util` package contains a number of utility classes (such as the `java.util.Hashtable` class) which by themselves aren't runnable, but which you can use from runnable applications or applets. To understand the power of class libraries, think about the Java runtime API; it's really just a set of interdependent Java class libraries and native libraries.

You may notice that most of the sample code provided with this book is part of the same package. Thus you can use all of the utility classes in the sample code (such as the hexadecimal manipulation classes) simply by importing the sample code package into your code.

Applet Model versus Application Model

Although the differences between applets and applications might seem blatantly clear, let's take a moment to explore how the two different types of Java code result in completely different computing models for communicating and networking applications. Once you truly understand the difference between these two models, you can make informed decisions about which model you choose to use.

First let's look at the model for a Java application, as shown in Figure 6–1. This is probably the client-server computing model you're most familiar with: the client is a network peer with any number of servers; the client has a significant amount of local persistent storage to store data between invocations of the application; and the application can link to native libraries.

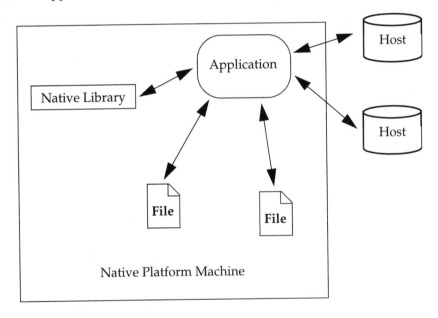

Figure 6–1 The Java Application Client-Server Computing Model.

Now let's look at the Applet client-server computing model. This model is a radical departure from the application model.

The `java.applet.Applet` subclass is wrapped up inside of an applet context shell. Typically, this is a Web browser, but it could also be something like Sun's *Applet Runner* or one of the debugging tools from Symantec, Borland, Natural Intelligence, and others that have the ability to run applets inside of a debugger shell.

A diagram of the Applet model is shown below in Figure 6–2.

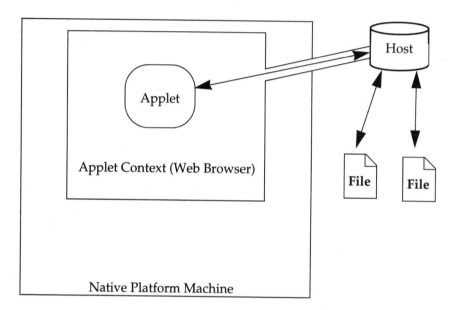

Figure 6–2 The Java Applet Client-Server Computing Model.

The Applet model starts with some radical assumptions:

- The client can only connect to a single Gateway server. It cannot connect to other servers on the Internet. However, it can have multiple connections open to the Gateway server.

- The client has no persistent local storage. All data that needs to be preserved between invocations of the applet is stored on the Gateway server.

What these assumptions translate into is:

- The Gateway server must provide all persistent storage. This removes any "identity" from the client, as login identity will have to be provided at runtime.

- The Gateway server must act as a funnel for all communications between the client and other hosts. If the client needs data from a fileserver, for instance, the Gateway will have to retrieve that data.

You can see why applets have some amount of appeal in Intranet situations— a network administrator can provide users with "thin," inexpensive Java clients with no local persistent storage (hard disks, etc.), low CPU cost, and have all of those clients funnel through a single Gateway server. This allows easy administration of the entire user equipment pool and explicitly prevents network security problems.

A Fourth Alternative: the Marimba "Channel" Model

If you're not familiar with Marimba and its technologies, it's worthwhile checking out `http://www.marimba.com/` for an introduction to Marimba. Marimba has attempted, and succeeded in many cases, to take the applet model further and make it useful for real applications.

Marimba has developed a system called "Castanet" in which servers ("transmitters") send out "channels" of code and content, and a client-side "Tuner" receives the code and content and executes the code inside a secure shell. The end user can configure their Tuner to receive only certain channels, and can control how often the tuner updates the code and content in the Channel.

The Marimba channel model is perhaps more useful than applets for the following reasons:

- Channel code running in the Tuner can allocate local, persistent file storage, subject to some security restrictions. (The tuner and the end user control where and how much space is allocated on the local client machine.) This overcomes perhaps the greatest limitation of applets.

- The Tuner provides the Channel code with a number of convenient hooks for online and offline transaction handling with the server-side Transmitter. This includes support for clients, such as laptops and PDAs, which are only periodically connected to the network.

- The Tuner provides a number of hooks for updating and synchronizing code and content. This is especially convenient for network applications where you need to synchronize content and code versions between the server and the local client.

- The Tuner provides the end user with some nice user interface for controlling the behavior of individual channels, such as the frequency of Channel updates.

- The Tuner provides the developer with some fantastic hooks for automatically updating code in the Channel. For instance, if you fix a bug in one class in your Channel, you can automatically update all your users to the latest version of the code the next time the user connects.

Some of the disadvantages of the Castanet model are:

- The interface to local persistent storage is still a bit ill-defined. Many of the "edge cases," such as nasty channels that wish to consume the user's entire disk drive, are still not handled in the most elegant manner. Also, code and content files are currently stored as ordinary files on the native platform. Marimba has announced that they plan to fix this by using a secure database to store data locally.

- Marimba is focused on IP network-based applications. This is only a problem if your users are unlikely to be connected to an IP network, or have poor access to the network.

- The Tuner, Transmitter, and other Castanet technologies are proprietary and owned by Marimba. Depending on your application, you may find it difficult to work the Marimba business model into your plans.

For some situations, the benefits of the Marimba model outweigh the disadvantages. In any case, the Marimba Channel model is certainly worth studying as an alternative client-server relationship.

Now that we've talked a bit about picking the right kind of Java project to build, let's talk about optimizing communications code.

Tips for Optimizing Throughput

Whenever you're developing a communicating application, there are a few basic trade-offs you need to consider. There is the runtime resource trade-off between speed and memory. You might be able to speed up your communications code if you allocate large buffers. But allocating this additional memory might put the squeeze on other parts of your application.

The other main trade-off to consider is development time versus performance. You might be able to optimize your communications code by very carefully hand-tweaking all of your code, but if a Java class already exists that does almost what you want, it might behoove you to utilize the existing class. A good example of this is streams. The Java streams classes do require some resource overhead and some of them aren't terribly fast; however, they are very useful and can save you a great deal of development time.

Let the Platform Do As Much of the Work As Possible

Java is an interpreted language, so it requires a bit of speed overhead to execute. With communications code you want to squeeze as much speed as you can out of the code. This makes Java nonoptimal for really low-level communications.

Fortunately, the Java API provides you with a number of ways to utilize the platform-native communications drivers. For instance, when you instantiate the `java.net.Socket` class, you're actually accessing the platform's built-in TCP/IP stack. Also, as we'll see in "Linking with the Natives" beginning on page -211, it isn't too difficult to link to system-native libraries that can perform difficult operations.

Whenever you can, you should allow the platform to do as much of the work of communications as you can, while balancing this with platform-independence and reusability.

Use Multithreading When Appropriate

Multithreading can speed up your code by avoiding blocking conditions and carrying out several operations simultaneously. For instance, if you're executing an interactive protocol where the client needs to send the server information in order to receive information back from the server, it might help to have separate threads deal with the input and output sides.

In some situations, multithreading can help your application *appear* faster to the user even if it doesn't actually speed up the application. For instance, you can progressively render information on the screen as data arrives from a remote host, which may appear faster to the user than if you waited for all of the data to arrive and rendered the screen in one shot.

Now that we've discussed good Java communications programming practices, let's implement an Internet chat application that works with existing chat servers.

Example: An Internet Chat Application

Internet Citizen's Band (ICB) is one of the many existing standards for interactive chat applications on the Internet. Another popular chat standard is Internet Relay Chat (IRC). Because the author finds ICB more user-friendly than IRC, we'll provide an implementation of an ICB client in this chapter, as an example of how to efficiently integrate data communications and user interface display.

Technical Overview of ICB

The ICB system is fairly simple: An ICB server listens on a well-known port, numerous ICB clients connect to the server, and the ICB server then acts as the pipeline for the clients to exchange messages.

Each server provides the ability to place several clients together in a "group." Clients can join and leave groups, but a client may only occupy a single group at a time. Placing users into groups is efficient because it limits how many messages you need to exchange to carry out a conversation.

Messages to the group you're currently in are referred to as "open messages." It is also possible to send a message to a specific user, regardless of that user's group. This type of message is referred to as a "private message."

ICB Message Exchange

Once the client connects to the ICB server, the two begin to exchange a series of messages. These messages carry text typed by the user as well as text provided by other users and by the server itself. There are 14 different ICB message types, as described below:

Table 6-1 ICB Messages

Message Type	Description
PACKET_TYPE_LOGIN	Login packet. Sent from client to server: carries username and initial group, nickname settings.
PACKET_TYPE_PROTO	Protocol version check message. Sent by server to client so that client can verify that it understands the version of the ICB protocol the server supports.
PACKET_TYPE_LOGINOK	A message sent from the server to the client in response to a MSGP_TYPE_LOGINOK once the user has successfully logged into the server.
PACKET_TYPE_OPEN	An open message to the entire group of which the user is currently a member. Both sent and received by client.
PACKET_TYPE_PERSONAL	A personal message for the user only. Sent and received by the client.
PACKET_TYPE_STATUS	System status update. Sent by server to client. Could transmit user's group status, group status, or server status.
PACKET_TYPE_COMMAND	Carries a command from the user to the server.
PACKET_TYPE_CMDOUT	Sent from server to client. Contains "stdout" result from server command user previously issued.
PACKET_TYPE_ERROR	Error message sent from server to client. Could indicate, for instance, that an error occurred while the user was trying to switch groups.

Table 6-1 ICB Messages (Continued)

Message Type	Description
PACKET_TYPE_EXIT	Message from server to client, telling the client to quit because of some error.
PACKET_TYPE_BEEP	A beep packet.
PACKET_TYPE_PING	Ping packet
PACKET_TYPE_PONG	Return for ping packet
PACKET_TYPE_IMPORTANT	Important notice sent by server to client. Rarely used.

Notice that some of these packet types are more commonly used than others. Later on this chapter we'll focus on implementing a client which only understands a small subset of this set of packets.

ICB Client Design

An ICB client application has a few core requirements:

1. Needs to be able to display lots of text quickly in a scrolling window. Messages arrive quickly from other users, and we need to display those messages in a timely manner.

2. Needs the ability to scroll back through received messages. Here we'll pick an arbitrary number of lines of scrollback buffer.

3. Needs to be able to collect lots of typed input from the user quickly. Our user needs to be able to quickly send messages to other users.

4. Needs to be able to recognize some common ICB keyboard shortcuts so that current ICB users won't find this new interface confusing.

5. Needs to be able to quickly send messages to and receive messages from a remote net server. This client should keep up with the speed of other clients that interact with the same servers.

In this section we'll look at how to meet these goals using the techniques we've learned so far, as well as by diving into pieces of the Abstract Window Toolkit.

Client User Interface

Here's a screenshot (Figure 6–3) of an ICB session running on a VT100 terminal attached to a Unix box.

```
▤□▦▦▦▦▦▦▦▦▦▦▦▦ shellx.best.com 1 ▦▦▦▦▦▦▦▦▦▦▦□▤
    Nickname      Idle  Sign-On  Account                              ⇧
   *PoohBear       30m   3:48pm  pvg@placenta.bigbook.com  (nr)
    Smartacus      15m   4:19pm  laurel@xanadu.cyborganic.net  (nr)
<stay> kagey :)
anyone reading any good books?
<Puma> *bite jamba*
<2Noj> bye for now...
<kagemusha> hi.
[=Sign-off=] kagemusha (brujah@alpha1.csd.uwm.edu) has signed off.
[=Depart=] 2Noj (WebMaster@user-168-121-21-65.dialup.mindspring.com) just left
<stay> what is reading?
<stay> what is a book?
is that a no?
<Puma> reading? I've got two I need to go finish...
<Puma> *fwap stay*
<stay> ouch *giggle*
<Puma> started 'em, need to finish 'em sometime...
what are you reading?
<stay> i read text books...do you think they are "good"? hehehe
<Puma> exciting stuff.... _The God Particle_ and _The Bell Curve_
<stay> the "bell curve"?
[=Sign-on=] neenja (neenja@digital.e-net.com) entered group
<neenja> hi
oh, are those books any good?█                                        ⇩
◁▭▭▭▭▭▭▭▭▭▭▭▭▭▭▭▭▭▭▭▭▭▭▭▭▭▭▭▭▭▭▭▭▭▭▭▭▭▭▭▭▭▭▭▭▭▭▭▭▭▭▭▷⊡
```

Figure 6–3 Sample ICB Chat Session.

The existing ICB client interface consists of a few parts:

1. Messages from other users are displayed in a scrolling text view. As new messages arrive from other users, they are displayed at the bottom of the screen, and travel up the screen as new messages arrive.

2. The main text view has a scrollback feature that allows the user to scroll back a number of lines to review messages that have already scrolled off the main screen. Currently the scrollback is limited by the VT100 terminal emulator used— in this case, NCSA Telnet for MacOS.

3. The user enters messages by simply typing. As the user types, her text appears at the bottom of the screen, and this blocks incoming messages until the user terminates her outgoing message. The user terminates a message by hitting the "return" or "enter" key. Hitting this key causes the message to be sent to the remote users.

4. The user has some keyboard shortcuts for inputting messages. For instance, Ctrl-U causes the current message to be erased completely.

In our implementation of an ICB client, we're going to build upon these features and add a new one:

• When you're typing a message in the existing ICB client interface, you block all incoming messages. In our implementation we'll separate the input view from the display view so that we can enter an outgoing message at our own pace and not block incoming messages.

A diagram of our implementation is shown in Figure 6–4 below.

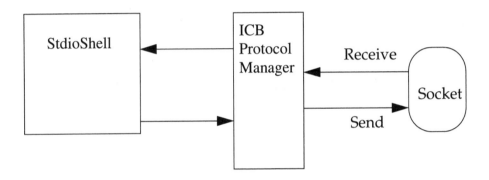

Figure 6–4 ICB Chat Client Implementation Block Diagram.

There are a few main pieces to the ICB client application:

1. Need some way to quickly display text to the user.

2. Need a way to quickly accept typed commands and text input from the user.

3. Need to connect to the ICB server in order to exchange messages.

4. Need to process special messages issued by the server.

To meet requirements 1 and 2 above, we will use the StdioShell utility class described in "Displaying Text and Obtaining User Input Quickly" beginning on page -297.

The implementation of the main `ICBProtocolManager` class is shown below.

Example 6-1 Chat Application: ICBProtocolManager Implementation

```
package JNC;


import java.net.*;
import java.util.*;
import java.io.*;

/**
 * Main class for managing an ICB client session
 */
public class ICBProtocolManager implements UserInputMonitor,
RemoteInputMonitor
{
//display constants
static final int
    MAX_DISPLAY_WIDTH = 740, //in pixels
    MAX_DISPLAY_HEIGHT = 500;


// ICB connection defaults
protected intfRemoteHostPort = 7326;//"SEAN"
protected StringfRemoteHostName = "icb.evolve.com";//default server


// ICB Packet types
static final char
    M_LOGIN      = 'a',// login packet
    M_LOGINOK    = 'a',// login response packet
    M_OPEN       = 'b',// open msg to group
    M_PERSONAL   = 'c',// personal msg
    M_STATUS     = 'd',// status update message
    M_ERROR      = 'e',// error message
    M_IMPORTANT  = 'f',// special important announcement
    M_EXIT       = 'g',// tell other side to exit
    M_COMMAND    = 'h',// send a command from user
    M_CMDOUT     = 'i',// output from a command
    M_PROTOVERS  = 'j',// protocol version information
    M_BEEP       = 'k',// beeps
    M_PING       = 'l',// ping packet
    M_PONG       = 'm';// response for ping packet

// ICB protocol info
static final int ICB_PROTOCOL_LEVEL= 1;// ICB protocol level known
static final char ICB_NULL    = '\001';// field divider used in packets

static final int MAX_NICKLEN= 12;// chars in a username
static final int MAX_PASSWDLEN = 12;// chars in a user password
static final int MAX_GROUPLEN= 8;// chars in a group name
static final int MAX_INPUTSTR= (250 - MAX_NICKLEN - MAX_NICKLEN - 6);
static final int MAX_FIELDS= 20;// fields in a packet
```

```java
//display formatting constants
static final String LBRACKET= "[=";
static final String RBRACKET= "=]";
static final String LANGLE= "<";
static final String RANGLE= ">";

//Default login information
protected String fUserID = "testuser";//default username (for
username@hostname)
protected String fNickName = "remus";//default nickname
protected String fGroup= "core";//default group to log into
protected String fPassword = "b0gu$";//to authenticate this testuser

//debugging
public int fDebugLevel = 1;
protected static final PrintStream fDebugOut = System.out;

public boolean fConnected = false;//state flag
//used to pull data from the server
protected byte[] fRawInputPacket;

protected SocketfRemoteHostSocket = null;
protected DataInputStream fRemoteHostInputStream = null;
protected OutputStream fRemoteHostOutputStream = null;
protected StdioShellfStdioShell = null; //interface to the user..

//used for reading commands from the user
protected DataInputStreamfInternalCmdInputStream;

//used for sending data to the user display
protected PrintStreamfInternalDisplayOutputStream;
//used to read user input
protected PipedInputStreamfUserDisplayStream;

//used to monitor input from the remote host
protected ICBRemoteInputMonitor fRemoteInputMonitor = null;

//used to monitor input from the user
protected ICBUserInputMonitor fUserInputMonitor = null;

//used for displaying time
Date fCurrentDate;

/**
* constructor
*/
public ICBProtocolManager()
{

    //we add some random info to the nickname to make it
    //less likely that novice's nicknames will collide
    Random tempRand = new Random();
```

```
    fNickName +=  tempRand.nextLong();
    if (fNickName.length() > 12) fNickName =
        fNickName.substring(0,11);//truncate
    tempRand = null;

    try {
        //allocate a pipe from protocol mgr to UI
        //the protocolmgr can write to screen with this
        PipedOutputStream displayOutputStream =
            new PipedOutputStream();
        fUserDisplayStream =
            new PipedInputStream(displayOutputStream);
        fInternalDisplayOutputStream =
            new PrintStream(displayOutputStream);
    }
    catch (IOException ioEx) {
        System.err.println("allocating streams failed: " + ioEx);
        return;
    }

    //now create the GUI
    fStdioShell = new StdioShell(
                    "WickedFastICB 1.0",fUserDisplayStream,
                    MAX_DISPLAY_WIDTH, MAX_DISPLAY_HEIGHT);
    fInternalCmdInputStream =
        new DataInputStream(fStdioShell.getInputStream());

    fStdioShell.resize(MAX_DISPLAY_WIDTH, MAX_DISPLAY_HEIGHT);
    fStdioShell.show();


    //preallocate our input buffer
    //(so we're not reallocating it on every read)
    fRawInputPacket = new byte[258];
    //get our login time (today's Date)
    fCurrentDate = new Date();

    //try to open the connection
    try {  openConnection(); }
    catch (Exception openEx) {
        System.err.println(
            "openConnection failed with ex: " + openEx);
        return;
    }

    //build and start the monitors...
    fRemoteInputMonitor = new ICBRemoteInputMonitor(this);
    fUserInputMonitor = new ICBUserInputMonitor(this);
    fUserInputMonitor.start();
    fRemoteInputMonitor.start();
} //ICBProtocolManager

/**
```

```
 * init connection to remote server
 */
protected void openConnection() throws Exception
{
    // Connect a new socket to the ICB server...
    fRemoteHostSocket =
        new Socket(fRemoteHostName, fRemoteHostPort);

    // Attach streams to the Socket
    fRemoteHostInputStream =
        new DataInputStream(fRemoteHostSocket.getInputStream());
    fRemoteHostOutputStream = fRemoteHostSocket.getOutputStream();

    if (fDebugLevel > 0)
        fDebugOut.println("openConnection OK!");
}//openConnection


/**
 * Shut down connection to the remote server
 */
protected void closeConnection()
{
    fRemoteHostInputStream = null;
    fRemoteHostOutputStream = null;

    if (fRemoteHostSocket != null)
        try {
            fRemoteHostSocket.close();
            if(fDebugLevel > 0) fDebugOut.println(
                "fRemoteHostSocket closed.");
        }
        catch(IOException ioEx) {
            fDebugOut.println("socket.close() threw: "+ ioEx);
        }


    fRemoteHostSocket = null;
}//closeConnection

/**
 * What follows are methods for dealing with data arriving from the
 * remote host.
 */


/**
 * read input from the remote host
 * this method will be called periodically by a driving thread
 */
public void readRemoteInput()
{
    String[] packet;
```

```java
        //read until we run out of incoming packets...
        while ((packet = readPacket()) != null ) {
            handlePacket(packet);
        }
}//readRemoteInput

/**
 * Gets a complete packet from the socket and splits it
 * into multiple fields,
 * delimited by  SOH (start-of-header, or ^A).
 * The packet type goes into packet[0],
 * the rest of the  packet in packet[1]...
 * @returns String[] A packet split into multiple fields.
 */
protected synchronized String[] readPacket()
{
    int packetLength = 0;
    int i = 0;
    int numTokens = 0;
    int bytesRead  = 0;

    fRawInputPacket[0] = 0;//clear the length?

    try {
        //read in packet length and packet type first
        bytesRead =
            fRemoteHostInputStream.read(fRawInputPacket, 0, 2);
        if(fDebugLevel > 1)
            fDebugOut.println("bytesRead: " + bytesRead);
        if (bytesRead <= 0) return null;


        packetLength = fRawInputPacket[0];
        if(packetLength < 0) {
            //overall data length > 255,
            //streamed over several packets.
            //adjust length to be *just* for this packet
            packetLength = packetLength + 256;
        }

        if (fDebugLevel > 1)
            fDebugOut.println("packetLength = " + packetLength);

        //push the packet type into fRawInputPacket[0]
        fRawInputPacket[0] = fRawInputPacket[1];
        if (fDebugLevel > 1)
            fDebugOut.println("packet type = '"+
                        (char) fRawInputPacket[0]+
                        "' (" + fRawInputPacket[0] + ")");

        // stuff in a fake delimiter for StringTokenizer
        fRawInputPacket[1] = '\0';
```

```
        fRemoteHostInputStream.read(fRawInputPacket,
                                2, packetLength - 1);

        if(fDebugLevel > 2)  fDebugOut.println(
            "rawPacket = '" +
            new String(fRawInputPacket, 0).substring(2,
                packetLength) + "'");
    }
    catch(IOException e) {
        System.err.println("readPacket ex: " + e);
        return null;
    }


    //create a new StringTokenizer to
    //break the raw packet into a series of delimited field Strings
    StringTokenizer strtok = new StringTokenizer(
                new String(fRawInputPacket, 0, 0, packetLength),
                ICB_NULL + "\0");

    //slurp all of the field tokens into the packet array
    numTokens = strtok.countTokens();
    String[] fieldList = new String[numTokens];

    for (i = 0; i < numTokens; i++) {
        fieldList[i] = (String)strtok.nextElement();
    }

    return fieldList;
}//readPacket


/**
 * Process an incoming packet
 */
public void handlePacket(String[] packet)
{

    if(packet.length == 0) {
        if (fDebugLevel > 0)
            System.err.println("handlePacket err: empty packet");
        return;
    }

    // Process incoming packet
    switch(packet[0].charAt(0)) {

        case M_PING:
            handlePacket_Ping(packet);
            break;

        case M_BEEP:
            handlePacket_Beep(packet);
```

```
                    break;

            case M_PROTOVERS:
                handlePacket_ProtoVersion(packet);
                break;

            case M_LOGINOK:
                handlePacket_LoginOkMsg(packet);
                break;

            case M_OPEN:
                handlePacket_OpenMsg(packet);
                break;

            case M_STATUS:
                handlePacket_StatusMsg(packet);
                break;

            case M_ERROR:
                handlePacket_ErrorMsg(packet);
                break;

            case M_IMPORTANT:
                handlePacket_ImportantMsg(packet);
                break;

            case M_EXIT:
                handlePacket_Exit(packet);
                break;

            case M_CMDOUT:
                handlePacket_CmdOutMsg(packet);
                break;

            case M_PERSONAL:
                handlePacket_PersonalMsg(packet);
                break;

            case ICB_PROTOCOL_LEVEL:
                //ignore
                break;

            default:
                fDebugOut.println("Unknown packet type: " + packet[0].charAt(0));
                return;
    } // switch(packet[0].charAt(0))


} /* handlePacket */

/**
* handle an important message packet
* @param packet The message packet received.
```

```java
*/
public void handlePacket_ImportantMsg(String[] packet)
{
    if(fDebugLevel > 1)
        fDebugOut.println("handlePacket_ImportantMsg()");

    if(packet.length != 3)
        fDebugOut.println("ImportantMsg length error");
    else
        display(LBRACKET+"*"+packet[1]+"*"+RBRACKET+" "+packet[2]);

} // handlePacket_ImportantMsg(String[] packet)


/**
 * Process an open message sent to the entire current group. (M_OPEN)
 * @param packet The message packet received.
 */
public void handlePacket_OpenMsg(String[] packet)
{
    if(fDebugLevel > 1) fDebugOut.println("handlePacket_OpenMsg()");

    if(packet.length != 3) fDebugOut.println("OpenMsg length error");
    else display(LANGLE+packet[1] + RANGLE +" " + packet[2]);

}//handlePacket_OpenMsg

/**
 * Process a private message sent just to me. (M_PERSONAL)
 * @param packet The message packet received.
 */
public void handlePacket_PersonalMsg(String[] packet)
{
    if(fDebugLevel > 1) fDebugOut.println("handlePacket_PersonalMsg()");

    if(packet.length == 2)
        display(LANGLE+"*"+packet[1]+"*"+RANGLE);
    else if(packet.length == 3)
        display(LANGLE+"*"+packet[1]+"*"+RANGLE+" "+packet[2]);
    else
        fDebugOut.println("PersonalMsg length error");
}//handlePacket_PersonalMsg

/**
 * handle a BEEP packet
 * @param packet The message packet received.
 */
public void handlePacket_Beep(String[] packet)
{
    if(fDebugLevel > 1) fDebugOut.println("handlePacket_Beep()");

    if(packet.length != 2) {
        fDebugOut.println("Beep length error");
```

```
            return;
    }

    //we can't beep easily, so we just tell the user
    display(LBRACKET+"Beep!"+RBRACKET+" "+ packet[1] +" sent you a beep.");

    return;
} // handlePacket_Beep(String[] packet)


/**
 * handle a a command output (result) packet
 * @param packet The message packet received.
 */
public void handlePacket_CmdOutMsg(String[] packet)
{
    if(fDebugLevel > 1) fDebugOut.println(
        "handlePacket_CmdOutMsg(" + packet.length +") " + packet[1]);

    if(packet.length < 2) {
        System.err.println("CmdOutMsg length err");
        return;
    }

    // Header for a group listing
    if(packet[1].equals("gh"))
    {
        return;
    } // else if(packet[1].equals("gh"))

    // Who group listing - is this ever sent?
    else if(packet[1].equals("wg"))
    {
        if(fDebugLevel > 0)
            fDebugOut.println("wg command output received");

        if(packet.length < 3) fDebugOut.println(
            "CmdOutMsg Who Group listing length err");
        else if(packet.length == 3) // group name from a who command
            display("Group: "+packet[2]);
        else
            display("Group: "+packet[2]+"  "+packet[3]);

        return;
    } // else if(packet[1].equals("wg"))

    // Header for a who listing
    else if(packet[1].equals("wh"))
    {
        // see below to line up header and text
        //display(" Nickname         Idle      Sign-On  UserID");
        return;
    } // else if(packet[1].equals("wh"))
```

```
// Who listing
else if(packet[1].equals("wl"))
{
    int idletime, idleh, idlem, idles;
    StringBuffer s = new StringBuffer(128);

    if(packet.length != 10)
    {
        fDebugOut.println("CmdMsgOut Who Listing length err");
        return;
    }

// "  Nickname           Idle      Sign-On  UserID
// " *munge        1:15:00  Jul19  08:46  vapid@rawthought.com (nr)"
//    23              4        6        7      8                    9
    s.append(" ");

    // prepend asterisk to group moderator's name
    if(packet[2].charAt(0) == 'm')
        s.append('*');
    else
        s.append(' ');

    // nickname
    //pad nickname out to 15 spaces
    int nickLen = packet[3].length();
    if (nickLen < 15) {
        for (int catCount = 0;
                catCount < (15 - nickLen); catCount++)
            packet[3] += " "; //append a space
    }

     s.append(packet[3]); //append the actual username

    // idle time
    idletime = Integer.parseInt(packet[4]);
    idleh = idletime / 3600;
    idlem = idletime / 60 % 60;
    idles = idletime % 60;
    if(idleh > 0)
    {
        s.append(idleh);
        s.append(':');
        if(idlem < 10) s.append('0');
    }
    else
    {
        s.append("   ");
        if(idlem < 10) s.append(' ');
    }
    s.append(idlem);   s.append(":");
    if(idles < 10) s.append('0');
```

```
        s.append(idles);
        s.append("   ");

        // packet[5] = response time, obsolete

        // login time
        s.append( dateToICBTimeStr(
            new Date( Long.parseLong(packet[6]) * 1000L)) );

        s.append("   ");

        s.append(packet[7]);   s.append('@');
        s.append(packet[8]);
        s.append("   ");

        // (nr) flag for not being registered
        s.append(packet[9]);

        display(s.toString());
        return;
    } // if(packet[1].equals("wl"))

    else if(packet[1].equals("c"))
    {
        if(fDebugLevel > 0)
            fDebugOut.println("c command output received");

        display("% "+ '/' +packet[2]);
        return;
    } // else if(packet[1].equals("c"))

    // Generic command output
    else if(packet[1].equals("co"))
    {
        if(packet.length == 3)
        {
            // "Group: foo       (pvl) Mod: (None)       Topic: bar"
            // becomes "foo       (pvl) Mod: (None)       Topic: bar" and
            //    user header is attached here instead of in "wh"
            if(packet[2].startsWith("Group: "))
            {
                display(packet[2].substring(7));
                display("  Nickname          Idle      Sign-On  UserID");
            }
            else
                display(packet[2]);
        }
        else display("");//blank line


        return;
    } // else if(packet[1].equals("co"))
```

```
    else
    {
        fDebugOut.println(
            "CmdOutMsg Unknown Command Type = "+packet[1]);
        return;
    }
} // handlePacket_CmdOutMsg(String[] packet)


/**
 * We received an error message from the ICB server.
 * @param packet The packet received. (M_ERROR: error message)
 */
public void handlePacket_ErrorMsg(String[] packet)
{
    if(fDebugLevel > 1)
        fDebugOut.println("handlePacket_ErrorMsg()");

    if(packet.length != 2) {
        //fDebugOut.println("ErrorMsg length err");
        return;
    }

    display( LBRACKET + "Error" + RBRACKET + " " + packet[1] );
}//handlePacket_ErrorMsg


/**
 * We received a packet from the ICB server telling us to exit
 * ( M_EXIT: exit message)
 * @param packet The packet received.
 */
public void handlePacket_Exit(String[] packet)
{
    if(fDebugLevel > 1)
        fDebugOut.println("handlePacket_ExitMsg()");

    if(packet.length != 1)
        fDebugOut.println("Exit msg length err");
    else   shutdown();

}

/**
 * The ICB server sent us a message letting us know we
 * logged in correctly. (M_LOGINOK: login packet receipt)
 * @param packet The packet received.
 */
public void handlePacket_LoginOkMsg(String[] packet)
{
    if(fDebugLevel > 1)
        fDebugOut.println("handlePacket_LoginOkMsg()");
```

```
    fConnected = true;

}//handlePacket_LoginOkMsg

/**
 * We received a ping message from the ICB server.(M_PING)
 * Respond with a pong message.
 * @param packet The packet received.
 */
public void handlePacket_Ping(String[] packet)
{
    if(fDebugLevel > 1) fDebugOut.println("handlePacket_Ping()");

    if(packet.length != 1) fDebugOut.println("Ping msg length err");
    else sendPacket("" + M_PONG);

}//handlePacket_Ping


/**
 * Process a packet containing ICB protocol version info.
 * @param packet The packet received.
 */
public void handlePacket_ProtoVersion(String[] packet)
{
    int proto_level = 0;

    if(fDebugLevel > 1) fDebugOut.println("handlePacket_Proto()");

    if(packet.length != 4) {
        fDebugOut.println("ProtoVersion msg length err");
        return;
    }

    try {
        proto_level = Integer.parseInt(packet[1]);
    }
    catch (NumberFormatException e) {
        fDebugOut.println("handlePacket_ProtoVersion ex: "+ e );
    }

    if(proto_level != ICB_PROTOCOL_LEVEL)
        fDebugOut.println("Bogus Protocol Level: "+ proto_level);
    else sendLogin();

    return;
}//handlePacket_ProtoVersion


/**
 * Process a system status message sent by the server.
 * @param packet The packet received.
 */
```

```java
public void handlePacket_StatusMsg(String[] packet)
{
    if(fDebugLevel > 1) fDebugOut.println("handlePacket_StatusMsg()");

    if(packet.length != 3) fDebugOut.println("StatusMsg length err");
    else {
//two status messages we filter for:
// 3:M_STATUS:Drop:Your connection will be dropped in 4 minutes due
// to idle timeout.:
// 3:M_STATUS:Drop:Your connection has been idled out.:
        if(packet[1].equals("Drop"))
        {
            if(packet[2].equals(
                    "Your connection has been idled out.")) {
                shutdown();
            }
            else {
                //ping the server to reset the idle?
                sendServerCommand("ping", "server");
            }
        }
        else
            display(LBRACKET+packet[1]+RBRACKET+" "+packet[2]);
    }

    return;
} // handlePacket_StatusMsg(String[] packet)




/**
 * What follows are methods for dealing with user input.
 */



/**
 * read some user input
 */
public void readUserInput()
{

    String userCmdStr = null;
    try { userCmdStr = fInternalCmdInputStream.readLine(); }
    catch (IOException ioEx) {
        System.err.println("readLine failed with: " + ioEx);
    }

    if (userCmdStr != null) {
        handleUserInput(userCmdStr);
    }
}//readUserInput

/**
```

```
 * Handle input from the user.
 */
public void handleUserInput(String inputStr)
{

    if (inputStr.length() > MAX_INPUTSTR) {
        //input string is too long...truncate it!
        inputStr = inputStr.substring(0,(MAX_INPUTSTR - 1));
    }

    if (inputStr.startsWith("/") ) {
        //user has issued a command -- handle it!
        sendCommand(inputStr);
    }
    else sendOpenMsg(inputStr); //send input to the current group

}//handleUserInput


/**
 * Process a user-supplied /command line and send it off.
 * @param text The command line to be processed.
 */
public void sendCommand(String text)
{
    String command = "";
    String args = "";

    if(fDebugLevel > 1)
        fDebugOut.println("sendCommand('"+text+"')");

    if(fConnected) {
        int space = -1;

        // [0] = '/', [1..space-1] = command, [space+1..] = args
        space = text.indexOf(' ');
        if(space == -1)
            command = text.substring(1).toLowerCase();
        else {
            command = text.substring(1, space).toLowerCase();
            args = text.substring(space+1);
        }

        if(fDebugLevel > 0) fDebugOut.println(
            "Sending command: '"+command+":"+args+"'");

        // Test for user command or send it on to the server
        handleUserCommand(command, args);

    } // if(fConnected)
    else fDebugOut.println("send cmd err: No connection.");

} // sendCommand(String text)
```

```
/**
* Deal with a command issued by the user.
* Tries to deal with commands locally first, then passes on to the server.
* Note that command is always lowercase, args is mixed-case.
* @param command A string which contains a  command.
* @param args  Parameters for the command.
*/
public void handleUserCommand(String command, String args)
{
    if(fDebugLevel > 1) fDebugOut.println(
        "handleUserCommand('"+command+"', '"+args+"')");

    //we currently only support one local ICB command:
    // the "quit" command ("/q" or "/quit")
    //everything else is forwarded to the server...

    if(command.equals("q") || command.equals("quit")) {
        shutdown();
    } // quit
    else {
    // pass it on to the server
    if(fDebugLevel > 1) fDebugOut.println("An actual icb command!");
    sendServerCommand(command, args);
    }
} // handleUserCommand(String command, String args)

/**
* What follows are methods for sending data to
* the remote server.
*/

/**
* Send an ICB packet out on the remote server output stream.
* ICB packets are comprised of:
* <OL>
* <LI>A single length byte.
* <LI>Length number of data bytes.
* </OL>
* @param dataStr A string to be sent.
*/
protected  void sendPacket(String dataStr)
{
    if(fDebugLevel > 1)
        fDebugOut.println("icbSendPacket('"+ dataStr +"')");

    int dataLen = dataStr.length();
    //convert to array of bytes..add space for null and length bytes
    byte[] packetBytes = new byte[dataLen + 2];
    packetBytes[0] = (byte) (dataLen + 1); //the length byte
    dataStr.getBytes(0,dataLen,packetBytes,1);
    packetBytes[dataLen + 1] = 0; //stuff in null
```

```
    try {
        fRemoteHostOutputStream.write(packetBytes);
        if (fDebugLevel > 1) fDebugOut.println("wrote OK");
    }
    catch (IOException ioEx) {
        System.err.println("sendPacket failed: " + ioEx);
        fConnected = false;
    }
}

/**
 * Send an open message to the entire current group.
 * @param msg The message to send.
 */
public void sendOpenMsg(String msg)
{
    if(fDebugLevel > 1) fDebugOut.println("sendOpenMsg('"+msg+"')");

    if(!fConnected) fDebugOut.println("Error: No connection.");
    else
        sendPacket(M_OPEN + msg);
}//sendOpenMsg


/**
 * Send a command directly to the ICB server.
 * @param command The command to send.
 * @param args Parameters for the command.
 */
public void sendServerCommand(String command, String args)
{
    sendPacket(M_COMMAND + command + ICB_NULL + args);
}//sendServerCommand


/**
 * Send a login packet to the ICB server
 * @param command A command to send.
 */
public void sendLogin()
{
    if(fDebugLevel > 1) fDebugOut.println("sendLogin()");

    if(fConnected) fDebugOut.println("Error: Already connected.");
    else
        sendPacket(M_LOGIN +
                    fUserID+ ICB_NULL +
                    fNickName+ICB_NULL +
                    fGroup+ ICB_NULL +
                    "login"+ICB_NULL +
                    fPassword);
}//sendLogin
```

```
/**
 * What follows is utility stuff for ICB
 */

//set up the month name table ahead of time

static String[] fMonthNameTable =
        { "Jan", "Feb", "Mar", "Apr", "May", "Jun",
          "Jul", "Aug", "Sep", "Oct", "Nov", "Dec" };

/**
 * Generate an appropriate timestamp string given a Date.
 * @param when Date to get time for...
 * @returns String The given time in the form "Jan01  00:00".."Dec25 23:59"
 */
public String dateToICBTimeStr(Date when)
{
    Date now = new Date();
    int date, hour, min;
    StringBuffer s = new StringBuffer(11);

    if(fDebugLevel > 1)
        fDebugOut.println("dateToICBTimeStr("+when+")");

    date = when.getDate();
    hour = when.getHours();
    min = when.getMinutes();

    //if date is same as fCurrentDate, don't display month/date
    if (fCurrentDate.getDate() == date) s.append("      ");
    else {
        s.append(fMonthNameTable[when.getMonth()]);
        if(date < 10) s.append('0');
        s.append(date);
    }
    s.append(' ');

    if(hour < 10) s.append('0');
    s.append(hour);

    s.append(':');

    if(min < 10) s.append('0');
    s.append(min);

    return s.toString();
} // dateToICBTimeStr(Date when)


/**
 * Display a string to the user
```

```
*/
public void display(String msg)
{
    if (fInternalDisplayOutputStream != null)
        fInternalDisplayOutputStream.println(msg);
}//display

/**
 * close down and clean up
 */
public void shutdown()
{
    if (fDebugLevel > 0) fDebugOut.println("shutdown...");
    closeConnection();//try to shut down our connection...
    System.exit(0);//close down the app

}//shutdown



} /* class ICBProtocolManager */
```

The final ICB chat client implementation user interface is shown in Figure 6–5 below.

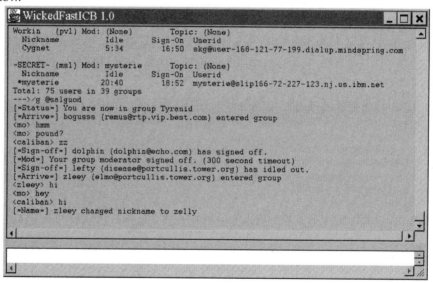

Figure 6–5 Java ICB Client User Interface.

Debugging Java Communications Code

As a rule, it's rare when communications and networking code runs right the first time— you almost always need to run through a series of tests and debug your communications code. On some platforms, using some languages and APIs, debugging communications can be very difficult. However, Java provides a number of facilities that make debugging easier.

Take Advantage of Exceptions

Make it a habit to wrap critical sections of your communications code that are likely to fail in `try...catch` exception handlers. Also, it's a good communications coding practice to handle nonfatal error conditions and try to recover. Because an exception handler can filter for specific exceptions, you can detect which error conditions are nonfatal and recover appropriately.

Be aware that adding exception handlers does add some runtime performance overhead to your code. Basically, every time you add an exception handler to your code, the Java runtime needs to allocate some memory for preserving the context before the `try`. However, on all of the platforms that currently run Java, you're unlikely to notice the performance hit.

One thing you might consider doing is throwing your own exceptions internally. This might allow you to track specific error conditions more easily.

Handle Exceptions at the Proper Level

If you're creating libraries of communications code that your clients will call, then by all means hide exceptions from your clients. For instance, let's say you're creating some kind of Web content transaction agent that searches for and downloads Web content automatically and provides the net result to your client. It's inappropriate to force your client to deal with IOExceptions. It would be better if your code handled such low-level exceptions and provided more appropriate exceptions to your higher-level clients. If your code has a set of high-level error conditions that make sense to pass back to the client, then by all means roll your own exceptions and do so.

Dump Debugging Info to System.err

Use System.err or your own output stream to display or log debug info. Typically `System.err` is for displaying fatal error conditions only, but if you're debugging, it might make it easier to separate your program's output from your debug output. Now, on some platforms `System.err` and `System.out` map to the same display area (such as under BC5 for Win32). On other platforms, such as the Mac JDK, each of these System output streams is provided its own separate display window and local-file logging facility.

Use Compile Time and Runtime Debug Flags in Your Code

In most of the sample code classes in this book you'll see a boolean instance variable called fDebugOn. This is a simple on-or-off approach to debugging—when fDebugOn is true, debug is turned on, and a series of debug messages will print to System.out. For more fine-grained control you might want to include an fDebugLevel integer variable in your classes and set the debug level to different levels as you debug. For instance, a debug level of 0 might mean debugging is turned off; a debug level of 10 might mean to dump every single condition you encounter to the debug log.

Prototype and Test Using Streams

Java provides an abundance of streams classes. You can use these classes to simulate data arriving from a remote host during a communications session. For instance, you can set up a file containing sample packet data, then read it in using a FileInputStream to simulate packets arriving from a remote host. You could also download actual packets from a remote host and dump them to a file using a FileOutputStream.

A useful tool for debugging communications code would be a stream class that inserts garbage data on your input or output streams. This would allow you to test your code's error handling and recovery with a known set of error conditions. For instance, you could create a subclass of FilterInputStream as follows:

Example 6-2 A FilterInputStream Subclass That Inserts Garbage

```
public class FlakyInputStream extends FilterInputStream
{
java.util.Random fRandomizer;
public FlakyInputStream(InputStream in)
{
    super(in);
    fRandomizer = new java.util.Random();
}
public int read() throws IOException
{
    if (Random().nextInt() > (Integer.MAX_VALUE/2)) {
        return Random.nextInt();
    }
}

//need to override read(byte[], int offset, int len) for completeness!
}
```

The basic idea here is that you can take your clean `InputStream` and run it through a filter that will insert garbage bytes at pseudorandom intervals. The `FlakyInputStream` simply returns a random value from `read` at random intervals. This is probably overkill if you're simply trying to test error recovery, but it can provide a good worst-case test scenario.

Use a Source-Level Debugger

The Java debugging tools for many platforms seem to be multiplying and increasing in strength. For instance, the Borland C++ 5.0 Java environment provides a good source-level debugging environment, as does the Metrowerks Java IDE for MacOS, and Symantec's Cafe product for MacOS and Win32. Even Unix addicts might find these environments more useful than the command-line debugger that comes with the JDK, *jdb*.

CHAPTER

7

- Overview of Datagrams

- The Domain Name Service (DNS) Protocol

- A Custom Datagram-Based Protocol

- A Datagram Client

- A Datagram Server

- New for JDK 1.1: Changes to `DatagramSocket`

- New for JDK 1.1: `MulticastSocket`

Datagrams A-Go-Go

We're now familiar with the streams-based interface that Socket provides. For many applications the convenience of the streams interface outweighs the overhead required. However, for certain applications it is much more efficient to utilize datagrams— small, fixed-length messages sent between nodes on a network.

Datagrams Can Be More Efficient

Let's look briefly at the overhead required for opening a TCP connection. First, you need to go through several stages of opening a connection. This takes quite a bit of time, as anyone who's ever tried to open a telnet or HTTP session to a busy host understands. Once the connection is open, sending and receiving data each involve several steps. Each one of these steps adds some time and data overhead to the transaction. If you're sending large amounts of data that absolutely must arrive at its destination, you should use the TCP protocol. However, if all you want to do is quickly send a simple, short message, all of this work may not be worthwhile.

What Are Datagrams?

The difference between datagrams and streams is like the difference between pagers and telephones. With a telephone, you make a connection to a specific telephone number (a telephone's "address"), if someone answers the phone you are able to talk for some period of time, exchanging arbitrary amounts of information, and then you close the connection. With a pager, you typically send a message via a radio tower one-way to a tiny radio receiver. Because of broadcast difficulties, and delays you cannot be certain if or when the paged party receives the message. The only way to tell is if you request and receive some kind of response (a phone call, email, a response page, etc.). You might retry several times if you get no response, then give up.

On an IP network such as the Internet, a protocol called UDP (the Unreliable Datagram Protocol) is used to transmit fixed-length datagrams. This is the protocol that Java taps into with the DatagramSocket class.

Overview of Datagrams

Datagrams are unreliable, so why would you ever want to use them? Datagrams have a couple of advantages.

- **Speed.** UDP involves low overhead. With TCP you have to go through the hassle of setting up and tearing down a connection, which takes time. For small amounts of data, it may not be worth it. The overhead time for setting up a connection may be greater than the amount of time it takes to send a small chunk of data. In many cases you could send and retry to send a datagram several times before a TCP connection could be opened.

- **Message-Oriented Instead of Stream-Oriented.** If you have a simple data structure such as a database record with fixed-length fields, it might be easier to simply send the chunk of bytes. The alternative is to slurp the record into a stream and go through all that hassle.

DatagramSocket and DatagramPacket

Two java.net classes define the heart of datagram-based messaging in Java: the DatagramSocket and the DatagramPacket.

The DatagramSocket is the interface through which DatagramPackets are transmitted. A DatagramPacket is simply an IP-specific wrapper for a block of data.

The DatagramSocket Class

In this section we'll take a look at the DatagramSocket class and API.

The DatagramSocket class provides a good interface to the UDP protocol. This class is responsible for sending and receiving DatagramPackets via the UDP protocol.

The most commonly used `DatagramSocket` methods are shown below.

Table 7-1 Commonly-Used `java.net.DatagramSocket` **Methods**

Method	Description
DatagramSocket	Constructor comes in two flavors: one where you specify the local port to be used, and one where the system picks an ephemeral local port for you.
receive	Receive a DatagramPacket from any remote server.
send	Send a DatagramPacket to the remote server specified in the DatagramPacket (see DatagramPacket constructors).
close	Tear down local communications resources. After this method has been called, release this object.
getLocalPort	Returns the local port this DatagramSocket is using. This should be the port you specified or the port the system picked if you didn't specify a port on instantiation.

Note that there are two flavors of `DatagramSockets`: those created to *send* `DatagramPackets`, and those created to *receive* `DatagramPackets`. A "send" `DatagramSocket` uses an ephemeral local port assigned by the native UDP implementation. A "receive" `DatagramSocket` requires a specific local port number.

These two different flavors of `DatagramSocket` can be created by calling one or the other constructor. The constructor that accepts a local port is meant for creating "receive" `DatagramSockets`.

The DatagramPacket Class

A `DatagramPacket` represents the datagram transmitted via a `DatagramSocket`. The most frequently-used methods of `DatagramPacket` are listed below.

Table 7-2 Commonly-Used `java.net.DatagramPacket` Methods

Method	Description
DatagramPacket	Constructor comes in two flavors: a "send" packet and a "receive" packet. For the send packet, you need to specify a remote InetAddress and port to which the packet should be sent, as well as a data buffer and length to be sent. For the receive packet, you need to provide an "empty" buffer into which data should be read, and the maximum number of bytes to be read.
getAddress	This method allows you to either obtain the InetAddress of the host that sent the DatagramPacket, or to obtain the InetAddress of the host to which this packet is addressed.
getData	This method allows you to access the raw binary data wrapped in the DatagramPacket.
getLength	This method allows you to determine the length of data wrapped in the DatagramPacket without getting a reference to the data block itself.
getPort	Returns either the port of the server to which this packet will be sent, else it returns the port of the server that sent this packet, depending on whether the packet was built to be sent or built to receive data.

Again, you need to be careful to distinguish between "send" `DatagramPackets` and "receive" `DatagramPackets`. Depending on whether the packet is sent or received, the information returned by `getAddress` and `getPort`, for instance, will vary.

How to Create a Datagram "Connection" Using the Socket Class, and Why You Shouldn't

It is possible to exchange data via datagrams using the `Socket` class. To do this, you must use one of the `Socket` constructors that includes the boolean `useStream` parameter, as in:

```
Socket(InetAddress, int port, boolean useStream)
```

and set useStream to false. This tells Socket to use the faster but unreliable UDP protocol (instead of the default TCP protocol) to exchange data with the remote host.

There are a couple of advantages to using this interface instead of a DatagramSocket/DatagramPacket combination. First, it provides a streams interface to datagrams. Second, you don't have to instantiate and manage a separate DatagramPacket to hold the data.

But there are significant disadvantages to using this interface as well. First, there's no way to detect if a particular datagram sent doesn't arrive at the remote host. Your streams interface can lie to you— the data goes out on the output stream, but you have no guarantee that it will arrive at the remote host in the correct order. You also have no guarantee that the data you're reading in on the input stream is arriving in the right order, or arriving at all.

Also, you still need to go through the hassle of setting up a "connection" with Socket in order to send connectionless datagrams. The Java runtime doesn't form any kind of connection, but you still need to go through the motions in order to be able to read/write data.

When you weigh the advantages and disadvantages of using a Socket over using a DatagramSocket, I think you'll conclude that DatagramSocket is the better interface for sending datagrams.

A Datagram Client Class

With most Internet protocols that are based on UDP datagrams, the client must implement the following behavior:

1. Send a request to a datagram server.
2. Wait for a response (acknowledgment).
3. If no response is received within X milliseconds, go to step 1.
4. Receive and process a response.

The critical step here is step 3. The datagram client needs to be capable of retrying its request simply because datagrams are unreliable. The only way to guarantee reliability with datagrams is through acknowledgments and retries.

In this section we'll look at writing a DatagramClient class that implements this core behavior.

Let's start by noticing that the DatagramClient must do two things: send and receive one datagram. It must send before it receives, but it should give up on receiving after a certain length of time so that it can resend if necessary.

Now, the DatagramSocket class does not provide an interface that says "Try to receive a datagram for X milliseconds." DatagramSocket only provides a single, synchronous receive method: Once you call DatagramSocket.receive, your thread is blocked indefinitely waiting for a datagram to arrive. So somehow we need to implement our DatagramClient such that the receive is carried out asynchronous to the send.

In order to do this, we'll define two helper classes for DatagramClient: DatagramReplySlave will be concerned with receiving datagrams, and the DatagramSendSlave will be charged with sending out our request datagram.

The DatagramReplySlave should set up a separate thread that simply starts waiting for a datagram to arrive, and times out if a datagram doesn't arrive within a certain length of time. The DatagramClient will set up and control the DatagramReplySlave. The implementation of DatagramReplySlave is shown below.

Example 7-1 **Implementation of DatagramReplySlave**

```
/**
 * A class for dealing with the problems of waiting
 * for a datagram response.
 */
class DatagramReplySlave extends Thread
{
private final static boolean fDebugOn = true;

DatagramPacket fRecvPacket;
DatagramSocket fRecvSocket;
DatagramClient fParent;
int fWaitTime = 50000;

public  int fReceivedState = 0;//neither received nor failed

/**
 * @param recvPacket The packet in which to stuff our results.
 * @param recvSocket The socket on which to receive data.
 * @param totalWaitTime The amount of time to wait for a response.
 */
public DatagramReplySlave(DatagramPacket recvPacket,
                          DatagramSocket recvSocket,
                          int totalWaitTime)
{
    fRecvPacket = recvPacket;
    fRecvSocket = recvSocket;
    fWaitTime = totalWaitTime;
}//DatagramReplySlave

/**
 * @returns int The receive status (fail or received)
```

```
*/
public synchronized int waitOnReply()
{
    try {wait(fWaitTime);}
    catch (InterruptedException intEx) {
        if (fDebugOn)
            System.out.println("waitOnReply interrupt!");
    }
    return fReceivedState;
} //waitOnReply

/**
 * perform all the useful stuff here
 */
public synchronized void run()
{
    if (fDebugOn)
        System.out.println("DatagramReplySlave running...");

    try {
        if (fDebugOn)
            System.out.println("DatagramReplySlave receiving...");
        fRecvSocket.receive(fRecvPacket);
        fReceivedState = 1;//received OK!
        System.out.println("DatagramReplySlave received OK!");
    }
    catch (IOException receiveEx) {
        System.err.println("receive failed! " + receiveEx);
        fReceivedState = -1;
    }; //receive failed!

    notify();//hey! we received or failed...
} //run

} /* class DatagramReplySlave */
```

Notice that all of the potentially blocking operations such as
DatagramSocket.receive are performed inside
DatagramReplySlave.run. This allows the DatagramReplySlave to
perform its potentially lengthy operations asynchronously from the
DatagramClient and DatagramSendSlave threads.

Notice also that a key method in DatagramReplySlave is waitOnReply. This
method causes the client caller to wait around for the state of the
DatagramReplySlave to change, or the timer to timeout. If the
DatagramReplySlave receives a datagram, it notifies any clients waiting via
waitOnReply. Alternatively, if the DatagramReplySlave doesn't receive a
datagram within the allotted period of time, the wait timer expires and the client
is notified.

Finally, notice that the DatagramReplySlave does not create its own
`DatagramSocket` on which to receive datagrams. Instead, the
DatagramReplySlave's master (`DatagramClient`) is expected to provide this
at instantiation. This allows the `DatagramClient` to share a single
`DatagramSocket` between its send and reply slaves.

The `DatagramSendSlave` should send the request datagram every few seconds
until told to stop. The `DatagramClient` will be in charge of telling the
`DatagramSendSlave` to start and stop sending.

The implementation of the `DatagramSendSlave` is shown below.

```
/**
 * a class for dealing with the problems of sending a datagrams
 */
class DatagramSendSlave extends Thread
{

protected final static boolean fDebugOn = true;

DatagramPacket fSendPacket;
DatagramSocket fSendSocket;
public  int fSendState = 0;//neither received nor failed
protected int fRetryInterval; //in msec

/**
 * @param sendPacket
 */
public DatagramSendSlave(DatagramPacket sendPacket,
                        DatagramSocket sendSocket,
                              int retryTime)
{
    fSendPacket = sendPacket;
    fSendSocket = sendSocket;
    fRetryInterval = retryTime;

}//DatagramSendSlave


/**
 * proceed with all of the time-consuming stuff here
 */
public void run()
{
    if (fDebugOn)
        System.out.println("DatagramSendSlave running...");

    while (fSendState == 0) {
        try {
          if (fDebugOn)
```

```
            System.out.println("DatagramSendSlave sending...");
          fSendSocket.send(fSendPacket);
          fSendState = 0;//sent OK!
      if (fDebugOn)
          System.out.println("DatagramSendSlave sent ok!");

          try {this.sleep(fRetryInterval);}
          catch (InterruptedException iEx) {
              if (fDebugOn)
                  System.err.println(
                      "DatagramSendSlave sleep interrupted!");
              fSendState = -1;
          };
      }
      catch (IOException sendEx) {
          if (fDebugOn)
              System.err.println("send failed! " + sendEx);
          fSendState = -1;
      };
   }

}//run

}/* class DatagramSendSlave */
```

The key method in the DatagramSendSlave is run, which simply sends a datagram, waits a fixed length of time, then resends and so on. This class's job is to keep sending the request datagram packet until told to stop. This class's run method is stopped by setting the fSendState to anything but 0.

Notice that once again the DatagramSendSlave does not create its own DatagramSocket on which to send datagrams; instead, the DatagramClient provides that socket at instantiation.

Building a DatagramClient class should now be straightforward. This class simply needs to:

- Create a DatagramReplySlave instance.

- Start the DatagramReplySlave listening for incoming datagrams.

- Create a DatagramSendSlave instance.

- Tell the DatagramSendSlave to start sending out a datagram.

- Wait on DatagramReplySlave.waitOnReply. When this method returns, we've either received a datagram or we've exceeded the amount of time we wanted to wait for a datagram.

The source for DatagramClient is shown below.

Example 7-2 Implementation of DatagramClient

```
/**
* A class that  forms the backbone of a basic
* send request/receive response datagram client
*/
public class DatagramClient
{

public final static boolean fDebugOn = true;

public final static int
    DEFAULT_MAX_DATAGRAM_SIZE = 512,//max size for an incoming datagram
    DEFAULT_MAX_RETRIES = 10;//number of times to resend if no response

protected DatagramSocket fSocket; //this is where we send/recv data
protected DatagramPacket
            fSendDatagram,
            fRecvDatagram;

protected byte[]
    fSendBuffer, //this is where the bytes are actually sourced
    fRecvBuffer; //this is where the bytes are actually stored

protected int
    fSendBufLength,
    fRecvBufLength;

protected int
    fSendPort,
    fRecvPort;

protected InetAddressfRemoteAddress;
protected int
    fRetryTimer = 5000, //in msec
    fRetryCount = 0;//number of times we've retried
protected DatagramReplySlave fReplySlave;
protected DatagramSendSlave fSendSlave;


/**
* This constructor should be used when the output
* buffer is known at instantiate time. However, you
* can always change the outputBuf later using
* setOutputBuf.
*
* @param inBufSizeSize of data buffer to return with recvd data.
* @param outBufA buffer of bytes to send to the remote host
* @param localPort The local port to use
*    (if 0, uses arbitrary local port).
* @param remotePort The remote port to which to send.
* @param remoteAddress The remote InetAddress to send data to.
* @param waitTime Milliseconds to wait for a reply.
```

```
*/
public DatagramClient(int inBufSize,
                      byte[] outBuf,
                      int localPort, int remotePort,
                      InetAddress remoteAddress,
                      int waitTime )
{
    fSendPort = remotePort;
    fRecvPort = localPort;
    fSendBuffer = outBuf;
    fSendBufLength = outBuf.length;
    fRecvBufLength =
        ((inBufSize > 0) ? inBufSize: DEFAULT_MAX_DATAGRAM_SIZE);
    fRecvBuffer = new byte[fRecvBufLength];

    fRemoteAddress = remoteAddress;
    fRetryTimer = ((waitTime > 0) ? waitTime: fRetryTimer);

    fRecvDatagram =
        new DatagramPacket(fRecvBuffer, fRecvBufLength);
    fSendDatagram =
        new DatagramPacket(fSendBuffer, fSendBufLength,
                           fRemoteAddress, fSendPort);
}//DatagramClient

/**
 * This constructor allows us to instantiate without
 * actually having an output buffer yet.
 * The output buf can subsequently be set with
 * setOutputBuf.
 * @param inBufSizeSize of data buffer to return w/rcvd data.
 * @param localPort The local port to use
 *    (if 0, uses arbitrary local port).
 * @param remotePort The remote port to which to send.
 * @param remoteAddress The remote InetAddress to send data to.
 * @param waitTime Milliseconds to wait for a reply.
 */
public DatagramClient(int inBufSize,
                      int localPort, int remotePort,
                      InetAddress remoteAddress,
                      int waitTime )
{
    fSendPort = remotePort;
    fRecvPort = localPort;
    fRecvBufLength =
        ((inBufSize > 0) ? inBufSize: DEFAULT_MAX_DATAGRAM_SIZE);
    fRecvBuffer = new byte[fRecvBufLength];

    fRemoteAddress = remoteAddress;
    fRetryTimer = ((waitTime > 0) ? waitTime: fRetryTimer);

    fRecvDatagram =
        new DatagramPacket(fRecvBuffer, fRecvBufLength);
```

```
}//DatagramClient


/**
* @param outBuf A buffer filled with data to be sent
*/
public void setOutputBuf(byte[] outBuf)
{
    fSendBuffer = outBuf;
    fSendBufLength = outBuf.length;
    fSendDatagram =
        new DatagramPacket(fSendBuffer, fSendBufLength,
                            fRemoteAddress, fSendPort);
}//setOutputBuf

/**
* This is where we manage the transaction
*/
public DatagramPacket handleTransaction()
    throws SocketException, IOException
{
    fRetryCount = 0;

    Bind();

    fSendSlave =
            new DatagramSendSlave(fSendDatagram, fSocket,
                                    fRetryTimer);

    fReplySlave =
            new DatagramReplySlave(fRecvDatagram, fSocket,
                        DEFAULT_MAX_RETRIES * fRetryTimer);
    fSendSlave.start();//start sending datagrams
    fReplySlave.start();//start waiting for incoming datagrams


    int recvState = fReplySlave.waitOnReply();//this blocks!

    if (fDebugOn)
        System.out.println("DatagramClient recvState: " + recvState);

    if (recvState != 1) fRecvDatagram = null;

    fSendSlave.fSendState = 1;//stop sender thread...

    //keep from running further...
    if (fReplySlave.isAlive())
    try {fReplySlave.stop(); } catch (Throwable tex) {}

    return fRecvDatagram;

}//handleTransaction
```

```
/**
* Bind the local resources we need
* (in this case, just the local  port)
*/
protected void Bind() throws SocketException
{
    //bind to the specific local port
    if (fRecvPort != 0) fSocket =
        new DatagramSocket(fRecvPort);
    else //get an arbitrary local port
        fSocket = new DatagramSocket();

    if (fDebugOn)
        System.out.println("Bound to: " + fSocket.getLocalPort());
}//Bind

/**
* dump all the allocated resources for this instance
*/
public void Dispose() //
{
    if (fSocket != null) fSocket.close();
    //be nice in preparing for GC
    fRecvDatagram = null;
    fSendDatagram = null;

    fSendBuffer = null;
    fRecvBuffer = null;

}//Dispose

}/* class DatagramClient */
```

The key method in the DatagramClient class is handleTransaction, which creates the necessary helper class instances and carries out the transaction. Notice that it is this method that creates a new DatagramSocket, creates the DatagramReplySlave and DatagramSendSlave, then synchronously blocks in DatagramReplySlave.handleTransaction waiting for the transaction to complete or fail within the allotted time.

A Datagram Server Class

Let's now implement the complement to the DatagramClient: a DatagramServer.

The `DatagramServer` is responsible for listening on a given port for a datagram request arriving from the client. This class is similar to the `DatagramReplySlave` we discussed previously since its main job is to simply wait for incoming datagrams.

The source for the `DatagramServer` is provided below.

Example 7-3 **Implementation of a DatagramServer**

```
package JNC;

import java.net.*;

/**
 * A base class for a server that receives datagram requests and
 * sends datagram responses
 */
public class DatagramServer
{
public final static int DEFAULT_MAX_DATAGRAM_SIZE = 512;//the default max
size we'll allow for an incoming datagram
protected DatagramSocket fRecvSocket; //this is where we receive/send data
from
protected DatagramPacketfRecvDatagram;
protected byte[]fRecvBuffer;
protected int   fRecvBufSize;
protected int   fRecvPort;

/**
 * @param port The port to listen on.
 * @param messageSize The size of the message to receive.
 */
public DatagramServer(int port, int recvBufSize)//(in) the port to listen on
{
    fRecvPort = port; //tuck away the port number we're going to listen on

    if (recvBufSize != 0) fRecvBufSize = recvBufSize; //allows our client to
set the buffer size if they so desire
    else fRecvBufSize = DEFAULT_MAX_DATAGRAM_SIZE;

}//DatagramServer

/**
 * Wait around for a datagram to arrive on the receive port.
 * Typically this blocks, waiting for data.
 * @returns DatagramPacket A received datagram packet
 */
public DatagramPacket waitForRequest() throws Exception
{
    fRecvBuffer = new byte[fRecvBufSize];
    fRecvDatagram = new DatagramPacket(fRecvBuffer, fRecvBufSize);

    fRecvSocket.receive(fRecvDatagram); //receive data into the datagram
```

```
     return fRecvDatagram;

}//waitForRequest


/**
 * Bind the local resources we need
 * (in this case, just the local static port)
 */
public void Bind() throws SocketException
{
    fRecvSocket = new DatagramSocket(fRecvPort);//bind to the local port
}//Bind


/**
 * dump all the allocated resources for this instance
 */
public void Dispose() //
{
    if (fRecvSocket != null) fRecvSocket.close();//## is there any harm in
calling this if Bind failed?
}//Dispose

}/* class DatagramServer */
```

Notice that the key `DatagramServer` method is `waitForRequest`. This
method is synchronous: that is, it blocks waiting for a request to arrive. Useful
subclasses of `DatagramServer` will likely want to set up a separate thread that
calls the `waitForRequest` method.

The `waitForRequest` method returns a `DatagramPacket`. We opted to return
the whole packet instead of just the enclosed data so you can obtain other useful
information from the packet such as the `InetAddress` and port of the requesting
client. This information is critical when you are replying to a client's request, as
we will see later in this chapter.

Datagram Applications

Now that we understand the basics of sending and receiving datagrams, let's look
at some applications of datagrams. Examples of critical Internet protocols that are
based on UDP datagrams include:

- BootP (Boot Protocol) and DHCP (Dynamic Host Configuration Protocol).
  These are protocols used to automatically configure hosts that have just
  booted on the network. These protocols help provide a newborn host with
  key information such as the address of the local DNS server.

- SNMP (Simple Network Management Protocol). This protocol is used to configure and manage various network devices such as routers, bridges, printers, and so forth.

- TFTP (Trivial File Transfer Protocol). This simple file-transfer protocol is used to transfer critical configuration files to a host that has just booted onto the network.

- DNS (Domain Name Service). This protocol is used to translate Internet domain names into IP addresses.

As you can see, datagram-based protocols are at the heart of the infrastructure of the Internet. Let's look at one of these protocols in detail.

The Domain Name Service (DNS) Protocol

The Internet DNS protocol, among others, uses datagrams for the most part. This helps keep host overhead and net traffic down. For small chunks of data, it is also faster.

The DNS protocol is a simple request-response protocol. A DNS client (known as a "Domain Name Resolver" or "DNR") asks questions of a DNS server. The DNS server responds with answers.

Currently, DNS is limited to a few categories of information. The most common is: Given a domain name (i.e., "www.rawthought.com"), what is the corresponding IP address? Other popular questions include: What's the mail server name for a given domain? Which server has authority over an entire domain? What's the hostname for a given IP address (reverse name lookup). There are other kinds of records (such as host info) but these are much less common and not guaranteed to be supported by all DNS servers.

In this section we'll look at implementing a DNS client using the DatagramClient class we implemented previously. This test application will query a DNS server and receive a response.

To understand how this example works, you have to understand a little bit about the DNS protocol. The way it works is that the DNR client first sends a datagram containing one or more "questions" to a known DNS server. Each question is completely independent from other questions in the packet. In our example, we'll send just a single question of a single type in a packet.

Each question consists of a domain name string in a special format, plus a question type code. The domain name string is broken up into a series of "labels," which are simply the dot-delimited tokens in a domain name string. For instance, the domain name "www.rawthought.com." consists of the labels "www", "rawthought", and "com" (as well as a zero-length terminating label).

Each label consists of a length byte followed by the label string, similar to the way strings are stored under the Pascal language. The final label in a domain name stored in this format is simply a label with a length byte of zero.

When the server responds to a client's query, it sends a datagram containing zero or more answers to the questions the client asked, plus an error code and some other status information. The response datagram also contains the original questions that the client sent. This allows the client to map answers to their corresponding questions. This might seem inefficient, but DNS uses a domain name compression scheme that reduces the overhead of echoing the questions in the response packet.

Without getting into too much detail, the compression scheme is this: Anywhere a domain name label can start, a pointer can be inserted that is a pointer to another label stored in the same packet. While the DNR is reading a response domain name label, it may be redirected by one of these pointers to read the tail end of the domain name from elsewhere in the packet. If the DNS query and response pertains to a single domain name, this can compress the space required to store several related domain names significantly. For instance, if the query pertains to the "rawthought.com" domain, and the response contains "ns.rawthought.com", "www.rawthought.com", "ftp.rawthought.com", and "shellx.rawthought.com", the space required to store these answers is the space required to store "rawthought.com", "ns", "www", "ftp", and "shellx", plus a few bytes of overhead, instead of the space required to store the four complete domain name strings.

Our sample implementation contains code for decompressing this compression scheme. The source for the DNS test application is shown below.

Example 7-4 DNS Test Code Implementation

```
import JNC.*;
import java.net.*;

/**
 * A class for demonstrating how the DNS protocol uses
 * UDP datagrams.
 */

public class DNSTest
{

public static void main(String[] args)
{
    byte[] outbuf = new byte[1024];
    int offset = 0;
```

```
try {
    //unfortunately, we can't even build an InetAddress
    //without, essentially, doing a DNS name lookup.
    //fortunately, most DNR implementations are smart
    //enough to translate a dotted-decimal string into
    //an IP address without actually doing a lookup
    InetAddress dnsHostAddress =
        InetAddress.getByName("204.156.128.10");
        //(replace with your own DNS server address)

    System.out.println("dnsHostAddress: " + dnsHostAddress);

    //build the outBuf
    offset = stuffHeader(outbuf, 0, 1);

    //use the domain name passed in, or a default
    String domainStr = "www.rawthought.com";
    if (args.length > 0) domainStr = args[0];

    offset = stuffDomainStr(outbuf, domainStr, offset);

    offset = stuffTypeAndClass(outbuf,offset);

    byte[] cleanOutBuf = new byte[offset + 1];
    System.arraycopy(outbuf,0,cleanOutBuf,0,offset + 1);



    DatagramClient DNSclient =
            new DatagramClient(1024,cleanOutBuf,
                               0, 53,
                               dnsHostAddress,
                               5000);

    DatagramPacket answerPacket =
        DNSclient.handleTransaction();

    if (answerPacket != null) {

        System.out.println("got return packet! " +
            answerPacket.getLength());

        //get the data from the datagrampacket
        byte[] inbuf = answerPacket.getData();

        //get the result code:
        int resultCode = getResultCode(inbuf);
        System.out.println("resultCode: " + resultCode);

        //how many answers did we receive?
        int totalAnswers = getAnswerRecordsCount(inbuf);
        offset = 12; //end of answer header...
```

```
            offset = dumpOneQuestion(inbuf,offset);

                //dump each answer....
                for (int recordCount = 0;
                        recordCount < totalAnswers;
                        recordCount++) {
                    offset = dumpOneRecord(inbuf,  offset);
                }

            }

        DNSclient.Dispose();

    }
    catch (Exception ex) {
        System.err.println("test threw: " + ex);
        return;
    }
}

/**
 * stuff the request header into the output buffer
 */
public static int
stuffHeader(byte[] outBuf, int offset, int numQuestions)
{
    //we skip identification...first 2 bytes
    outBuf[offset + 2] = 1; //sets RD (recursion desired) flag
    //we skip all other flag fields
    //up to 4 bytes now

    //stuff in num questions, 255 max
    outBuf[offset + 5] = (byte)numQuestions;

    return (offset + 12);//header is fixed at 12 bytes length
}//stuffHeader

/**
 * stuff in the domain name string we're querying for
 */
public static int
stuffDomainStr(byte[] outbuf, String domainStr, int offset)
{
    int byteIdx = offset;
    int charIdx = 0;
    int domainStrLen = domainStr.length();
    //create a buffer to hold all the labels and label
    //lengths. this will be longer than the incoming
    //domainStr by the extra first labellen and the
    //end null
    byte[] labelsBuf = new byte[domainStrLen + 2];
```

```
    //dump the basic bytes into the temp buffer
    domainStr.getBytes(0,domainStrLen,labelsBuf,1);
    labelsBuf[domainStrLen + 1] = 0;//end null

    int lastDotIdx = 0;
    //now walk through the outbuf replacing dots with
    //Pascal-String-style label lengths
    while( charIdx < domainStrLen)
    {
        int dotIdx = domainStr.indexOf(".",charIdx);
        if (dotIdx < 0) dotIdx = domainStrLen;
        System.out.println("dotIdx: " + dotIdx);

        //how many chars between start and dot?
        int labelLen = dotIdx - charIdx;
        System.out.println("labelLen: " + labelLen);

        labelsBuf[lastDotIdx] = (byte)labelLen;
        lastDotIdx = dotIdx + 1;
        charIdx = dotIdx + 1;
    }


    for (int idx = 0; idx < labelsBuf.length; idx++) {
        System.out.print((char)labelsBuf[idx] +
            "(" + labelsBuf[idx] + ")" +",");
    }
    System.out.print("\n");

    System.arraycopy(labelsBuf,0,outbuf,offset,labelsBuf.length);

    return (offset + labelsBuf.length);
}//stuffDomainStr

/**
* stuff in the query type and class
*/
public static int stuffTypeAndClass(byte[] outbuf,int offset)
{
    //stuff the A type
    outbuf[offset + 1] = 1;

    //stuff the IN class
    outbuf[offset + 3] = 1;

    return (offset + 4);
}//stuffTypeAndClass


//--- The following are methods for processing the response -----

/**
* get the response result code
```

```
*/
public static int getResultCode(byte[] inbuf)
{
    return inbuf[1] & 15; //just the first four bits

}//getResultCode

/**
* get a count of the number of records
*/
public static int getAnswerRecordsCount(byte[] inbuf)
{
    //answer records count is sum of answer RRs count,
    //authority RR count, additional RRs count
    int numAnswerRRs = (inbuf[6] << 8 ) + inbuf[7];
    int numAuthorityRRs = (inbuf[8] << 8) + inbuf[9];
    int numAdditionalRRs = (inbuf[10] << 8) + inbuf[11];
    int retVal = (numAnswerRRs + numAuthorityRRs + numAdditionalRRs);

    System.out.println("total answers: " + retVal);

    return retVal;

}//getAnswerRecordsCount

/**
* slurp one domain name string from the response buffer
*/
public static int pullOneDomainStr(byte[] inbuf, int offset)
{
    int labelLen = 0;
    String labelStr, domainNameStr;
    int startOffset = offset;
    int byteIdx = offset;

    domainNameStr = "";

    while (byteIdx < inbuf.length)
    {
        labelLen = inbuf[byteIdx];
        if (labelLen < 0) labelLen = -labelLen;
        System.out.println("labelLen: " + labelLen);

      if (labelLen > 63) {
      //handle compression scheme!
        //current two bytes are a 14 bit ptr
        byteIdx = ( (labelLen & 63) << 8) + inbuf[byteIdx+1];
        //clear two high bits of ptr

        labelLen = inbuf[byteIdx];
      }
```

```
        if (labelLen > 0) {
            labelStr =
                new String(inbuf, 0,byteIdx + 1,labelLen);
             System.out.println("labelStr: " + labelStr);
            domainNameStr += labelStr + ".";
            byteIdx += labelLen + 1;
        }
        else {
            byteIdx++;//get beyond the end null
            break;
        }
    }

    System.out.println("domainNameStr: " + domainNameStr);

    //skip beyond the ptr now
    if (byteIdx <= startOffset) byteIdx = startOffset + 2;
    return byteIdx;

}//pullOneDomainStr

/**
 * Print a single question's contents to stdout
 */
public static int dumpOneQuestion(byte[] inbuf, int offset)
{
int byteIdx = pullOneDomainStr(inbuf,offset);
  int queryType = (inbuf[byteIdx] << 8) + inbuf[byteIdx + 1];
  byteIdx += 2;
  int queryClass = (inbuf[byteIdx] << 8) + inbuf[byteIdx + 1];
  byteIdx += 2;

  System.out.println("query type: " + queryType +
                        " class: " + queryClass);
  return byteIdx;

}//dumpOneQuestion

/**
 * Print a single record's contents to stdout
 */
public static int dumpOneRecord(byte[] inbuf, int offset)
{
    int byteIdx = pullOneDomainStr(inbuf,offset);

    int type = (inbuf[byteIdx] << 8) + inbuf[byteIdx + 1];
    byteIdx += 2;
    int recClass = (inbuf[byteIdx] << 8) + inbuf[byteIdx + 1];
    byteIdx += 2;

    System.out.println("type: " + type + " class: " + recClass);

    //extract the 4-byte timeToLive value
```

```
    int timeToLive =
        (inbuf[byteIdx] << 24) + (inbuf[byteIdx + 1] << 16) +
        (inbuf[byteIdx + 2] << 8) +  inbuf[byteIdx + 3];

    byteIdx += 4;
    System.out.println("Time To Live (secs): " + timeToLive);

    int resourceDataLength =
        (inbuf[byteIdx] << 8) + inbuf[byteIdx+1];
    byteIdx += 2;

    System.out.println(
        "resource data length: " + resourceDataLength);


    if (resourceDataLength == 4) { //assume it's an IP address?
        System.out.println("possible IP address: " );

        for (int off = 0; off < 4; off++) {
            int octet = inbuf[byteIdx + off];
        if (octet < 0) octet += 256;
            System.out.print(octet + ".");
        }
      System.out.println("\n");//flushes output

    }

    byteIdx += resourceDataLength;//step beyond current record

    return byteIdx;

}//dumpOneRecord



}/* class DNSTest */
```

Notice a few things about this code:

- We use a trick to build an `InetAddress` from the known 4-byte IP address of our DNS server. Since the `InetAddress` class doesn't provide a constructor that accepts a four-byte IP address, we must trick the `InetAddress` into building the address we want. Therefore, what we do is build call `InetAddress.getByName` with the IP address in a dotted-decimal string format. thus, the IP address array `[165,227,67,1]` becomes the String "`165.227.67.1.`" Now, typically `InetAddress.getByName` uses the DNR native to a particular platform to translate a string into an IP address. However, most platform's DNRs are smart enough to know that a dotted-decimal format string can be translated into an IP address locally, without having to query a DNS server. In this case, we're taking advantage of that intelligence to overcome a limitation of the `InetAddress` interface.

- In this test code, we've implemented all of the methods as static methods. If you were really going to implement a DNR, you'd probably roll these methods into a separate `DatagramClient` subclass.

In this section we've glossed over some of the gritty details of implementing a DNS client. For a solid reference on the DNS protocol see Stevens, W. Richard, and Gary R. Wright, Tcp/Ip Illustrated: The Implementation. Addison-Wesley, 1995, ISBN: 020163354X

Writing a Custom Datagram Protocol

While it is interesting and useful to examine an existing datagram-based protocol such as DNS, it is even more instructive to create and implement our own datagram-based protocol, including both a client, server, and perhaps an interserver protocol.

In this section we'll look at an example of implementing your own datagram-based protocol. We'll create a new protocol called the Switchboard protocol. This protocol will provide a service directory. Clients will connect to Switchboard servers in order to discover which services are available to them on a network.

The Switchboard protocol takes the idea of DNS one step further. With DNS, you have to know the named host to which you want to connect. This imposes several harsh restrictions:

- Your server must use a domain name registered with InterNIC, the Internet domain name registration authority. As anyone who's registered a name before knows, registration takes time and money.

- Your potential clients must know the name of the server they wish to contact. In order for users to find your domain, someone has to tell them that it exists.

- Your server must have one or more fixed IP addresses: the addresses assigned when your domain name was registered. This precludes you from offering service from dynamic IP addresses (those assigned on-the-fly to most dial-in PPP and SLIP connections, for instance).

The Switchboard protocol attempts to overcome these restrictions in the following manner:

- It only requires that the client know the address of the Switchboard server itself. This is similar to DNS's requirement that DNRs know the address of one or more DNS servers.

- The service records that the Switchboard system collects and distributes are independent of domain names, based instead on "service type". Switchboard clients need only know the service type they're looking for, and the Switchboard server will provide the appropriate records.

- The Switchboard protocol relies on service providers registering themselves with the Switchboard server. As soon as the service provider registers itself with a Switchboard server, all of the clients that talk to that server will then immediately "know" about the service provider.

- Since the protocol relies on service providers being proactive and registering themselves, a service provider can provide service from a dynamically-assigned IP address. For instance, you might have a part-time Internet connection and wish to provide a part-time service from your machine. The way to do this is: As soon as you wish to provide services, simply register with the Switchboard server.

In order to implement this system, we're going to break it up into three generic entities: a Switchboard Server, a Switchboard Client, and a Service Provider.

A Switchboard Server is a repository for service records— records that describe which services are available on the network, and where. A Switchboard Client connects to a Switchboard Server and asks for service records of different types.

A Service Provider is a third-party server on the network that wishes to register its services with a Switchboard Server so that potential Switchboard Clients can access its services. A diagram illustrating the relationship between the three entity types is shown below.

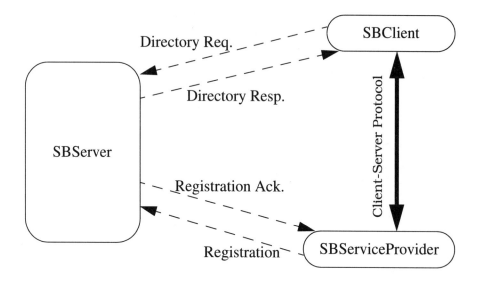

Figure 7–1 Switchboard Data Flow Diagram.

Let's give a solid example of how this protocol might be used. Let's say you want to provide check-verification services with your server. So your server registers its services (with the appropriate "check verification" service type) with a known Switchboard server. Then, a client who is looking for a check verification service asks the Switchboard server which servers provide such a service. The Switchboard server passes along your server's contact information to the client. The client then contacts your server directly to carry out check verification transactions using the "check verification protocol." Note that the client needn't perform any DNS lookups or know any of the host names involved. In a way, this keeps the Switchboard system more appropriately abstract than DNS.

Now let's implement the core Switchboard Client, Switchboard Server, and Switchboard Service Provider classes. Other applications can use these classes depending on which role they wish to play.

The Switchboard Client

We'll start by approaching this protocol from the Client's point of view. From the Client side, there are a few basic steps to the Switchboard protocol:

1.   The Client needs to locate a Switchboard Server. He can either do that by punching in an IP address manually (as is often done with DNS), or via

some other means. For this example we're going to assume that the IP address of the server is known ahead of time, and the client simply makes requests of that server. Later on we'll talk a bit about how this system could be extended to allow more automatic discovery of a Switchboard Server.

2. The Client needs to send a request to the Switchboard Server. The request will be a single `DatagramPacket` that contains a single question, for a single service type. We'll talk about the packet format in a bit.

3. The Client waits for a response. Because datagrams are unreliable, if the client does not receive a response within about five seconds, it should resend the original request. It should also keep a count of the number of times it retries, and give up after some reasonable count.

If things go well, the Client receives a response and must process it. The response will consist of a single DatagramPacket that contains zero or more response records, and an error code. We'll talk about the record format in a moment.

Let's look at the format of the two messages that the Client exchanges with the Server: the Request format and the Response format.

Switchboard Request Format

The Request the client sends to the Server is very simple. It consists of the following fields:

Table 7-3 Fields in a Switchboard Request

Field	Length (Bytes)	Description
packet type	1	For a request, this value is always fixed.
unique ID	2	The client sets this field to some arbitrary value; the server returns the same value in the associated Response.
service type	8	The service type for which the client is searching.

Notice that we've allotted eight bytes for service type. This might seem overkill at first, but it has a couple of advantages:

• It provides plenty of room for a possible future proliferation of service types. Unlike IP addresses, which were chosen to be big yet not big enough at 4 bytes, we're allocating plenty of room to grow.

- It allows semi-human-readable type "strings" to be used. For instance, if I provided a "Courtois" service, I could publish a service type of COURTOIS, and this would fit into eight bytes. Folks who are familiar with the "8.3" filename format of MS-DOS files should find this eight-byte name space familiar.

- We're implementing our own custom datagram protocol here for the sake of learning— so why not use eight bytes?

Now let's look at the Response packet format that the Server returns to the Client in response to a Request.

Switchboard Response Format

The Response that the Server sends to the Client consists of an initial header followed by zero or more Service Records. The format of the Response Header is as follows:

Table 7-4 Fields in a Switchboard Response

Field	Length (Bytes)	Description
packet type	1	For a response, this value is always fixed.
unique ID	2	The Client sets this field to an arbitrary value in a Request, the Server returns the same value in the associated Response.
error code	1	The response result code. This could be an error code, or zero for no error.
record count	1	The number of records stored in the packet following the header. Note that at about (18?) bytes per record, you can only store about (25?) records in the remainder of a datagram that is 512 bytes long.

The Response header is immediately followed by the number of Service Records given in the "record count" field of the header. We'll assume that the maximum size of a datagram packet is 512 bytes, and send only as many Service Records in the Response as will fit within that packet size limitation.

Now that we know the format of the basic Request and Response, let's look at the format of Service Record transmitted over the network.

Switchboard Service Record Format

A Service Record consists of the type of service, the expected lifetime (Time-to-Live or TTL) of the service, and the critical service provider's contact information, including IP address and port number.

The fields in the Service Record are shown below.

Table 7-5 Fields in a Switchboard Service Record

Field	Length (Bytes)	Description
service type	8	What type of service is this record for?
TTL	4	The amount of time remaining for which this record should be valid. This time value is a delta value from the current time. Note that this time is estimated by the Service Provider; it is not guaranteed. The Switchboard Client should be prepared to deal with Service Providers that have disappeared.
IP Address	4	The IP address of the service provider. This is a four-byte IP address array (e.g. [165,227,67,1] for 165.227.67.1).
Port	2	The port number on which the service provider resides. This is simply the IP port number, a 16-bit integer value.

Note that the TTL field is absolutely essential to the operation of the Switchboard system. It allows a Service Provider to provide a reasonable estimate as to how long they will be able to provide service. It also allows Switchboard Servers to decide whether they will cache and distribute a given Service Record; if the TTL is too small, the Server might not bother to cache the record because the overhead of storing the record and distributing it to clients isn't worthwhile. If the TTL is too large, the Server might opt not to store the record, since it might want to give a variety of Service Providers an opportunity to register.

Because of the dynamic nature of this protocol, Clients should be careful to cache Service Records they receive only for the expected TTL, and be aware that the TTL is not guaranteed.

The SBServiceRecord Class

First let's build a class that encapsulates a Switchboard Service Record and provides methods for manipulating the data.

Example 7-5 Implementation of the SBServiceRecord class

```
package JNC;

import java.util.*; //for Date and such
import java.net.*; //for InetAddress and such

/**
* A record class for storing service records.
*
```

```
 * A service record contains:
 *
 * service type (8-char type value "COURTOIS")
 * estimated time-to-live (TTL) (4-byte int value)
 * IP address (four bytes)
 * port (two bytes)
 */

public class SBServiceRecord
{
public byte[]fRawServiceType; //shipped as 8 bytes
protected  intSERVICE_OFFSET = 0;
public long
    fServiceType = 0,//8 byte-value condensed from bytes
    fExpireTime = 0;//date in long format, delta shipped as 4 bytes
protected int EXPIRE_OFFSET = 8;

public InetAddress fAddress; //shipped as 4 bytes
protected int ADDRESS_OFFSET = 12;
public shortfPort = 0;//shipped as 2 bytes
protected int PORT_OFFSET = 16;

public static final int RECORD_LENGTH = 18;


/**
 * Convert an array of bytes to a long service type
 */
public static long convertBytesToServiceType(byte[] rawBytes, int offset)
{
    long retVal = 0;
    retVal =((rawBytes[0 + offset] << 24 |
                rawBytes[1 + offset] << 16|
                rawBytes[2 + offset] << 8 |
                rawBytes[3 + offset]  ) << 32) |
                (rawBytes[4 + offset] << 24|
                rawBytes[5 + offset] << 16|
                rawBytes[6 + offset] << 8 |
                rawBytes[7 + offset] );
    return retVal;
}//convertBytesToServiceType

/**
 * convert long service type to an array of bytes
 * slam the bytes into the given destination array
 */
public static void convertServiceTypeToBytes(long serviceType, byte[] dst,
int offset)
{

    for (int byteIdx = 0; byteIdx < 8; byteIdx++) {
        dst[byteIdx + offset] =
            (byte) ((serviceType >> (8*(7 - byteIdx))) & 255);
```

```
    }

}//convertServiceTypeToBytes

/**
 * convert to an array of bytes
 * ordering of output is:
 * service type (8-char type value "COURTOIS")
 * estimated time-to-live (TTL) (4-byte int value)
 * IP address (four bytes)
 * port (two bytes)
 */
public byte[] toByteArray()
{
    byte[] retVal = new byte[RECORD_LENGTH];//holder array

    //first copy in the service type
    try {
        System.arraycopy(fRawServiceType,0,retVal,0,fRawServiceType.length);
    }
    catch (Exception ex) {};

    //next, copy in the TTL delta
    long curDate = (new Date()).getDate();
    int TTL = (int)(fExpireTime - curDate);
    retVal[8] = (byte) ((TTL >> 24) & 255); //just the top 8 bits
    retVal[9] = (byte) ((TTL >> 16) & 255); //just the next 8 bits
    retVal[10] = (byte) ((TTL >> 8) & 255); //just the next 8 bits
    retVal[11] = (byte) (TTL  & 255); //just the bottom 8 bits

    //copy the address in
    byte[] addrArray = fAddress.getAddress();//get the 4 bytes
    try {
        System.arraycopy(addrArray,0,retVal,0,addrArray.length);
    }
    catch (Exception ex) {};

    //copy the port in
    retVal[16] = (byte) ((fPort >> 8) & 255);//top 8 bits
    retVal[17] = (byte) (fPort & 255);

    return retVal;
}//toByteArray

/**
 * instantiate a new record with the given data
 */
SBServiceRecord(byte[] rawServiceType, long expireTime,
                short port, InetAddress addr)
{
    fRawServiceType = rawServiceType;
    fServiceType = convertBytesToServiceType(fRawServiceType,0);
    fExpireTime = expireTime;
```

```
        fAddress = addr;
        fPort = port;
    }//SBServiceRecord


    /**
     * Instantiate a new record from a block of bytes
     */
    SBServiceRecord(byte[] srcData, int startOffset)
    {
        //build the service type
        fRawServiceType = new byte[8];
        try {
            System.arraycopy(srcData,startOffset + SERVICE_OFFSET,
                        fRawServiceType,0,fRawServiceType.length);
        }
        catch (Exception ex) {};

        fServiceType = convertBytesToServiceType(fRawServiceType,0);

        //build the TTL
        int TTL  = (srcData[startOffset + EXPIRE_OFFSET] << 24) |
                    (srcData[startOffset + EXPIRE_OFFSET + 1] << 16) |
                    (srcData[startOffset + EXPIRE_OFFSET + 2] << 8) |
                    srcData[startOffset + EXPIRE_OFFSET + 3];
                    ;
        fExpireTime = (new Date()).getDate() + TTL;



        //build a dotted-decimal string that we
        //can use to build an InetAddress.
        String fakeDomainStr = "";
        //add a single octet plus a dot to the string at a time
        for (int octetIdx = 0; octetIdx < 4; octetIdx++)
            fakeDomainStr +=
                srcData[startOffset + ADDRESS_OFFSET + octetIdx] + ".";

        //we should now have a dotted-decimal string of the
        //form "165.227.67.1."
        //InetAddress can translate this into an IP address without
        //actually connecting to a DNS server
        //(depending on the Java runtime implementation)
        try {fAddress = InetAddress.getByName(fakeDomainStr);}
        catch (UnknownHostException unhEx) {
            System.err.println("InetAddress.getByName threw: " + unhEx);
        }

        //build the port
        fPort = (short) ( (srcData[startOffset + PORT_OFFSET] << 8) |
                    srcData[startOffset + PORT_OFFSET + 1] );

    }//SBServiceRecord
```

```
/**
 * return a string representation of this record
 */
public String toString()
{
    String retVal = "type: ";
    for (int idx = 0; idx < 8; idx++) {
        retVal += (char)fRawServiceType[idx] +
                    "(" + fRawServiceType[idx] + ")";
    }
    retVal += "{" + fServiceType + "}";

    retVal += " expire: " + (new Date(fExpireTime)).toString();

    retVal += " address: " + fAddress;
    retVal += " port: " + fPort;

    return retVal;
}//toString

}/* class SBServiceRecord */
```

Notice we've implemented a few of the SBServiceRecord methods as static methods. This is because those methods are useful to other classes in the Switchboard system: thus, SBServiceRecord can act as a utility class for those other classes.

The Switchboard Client Implementation

Let's now look at the implementation of the Switchboard Client, the SBClient class. This class is based upon the DatagramClient class we constructed earlier, so it automatically contains code for send, receive, and retry of datagrams.

The source code for SBClient is shown below.

Example 7-6 SBClient Implementation

```
package JNC;

import java.io.*;
import java.net.*;
import java.util.*;


/**
 * This class implements a client to the Switchboard protocol.
 * The client requests records on a certain kind of service,
 * waits for a response
 * @author Todd Courtois
 */
class SBClient extends DatagramClient
{
```

```java
public final static int DEFAULT_PORT = 6969;
public final static int REQUEST_LENGTH = 11;

public boolean fDebugOn = true;
//data we've received from remote client
public DatagramPacket fCurReceivedPacket = null;
protected Random fIdGenerator = null;
protected short  fCurReqUniqueID = 0;


/*
*    Instantiate and init the core
*/
public SBClient(int remotePort, InetAddress serverAddress) {

    super(0,//use default inbuf size
        0, //use default local port
        ((remotePort != 0) ? remotePort: DEFAULT_PORT),
        serverAddress,
        0); //use default wait time

    fIdGenerator = new Random((new Date()).getDate());

}/* SBClient() */


/**
* get some answers for the given type of service
*/
public synchronized SBServiceRecord[] getByServiceType(long serviceType)
{
    SBServiceRecord[] answers = null;

    super.setOutputBuf(buildRequest(serviceType));

    try {
        fCurReceivedPacket = super.handleTransaction();
        answers = processResponse();
    }
    catch ( SocketException sockEx) {
        System.err.println("handleTransaction threw: " + sockEx);
    }
    catch( IOException ioEx) {
        System.err.println("handleTransaction threw: " + ioEx);
    }

    return answers;
} /* getByServiceType */


/**
* process received answers...
*/
```

```java
protected SBServiceRecord[] processResponse()
{
    //(in) fCurReceivedPacket
    /*
    the header consists of:
    response flag (one byte)
    unique ID (two bytes)
    error code (one byte)
    record count (one byte)
    */

    byte[] responseData = fCurReceivedPacket.getData();

    short responseUniqueID =
        (short) ((responseData[1] << 8) + responseData[2]);
    if (responseUniqueID != fCurReqUniqueID) {
        if (fDebugOn)
            System.err.println("unique IDs not equal!");
    }

    int errCode = responseData[3];//
    if (errCode != 0 ) {
        if (fDebugOn)
            System.err.println("got error code: " + errCode);
        return null; //no answers...
    }

    int recordCount = responseData[4];
    SBServiceRecord[] answers = new SBServiceRecord[recordCount];
    int totalOffset = 5;
    for (int recordIdx = 0; recordIdx < recordCount; recordIdx++)
    {
        answers[recordIdx] =
            new SBServiceRecord(responseData,totalOffset);
    }

    return answers;
} //processResponse


/**
 * build the request packet
 */
protected byte[] buildRequest(long serviceType)
{
    //get a 16 bit "unique" ID
    fCurReqUniqueID = (short) (fIdGenerator.nextInt() >> 16);
    byte[] sendBuf = new byte[REQUEST_LENGTH];

    /*
    A request contains:
    type (request, one byte)
    uniqueID (two bytes)
```

```
        serviceType (eight bytes)
    */

    sendBuf[0] = SBServer.BASIC_REQUEST;
    sendBuf[1] = (byte) (fCurReqUniqueID >> 8 );
    sendBuf[2] = (byte) (fCurReqUniqueID & 255);
    SBServiceRecord.convertServiceTypeToBytes( serviceType, sendBuf,  3);

    return sendBuf;

} //buildRequest


} /* class SBClient */
```

The key methods to look at in `SBClient` are:

- `getByServiceType` is used by `SBClient`'s clients to get a set of `SBServiceRecords` for a given service type. Notice how this method uses the inherited method `DatagramClient.handleTransaction` to handle the dirty work of the request/response protocol.

- `buildRequest` builds a Switchboard Request packet given only a service type.

- `processResponse` takes the raw Switchboard Response packet and culls any useful SBServiceRecords from it.

Implementing a Switchboard Service Provider

A Switchboard Service provider registers services with a Switchboard Server. The protocol that the Service Provider exchanges with the Server is similar to the protocol the Server exchanges with the Client.

The Service Provider connects to the Server and "posts" a packet format similar to the Response format the Server sends to the Client. The Server then modifies the post slightly and then returns it back to the Service Provider.

In this protocol, the `SBServiceProvider` does the following:

1. The `SBServiceProvider` needs to locate a switchboard server in his domain. He can either do that by punching in an IP address directly (that's what we'll assume here), or we could add another record type to DNS to supply the address using a simple DNS lookup (more about this later).

2. The SBServiceProvider needs to connect to his Switchboard Server and make a registration request. The request is in the same format as an ordinary SBServer Response record, except that the "request/response" flag is flipped.

3. The SBServiceProvider waits for a response. If the SBServicePro- vider does not receive a response within a few seconds, it should retry. Because there is no guarantee that the SBServer receives the request, and there's no guarantee that any SBServer responses will reach the SBServi- ceProvider, retry ensures that the transaction will complete. If the SBSer- viceProvider doesn't receive a response within about 60 seconds, it should probably give up and assume the SBServer is no longer active.

4. The SBServiceProvider receives a response and processes it. The response should just echo the request, but with the request/response flag flipped once more. Note that the SBServiceProvider can register multi- ple services and receive multiple verifications simultaneously by simply including more than one SBServiceRecord in the initial post.

The SBServiceProvider should provide in its records an estimated time-to- live. This information helps the SBServer determine how long to hold onto a registration record in its database cache before purging it

Note that an SBServiceProvider can only register services that exist on its own IP address. That is, the SBServer does a check to make certain that the SBServiceProvider's address corresponds to the services being registered. If it doesn't match, the SBServer simply ignores the request. This is a minor security/sanity check to ensure that people don't accidentally or intentionally register nonexistent services (with perhaps large TTLs) for other hosts.

The source code for the SBServiceProvider is provided below.

Example 7-7 Implementation of **SBServiceProvider**

```
package JNC;

import java.io.*;
import java.net.*;
import java.util.*;


/**
 * This class implements a service provider to the Switchboard protocol.
 * The client requests records on a certain kind of service,
 * waits for a response
 * @author Todd Courtois
 */
class SBServiceProvider extends DatagramClient
{
```

```java
public final static int DEFAULT_PORT = 6969;
public final static int POST_LENGTH = 11;

public boolean fDebugOn = true;

//data we've received from remote client
public DatagramPacket fCurReceivedPacket = null;
protected Random fIdGenerator = null;
protected short  fCurReqUniqueID = 0;


/**
 *   Instantiate and init the core
 */
public SBServiceProvider(int remotePort, InetAddress serverAddress) {

    super(0,//use default inbuf size
        0, //use default local port
        ((remotePort != 0) ? remotePort: DEFAULT_PORT),
        serverAddress,
        0); //use default wait time

    fIdGenerator = new Random((new Date()).getDate());

}// SBServiceProvider


/**
 * get some answers for the given type of service
 * @param serviceType The service type to register.
 * @return boolean Was the service registered?
 */
public synchronized boolean registerService(long serviceType)
{
    boolean didRegister = false;

    super.setOutputBuf(buildRequest(serviceType));

    try {
        fCurReceivedPacket = super.handleTransaction();
        didRegister = processResponse();
    }
    catch ( SocketException sockEx) {
        System.err.println("handleTransaction threw: " + sockEx);
    }
    catch( IOException ioEx) {
        System.err.println("handleTransaction threw: " + ioEx);
    }

    return didRegister;

} // registerService
```

```
/**
* process received answers...
*/
protected boolean processResponse()
{
    //(in) fCurReceivedPacket
    /*
    the header consists of:
    response flag (one byte)
    unique ID (two bytes)
    error code (one byte)
    record count (one byte)
    */

    byte[] responseData = fCurReceivedPacket.getData();

    short responseUniqueID =
        (short) ((responseData[1] << 8) + responseData[2]);
    if (responseUniqueID != fCurReqUniqueID) {
        if (fDebugOn)
            System.err.println("unique IDs not equal!");
    }

    int errCode = responseData[3];//
    if (errCode != 0 ) {
        if (fDebugOn)
            System.err.println("got error code: " + errCode);
        return false; //couldn't register
    }
    else return true; //no error, registered OK
    //To be thorough, we would verify that records sent
    //in the response are the same as the ones sent
    //in the initial registration packet.
} // processResponse


/**
* build the request packet
*/
protected byte[] buildRequest(long serviceType)
{
    //get a 16-bit "unique" ID
    fCurReqUniqueID = (short) (fIdGenerator.nextInt() >> 16);
    byte[] sendBuf = new byte[REQUEST_LENGTH];

    /*
    A request contains:
    type (BASIC_POST, one byte)
    uniqueID (two bytes)
    serviceType (eight bytes)
    */
```

```
sendBuf[0] = SBServer.BASIC_POST;
sendBuf[1] = (byte) (fCurReqUniqueID >> 8 );
sendBuf[2] = (byte) (fCurReqUniqueID & 255);
SBServiceRecord.convertServiceTypeToBytes(
    serviceType, sendBuf,  3);

    return sendBuf;

} // buildRequest

} /* class SBServiceProvider */
```

The key methods of `SBServiceProvider` are:

- `registerService` is the main method that `SBServiceProvider` clients use to interface with the `SBServiceProvider`. This method attempts to register a single service type with the `SBServer` given at instantiation.

- `buildRequest` is used to build the registration post packet given a service type.

- `processResponse` is used to verify that the registration post was accepted by the `SBServer`.

The Switchboard Server Implementation

There are two parts to the `SBServer`: front-end (client) access and back-end (service provider) access. Since the two parts are fairly separate, we'll look at implementing them separately.

Implementing SBServer Front-End (SBClient) Access

In this section we'll look at an implementation of front-end access to `SBServer`. This code provides the interface in na `SBServer` that an `SBClient` sees.

This portion of the `SBServer` receives requests from clients and responds to those requests using information stored in its local cache database. In our example we'll assume the database of records has already been built.

To implement the front-end, we need to do the following:

- Create a `DatagramSocket` and wait for incoming requests, similar to what we did in the `DatagramServer`.

- When a request arrives, look up the request in the database.

- Build a response in a `DatagramPacket`.

- Send the response back to the client.

- Repeat

Implementing SBServer Back-End (SBServiceProvider) Access

In this section we'll look at the implementation of back-end access in SBServer. This is the code that presents the interface that SBServiceProviders see. This is where the SBServer receives registration posts from other servers, servers that provide services. These servers would like to register their services with the SBServer so that it can stuff the appropriate record into its database. As we'll see, this protocol is related to the protocol the SBServer talks to SBClient, but is not exactly the same.

A summary of the implementation is this:

- Use the same DatagramSocket to wait for incoming requests.

- Receive a POST request.

- Process the POST and slam the given information into the local cache database.

- Confirm the POST by echoing it back to the SBServiceProvider with the packet type set to RESPONSE.

- Repeat.

The source code for the SBServer is given below.

Example 7-8 SBServer Implementation

```
package JNC;

import java.io.*;
import java.net.*;


/**
 * main SBServer class
 */
public class SBServer extends DatagramServer implements Runnable
{

//packet type constants
public final static byte
    BASIC_REQUEST = 2,
    BASIC_RESPONSE= 4,
    BASIC_POST = 8,
    BASIC_POST_VERIFY = 16;

//error codes
```

```
public final static  byte
    ERROR_NO_ERROR = 0,
    ERROR_NO_RECORDS_FOUND = 2,
    ERROR_NOT_AUTHORIZED = 4,
    ERROR_TTL_TOO_SMALL = 8,
    ERROR_TTL_TOO_BIG = 16;

/*
the header consists of:
response flag (one byte)
unique ID (two bytes)
error code (one byte)
record count (one byte)
*/
public final static int RESPONSE_HEADER_LENGTH = 5;
//post header is same as response header...
public final static int POST_HEADER_LENGTH = 5;

public final static int DEFAULT_PORT = 6969;

public boolean fContinueListening = true;

protected Thread fBackboneThread;

//instance vars for holding database file info
protected SBRecordDatabase fRecordCache;

//stuff for debugging
public boolean fDebugOn = true;

//statistics
public  int fTransactionCount = 0;//Transaction achieved


/**
* Create a new instance
*/
public SBServer(int port)
{
    //create a new datagram server
    super( ((port == 0)? DEFAULT_PORT : port),
        DatagramServer.DEFAULT_MAX_DATAGRAM_SIZE);

    //create a new database
    fRecordCache = new SBRecordDatabase();

    try {
        this.Bind();//bind to the local port

        fBackboneThread = new Thread(this,"SBServer Core");
        fBackboneThread.start();
    }
    catch (Exception ex) {
```

```
            System.err.println("SBServer constructor threw: " + ex);
    }

} /* SBServer */


/**
 * The core method of this class
 * loop waiting for incoming requests
 * when a request arrives, hand it off to be processed
 */
public void run()
{
    try {

        while (fContinueListening) {
            //the following usually blocks for awhile
            DatagramPacket transReq = super.waitForRequest();
            fTransactionCount++;
            //hand off this transaction request to the right place
            routeTransaction(transReq);
        }

        this.Dispose();
    }
    catch (Exception runEx) {
        System.out.println("SBServer run threw: " + runEx);
        //bail out!
    }

} /* run */

/**
 * route a single transaction to the correct type of handler
 */
public void routeTransaction(DatagramPacket packet)
{
    int packetType = BASIC_REQUEST;
    //first, find out what type of packet this is
    byte[] packetData = packet.getData();
    packetType = (int)packetData[0]; //first byte is the type...

    if (packetType == BASIC_REQUEST) {
        //add a new basic request handler
        SBBasicRequestHandler reqHandler =
            new SBBasicRequestHandler(packet, fRecordCache);
    }
    else if (packetType == BASIC_POST) {
        //add a new basic response handler
        SBBasicPostHandler postHandler =
            new SBBasicPostHandler(packet, fRecordCache);
    }
```

```
}/* routeTransaction */

} /* class SBServer */




/**
* Class for dealing with requests from SBClients
*/
class SBBasicRequestHandler extends Thread
{

protected SBRecordDatabase fRecordDatabase;

protected DatagramPacketfRequest;
protected shortfReqUniqueID;
protected long fReqServiceType;

protected SBServiceRecord[] fAnswers;
protected DatagramClient fResponder;
protected byte[]fResponseBuf;
protected DatagramPacketfResponsePacket;


/**
* minimal constructor
* takes request packet and tucks it away
* @param transactionRequest The packet containing the client's request
* @param database The database which contains possible answers to the
request.
*/
public SBBasicRequestHandler(DatagramPacket transactionRequest,
                                   SBRecordDatabase database)
{
    fRequest = transactionRequest;
    fRecordDatabase = database;
    this.start();
}


/**
*do all of the compute-intensive and network I/O stuff from here
*/
public void run()
{
    slurpReqInfo();
    findAnswers();

    buildResponsePacket();
    sendResponse();
}
```

```
/**
 * pull the basic request into from the request packet data
 */
protected void slurpReqInfo()
{
    /*
    read the header info
    A packet contains:
    type (request, one byte)-- we skip this
    uniqueID (two bytes) -- we save this & return it to the client
    serviceType (eight bytes) -- we use this to filter records
    */

    //first, get the source data
    byte[] reqData = fRequest.getData();
    //get the unique ID-- two bytes at offset 1
    fReqUniqueID = (short) ( (reqData[1] << 8) + reqData[2] );
    //get the service type-- eight bytes at offset 3
    fReqServiceType =
        SBServiceRecord.convertBytesToServiceType(reqData,3);

} /* slurpReqInfo */

/**
 * find some answers for the request
 */
protected void findAnswers()
{
    fAnswers = fRecordDatabase.retrieveRecords(fReqServiceType);
}//findAnswers


/**
 * build a response datagram packet to send to the client
 */
protected void buildResponsePacket()
{
    int numRecords =  ((fAnswers != null) ? fAnswers.length : 0);
    fResponseBuf = new byte[ SBServer.RESPONSE_HEADER_LENGTH +
                    numRecords * SBServiceRecord.RECORD_LENGTH] ;

    /*
    the header consists of:
    response flag (one byte)
    unique ID (two bytes)
    error code (one byte)
    record count (one byte)
    */

    fResponseBuf[0] = SBServer.BASIC_RESPONSE;
    fResponseBuf[1] = (byte)(fReqUniqueID >> 8);
    fResponseBuf[2] = (byte)(fReqUniqueID & 255);
    fResponseBuf[3] = (numRecords > 0) ?
```

```
                        SBServer.ERROR_NO_ERROR :
                        SBServer.ERROR_NO_RECORDS_FOUND;
    fResponseBuf[4] = (byte) numRecords;

    int totalOffset = 5;
    byte[] curRecordData = null;
    for (int recordIdx = 0; recordIdx < numRecords; recordIdx++)
    {
        curRecordData = fAnswers[recordIdx].toByteArray();
        try {
            System.arraycopy(curRecordData,0,fResponseBuf,
                totalOffset,curRecordData.length);
        }
        catch (Exception ex) {};
        totalOffset += curRecordData.length;
    }

    //we've finished building the response data,
    //now we need to build the actual packet
    fResponsePacket =
        new DatagramPacket(fResponseBuf,fResponseBuf.length,
                           fRequest.getAddress(),fRequest.getPort());


} /* buildResponsePacket */


/**
 * send a response back to the client
 */
protected void sendResponse()
{
    try {
        DatagramSocket clientSocket = new DatagramSocket();
        clientSocket.send(fResponsePacket);
        clientSocket.close();
    }
    catch (SocketException socketEx) {
        System.err.println("sendResponse DatagramSocket() threw: " +
socketEx);
    }
    catch (IOException ioEx) {
        System.err.println("sendResponse send() threw: " + ioEx);
    }
} /* sendResponse */


}/* class SBBasicRequestHandler */


/**
 * class for dealing with posts from SBServiceProviders
```

```
*/
class SBBasicPostHandler extends Thread
{

protected SBRecordDatabasefRecordDB;
protected DatagramPacket fPost;
protected byte[]fPostData;
protected int   fPostRecordCount;
protected int   fErrCode = SBServer.ERROR_NO_ERROR;


SBBasicPostHandler(DatagramPacket postPacket, SBRecordDatabase recordDB)
{
    fPost = postPacket;
    fRecordDB = recordDB;
    this.start();
} /* SBBasicPostHandler */

/**
 * do all the real work from here
 */
public void run()
{
    slurpPostInfo();
    storeRecords();

    sendVerification();
}/* run */


/**
 * pull the basic post into from the packet data
 */
protected void slurpPostInfo()
{
    /*
    read the header info
    A packet contains:
    type (post, one byte)-- we skip this
    uniqueID (two bytes) -- we save this and return it to the client
    error code (one byte) -- we skip this, because we don't care
    record count (one byte) -- we record this
    */

    //first, get the source data
    fPostData = fPost.getData();

    //get the number of records contained in the packet
    fPostRecordCount = (int) fPostData[4];
}/* slurpPostInfo */

/**
 * store away the records provided, watch for errors
```

```
*/
protected void storeRecords()
{
    int totalOffset = SBServer.POST_HEADER_LENGTH;

    for (int recordCount = 0;
            recordCount < fPostRecordCount; recordCount++) {
        //read a record from the post data stream
        //slam the new record into the database
        SBServiceRecord curRecord =
            new SBServiceRecord(fPostData,totalOffset);
        totalOffset += SBServiceRecord.RECORD_LENGTH;
        fErrCode = fRecordDB.storeRecord(curRecord);
        //if we got some error, give up immediately
        if (fErrCode != SBServer.ERROR_NO_ERROR) return;
    }
} /* storeRecords */


/**
 * send an "echo" back to the SBServiceProvider so
 * they'll know we got the post
 */
protected void sendVerification()
{
    //neat trick here:
    //simply take the post data, modify the packet type and
    //error code fields
    //and hand it back to the SBServiceProvider

    fPostData[0] = SBServer.BASIC_POST_VERIFY;//was BASIC_POST
    fPostData[3] = (byte)fErrCode;

    //we've finished building the response data,
    //now we need to build the packet
    DatagramPacket verifyPacket =
        new DatagramPacket(fPostData,fPostData.length,
                            fPost.getAddress(),fPost.getPort());

    try {
        DatagramSocket clientSocket = new DatagramSocket();
        clientSocket.send(verifyPacket);
        clientSocket.close();
    }
    catch (SocketException socketEx) {
        System.err.println(
            "sendVerification DatagramSocket() threw: " + socketEx);
    }
    catch (IOException ioEx) {
        System.err.println("sendVerification send() threw: " + ioEx);
    }

}/* sendVerification */
```

```
} /* class SBBasicPostHandler */
```

Fancy Switchboard Extensions (Exercises for the Reader)

There are a number of ways the Switchboard protocol could be improved; let's examine one of those ways.

There are ways to spoof a source IP address so that someone could potentially register services for a host they don't own. That is, they could make the SwitchboardServer believe that a given server provides services it doesn't provide. If this happens, SBClients would be constantly directed to a bogus SBServiceProvider address. This isn't especially dangerous, but it would be bothersome. To work around this problem, the SBServer could carry out some kind of verification protocol with the SBServiceProvider. For instance, after the SBServer receives a registration from a potential SBServiceProvider, it could send a "Is this correct?" query packet back to the SBServiceProvider, and the SBServiceProvider could then send a confirmation packet. In this way, only the host with the correct IP address would be able to register services.

New for JDK 1.1: Options for DatagramSocket

You can now set a single BSD-style option (socket timeout) on a DatagramSocket using the special configuration method setSoTimeout.

Table 7-6 New DatagramSocket Configuration Methods

Method	Description
setSoTimeout(int msec)	Specify milliseconds to wait on blocking socket operations (such as read). If operation doesn't complete within the time period, an exception is thrown but the DatagramSocket remains useful.
int getSoTimeout	Get the number of milliseconds for the timeout. A value of 0 means no timeout.

Depending on your particular application, you may find that adjusting the socket timeout results in higher performance. For instance, for a server application, you may find that by adjusting SO_TIMEOUT via setSoTimeout, you can optimize service for the fastest clients by spending less time waiting for slower clients to send data.

DatagramSockets Can Now Specify Local Address and Port

Under JDK 1.0 there was no way for a DatagramSocket to specify the local IP address to be used. This critical flaw assumed that the machine on which the DatagramSocket was running would only ever have one IP address. However, as we mentioned previously, some high-traffic servers are linked to several IP addresses.

Under JDK 1.1 this has been fixed by creating an overloaded constructor for DatagramSocket that allows you to specify which particular local IP network interface and port to use.

New for JDK 1.1: MulticastSocket

JDK 1.1 has added a subclass of DatagramSocket that allows you to send the same message to multiple recipients, or to receive datagrams from a "group" of transmitters. This kind of socket is called a MulticastSocket.

Overview of UDP Multicasting

MulticastSocket is based on UDP multicasting. UDP multicasting works by reserving a certain set of IP addresses specifically as "group" addresses. A group address can be used to broadcast UDP packets to a group of network hosts.

Multicast IP addresses fall into a special range: 224.0.0.1 through 239.255.255.255. No Internet host may have an address in this range— these addresses are reserved for multicast channels.

It should be noted that this kind of multicasting only works on networks that support it. In general, the broader Internet *does not* support multicasting. The reasons for this are numerous, but they boil down to the fact that many Internet routers and subnets could become quickly overloaded if they handled multicast traffic.

UDP multicast tries to alleviate some of the problems associated with multicasting by allowing for a "time-to-live" (TTL), which specifies how many networks (routers) the packet should traverse before "dying..

Thus, multicasting may only be useful in situations where you know the network upon which your application will be running. For instance, it's typically safe to use multicasting on a single ethernet-based IP network.

A good example of where multicast is currently used is in the Internet Multicast Backbone (MBONE) project. Here, various "channels" are created, and data is streamed out via multicast UDP on the channels. Each channel corresponds to a multicast address. MBONE is currently used for concerts and similar multimedia and music events.

MulticastSocket Interface

`MulticastSocket` introduces the concept of a "group" to quantify membership in a multicast channel. `MulticastSocket`s that are members of a group can listen to transmissions on that group. A `MulticastSocket` can also send transmissions to a multicast group, but they need not be a member of that group to do so.

It's helpful to understand that joining a group really causes the underlying implementation to listen for UDP datagrams on the given multicast IP address. Also, a `MulticastSocket` can join several groups simultaneously and receive packets from all of those groups.

It should be noted that under JDK 1.1, Applets are not allowed to instantiate `MulticastSocket`. One reason for this is that there is no way to restrict the applet from broadcasting information to a host other than the host from which the applet was downloaded— any member of the multicast address can listen in. This violates the one-to-one network relationship between the applet and the host that provides the applet.

The most commonly used methods of `MulticastSocket` are shown below.

Table 7-7 Commonly Used MulticastSocket Methods

Method	Description
`MulticastSocket(int)`	This version of the constructor allows you to specify the local port that should be used for sending datagrams.
`setInterface(InetAddress)`	Set the IP address interface to be used to send the packet. Useful for hosts with multiple network interfaces.
`InetAddress getInterface()`	Get the InetAddress of the network interface being used by the MulticastSocket to send packets.
`joinGroup(InetAddress)`	Join a particular multicast group. Note that multiple groups can be joined— a MulticastSocket can be a member of more than one group simultaneously.
`leaveGroup(InetAddress)`	Leave a particular multicast group.

Table 7-7 Commonly Used MulticastSocket Methods *(Continued)*

Method	Description
send(DatagramPacket, byte)	Send a DatagramPacket from the MulticastSocket, with a given time-to-live. To send a packet with the default TTL, use the inherited send method.
setTTL(byte)	Set the time-to-live for packets sent from the MulticastSocket. This specifies how many network hops a packet can traverse before it must die.
byte getTTL()	Get the time-to-live for packets sent from the MulticastSocket.
setSoTimeout(int msec)	Specify milliseconds to wait on blocking socket operations (such as read). If operation doesn't complete within the time period, an exception is thrown but the DatagramSocket remains useful.
int getSoTimeout	Get the number of milliseconds for the timeout. A value of 0 means no timeout.

In practice the MulticastSocket can be used very much like the DatagramSocket, except that instead of sending and receiving datagrams peer-to-peer, with MulticastSocket you can set up a client-to-group relationship.

Summary

In this chapter we've seen how datagrams can be used for a wide variety of network applications. The next time you are creating a network application, you might look at whether datagrams would meet your needs better than a streaming socket-based implementation.

CHAPTER
8

Linking with the Natives

While there are many advantages to writing communicating applications in Java, there are some situations where, for performance or other reasons, you'll want to link into platform-native code written in a language other than Java. For instance, you might have a legacy of highly optimized, platform-specific communications driver code written in C that might be difficult or impossible to port to Java. Also, you may want to link to platform-specific native code that you don't own, so you can't port them to Java.

Fortunately, Java provides a facility for linking to these platform-specific native libraries.

In this chapter we'll explore how to link Java code to platform-specific native libraries written in C. We'll also explore how to define a platform-independent "abstraction layer" to make it easier to port Java code that depends on native libraries between platforms.

How to Link Native Libraries into Your Java Code

Let's examine the basic steps involved in linking native libraries into your Java code.

Create a Java Class That Includes Native Methods

You first create a Java class that includes some static native methods, like so:

Example 8-1 A Simple Class That Contains Native Methods

```java
/**
 * NativeGlueExample.java
 * Class that demonstrates how various data types are exchanged
 * with the native world.
 */
public class NativeGlueExample
{

public native void
    dumpIntegers(byte myByte, short myShort, int myInt, long myLong);
public native void
    dumpFloats(float myFloat, double myDouble);
public native void
    dumpString(String myString);
public native void
    dumpByteArray(byte[] myByteArray, int length);
public native void
    dumpInstanceVars();
protected native void
    updateInstanceVars();//native can be protected

static {
    //let the Java runtime know our class will need
    //the following native library
    System.loadLibrary("NativeJavaGlueExample");
};

//Instance vars
public int fInstanceInt = 3;
public float fInstanceFloat = (float)5.5;
public String fInstanceString = "Helloooo nurse!";

//Constants for our convenience
public static final float MAX_FLOAT = java.lang.Float.MAX_VALUE;
public static final double MAX_DOUBLE = java.lang.Double.MAX_VALUE;
public static final byte MAX_BYTE = (byte)127;
public static final short MAX_SHORT = (short)32767;
public static final int MAX_INT = java.lang.Integer.MAX_VALUE;
public static final long MAX_LONG = java.lang.Long.MAX_VALUE;


/**
 * Run the demo
 * @param args A (possibly empty) array of strings.
 */
public static void main(String[] args)
{
    //create a new instance of this class since this
    //is a static method
    NativeGlueExample exampleObj = new NativeGlueExample();
```

```
    //if the user handed us a string, use it!
    if (args.length > 0)
        exampleObj.fInstanceString = args[0];

    //provide a bunch of integers to the native code
    System.out.println("myByte: " + MAX_BYTE +
                      " myShort: " + MAX_SHORT +
                      " myInt: " + MAX_INT +
                      " myLong: " + MAX_LONG);
    exampleObj.dumpIntegers(MAX_BYTE, MAX_SHORT, MAX_INT, MAX_LONG);

    //provide floating-point numbers to the native code
    System.out.println("myFloat: " + MAX_FLOAT +
                      " myDouble: " + MAX_DOUBLE);
    exampleObj.dumpFloats(MAX_FLOAT,MAX_DOUBLE );

    //hand off a string to the native code
    exampleObj.dumpString( exampleObj.fInstanceString);

    //hand off an array of bytes to the native code
    byte[] testByteArray = {'h','e','L','L','o','!'};
    exampleObj.dumpByteArray( testByteArray, testByteArray.length);

    //now, have the native code display all of the instance vars
    exampleObj.dumpInstanceVars();
    //have the native code tweak the instance vars somewhat
    exampleObj.updateInstanceVars();
    //redisplay the instance vars
    exampleObj.dumpInstanceVars();

} /* NativeGlueExample.main */

}/* class NativeGlueExample */
```

Notice that the native methods declared are special in two ways. First, they're labeled with the `native` keyword. Second, even though the methods aren't marked `abstract`, no implementation for the methods is provided. Normally this isn't possible unless we declare an interface. The `native` keyword allows you to separate the declaration of a Java native method from the native implementation of that method. In this sense, it's similar to C's `extern` keyword.

Notice also the static code block included in the class that calls `System.loadLibrary`. This code block will be called when an instance of the `NativeGlueExample` class is created. The `System.loadLibrary` method is responsible for linking platform-dependent native libraries with Java code. If you do not call this method, the Java runtime will not be able to find and call your native code. To become familiar with the kind of runtime errors you're likely to encounter with native linking, you might try commenting-out or removing this call to `System.loadLibrary`, compiling the Java code, and running it.

Java Networking and Communications

Run the Class File through the javah Tool

Once you've compiled the Java code into a class file, you need to run the class file through the *javah* tool. The *javah* tool generates two files from the class file you provide to it: a C source file (called the "native stubs" file) and a C header file. Currently *javah* only provides support for generating native header files in the C language.

Let's look at the header and source file that *javah* generated for our example class. The text of the header file is shown below.

Example 8-2 Native C Header File Generated by the *javah* Tool under MacOS

```
#include <native.h>

/* header for class NativeGlueExample */
#ifndef _Included_NativeGlueExample
#define _Included_NativeGlueExample
#ifdef __cplusplus
extern "C" {
#endif
typedef struct ClassNativeGlueExample {
    long fInstanceInt;
    float fInstanceFloat;
    struct Hjava_lang_String* fInstanceString;
#define NativeGlueExample_MAX_FLOAT3.40282e+38F
#define NativeGlueExample_MAX_DOUBLE1.79769e+308D
#define NativeGlueExample_MAX_BYTE127
#define NativeGlueExample_MAX_SHORT32767
#define NativeGlueExample_MAX_INT2147483647
#define NativeGlueExample_MAX_LONG9223372036854775807L
} ClassNativeGlueExample;

HandleTo(NativeGlueExample);

extern void NativeGlueExample_dumpIntegers(
    struct HNativeGlueExample*, /*char*/ long, /*short*/ long, long,
int64_t);
extern void NativeGlueExample_dumpFloats(
    struct HNativeGlueExample*, float, double);
extern void NativeGlueExample_dumpString(
    struct HNativeGlueExample*, struct Hjava_lang_String*);
extern void NativeGlueExample_dumpByteArray(
    struct HNativeGlueExample*, struct HArrayOfByte*, long);
extern void NativeGlueExample_dumpInstanceVars(
    struct HNativeGlueExample*);
extern void NativeGlueExample_updateInstanceVars(
    struct HNativeGlueExample*);
#ifdef __cplusplus
}
#endif
```

```
#endif /* _Included_NativeGlueExample */
```

There are several major parts to this file:

- A `ClassNativeGlueExample` struct definition that maps out the Java class's instance vars, and a HandleTo() for the class, which typedefs handles for the struct. You'll notice that the name of the struct is simply the name of the class with the word "Class" prepended.

- `#defines` for `static final` fields defined in the class. Note that for efficiency's sake these are transformed into #defines rather than being stored in the struct itself. Also notice that the various Java numeric type max values (such as `java.lang.Float.MAX_VALUE`) have been mapped to the appropriate native platform C value.

- A set of `extern` function declarations for each of the native methods in the Java class. (Note that the one nonnative method, `main`, isn't included.) You can use these as prototypes for the native functions you'll have to write. You'll note that the name of each function is a "mangled" name that includes the name of the Java class that contains the associated method. Thus, a `Vegetable` class would map to a C `struct` with the name `ClassVegetable`, and the native method `Vegetable.cook()` would map to the function definition `H_Vegetable_cook(H_Vegetable*)`. Notice that the first parameter to every function definition is a handle to the struct based on the main class you defined (`HNativeGlueExample` in the above example). This convention allows every function defined to access the context of the Java class instance itself. This provides you a way to set and get local variables in the Java class instance. It also generates a handle definition for that C struct. Thus the `java_lang_String.h` file will define an `H_java_lang_String` handle that provides access to a Java `String`. As we'll see in a moment, you can use the Java-runtime-provided unhand macro to access the Java object via these handles.

You need to `#include` this C header file in your native code source files. If you don't, your C compiler will complain at compile time that none of your functions have prototypes, many of your constants are undefined, and so on.

Now here's the C stubs file *javah* generated for our example class:

Example 8-3 C "Stubs" Source File for NativeGlueExample Class under MacOS

```
/* stubs for class NativeGlueExample */
/* DO NOT EDIT THIS FILE - it is machine generated */

stack_item* Java_NativeGlueExample_dumpIntegers_stub(
```

```
        stack_item* _P_, struct execenv* _EE_) {
    extern void NativeGlueExample_dumpIntegers(
    void*, /*char*/ long, /*short*/ long, long, int64_t);
    (void) NativeGlueExample_dumpIntegers(
    _P_[0].p, _P_[1].i, _P_[2].i, _P_[3].i, *(int64_t*) (_P_ + 4));
    return _P_ + 0;
}


stack_item* Java_NativeGlueExample_dumpFloats_stub(
        stack_item* _P_, struct execenv* _EE_) {
    extern void NativeGlueExample_dumpFloats(void*, float, double);
    (void) NativeGlueExample_dumpFloats(
    _P_[0].p, _P_[1].f, *(double*) (_P_ + 2));
    return _P_ + 0;
}


stack_item* Java_NativeGlueExample_dumpString_stub(
        stack_item* _P_, struct execenv* _EE_) {
    extern void NativeGlueExample_dumpString(void*, struct
Hjava_lang_String*);
    (void) NativeGlueExample_dumpString(_P_[0].p, _P_[1].p);
    return _P_ + 0;
}


stack_item* Java_NativeGlueExample_dumpByteArray_stub(
        stack_item* _P_, struct execenv* _EE_) {
    extern void NativeGlueExample_dumpByteArray(
    void*, struct HArrayOfByte*, long);
    (void) NativeGlueExample_dumpByteArray(_P_[0].p, _P_[1].p, _P_[2].i);
    return _P_ + 0;
}


stack_item* Java_NativeGlueExample_dumpInstanceVars_stub(
        stack_item* _P_, struct execenv* _EE_) {
    extern void NativeGlueExample_dumpInstanceVars(void*);
    (void) NativeGlueExample_dumpInstanceVars(_P_[0].p);
    return _P_ + 0;
}


stack_item* Java_NativeGlueExample_updateInstanceVars_stub(
        stack_item* _P_, struct execenv* _EE_) {
    extern void NativeGlueExample_updateInstanceVars(void*);
    (void) NativeGlueExample_updateInstanceVars(_P_[0].p);
    return _P_ + 0;
}
```

Notice several important things about this file:

- It contains only declarations for each native method. There are no constants defined.

- These declarations contains types such as `stack_item` and `execenv` that you probably haven't heard of and wouldn't want to know about unless you're implementing or porting a Java runtime to a particular OS. Suffice it to say that these stub functions interface between the Java runtime and your native code.

- The stubs file that javah generates contains C glue code that you will need to link into your native library in order to make it compatible with the Java runtime environment

Note that the format of this file may vary greatly from platform to platform. These declarations are only useful on the current native platform for allowing the Java runtime to link in this code at runtime. For this reason, the format will vary with the native library sharing mechanism.

> The format of the files *javah* generates has changed several times since Java 1.0 alpha, and it will probably continue to evolve as Sun and its licensees optimize the Java runtime environment. Furthermore, the format varies from platform to platform, and it will undoubtedly vary when native languages other than C are supported. Be aware that as the Java runtime environment evolves, you may need to regenerate your native header and stubs files and modify and recompile your native code.

Now that we've briefly reviewed the initial steps to linking to a native library, let's look at some utility functions you might use from within your native library to interact smoothly with the Java runtime and your own Java code.

Utility Functions for Gluing Native Code to Java

All of the Java Development Kits (JDKs) provide a set of C header files, and until now you might have been wondering why. One of the reasons is that they allow you access to some handy C utility functions contained within the Java runtime. These utility functions make it easier to exchange data between platform-specific native code and Java code.

By including the native header file *native.h* in your native project, your native code gets access to a number of useful utility functions in several different header files. Here are a few of the most useful utility functions by category:

Java Object Access

- unhand

`unhand(HObject*)`, defined in *interpreter.h*

This macro allows you to access the Java-like C `struct` behind an object handle. You can pass in any object handle, and then access the fields of the object's C `struct`.

- EE

`EE()`, defined in *interpreter.h*

This function allows you to get a reference to the current Java "execution environment" (`execenv struct`). While this reference isn't explicitly useful to you as a developer, it is useful for calling functions (such as `SignalError`) which require it. If you want to sneak a peek at what `execenv` and `stack_item` look like, look in *interpreter.h*.

Native Java String Manipulation

The Java runtime provides a number of useful string manipulation and translation functions that allow you to move strings between the Java world and the native C world.

There are generally two ways these functions work. One way is to make a copy of the data when moving it between the two worlds. The other approach is to share the actual data buffer between the two worlds.

This sharing approach is made possible by two factors. First, the implementation of the Java `String` class is fairly well hidden from the Java programmer. The `String` class API hides whether the string is null terminated, begins with a length byte, et cetera., but it's easy to see how you could implement the class using either C-style strings or Pascal-style strings. Second, even though the `String` class could be implemented in any number of ways, it is currently implemented using C strings in the Java runtime. This means that it's relatively easy to share strings between the C and Java worlds.

When you're using these string manipulation functions, keep in mind which approach you want to take. Do you want to have the memory overhead of making a copy of the strings? If you are working with fairly long strings, this can cause a significant memory impact. Also, making a copy of the string can take time. Sharing the data buffer can be faster and take less space, but you need to be careful about modifying and manipulating the string buffer.

String Methods That Share Buffers

- `makeJavaString`

`Hjava_lang_String *makeJavaString(char *, int)`, defined in *javaString.h*

This function creates a new Java `String` object, initializes the `String` with the C-string value given, and returns the new `String`.

- `MakeString`

`HArrayOfChar *MakeString(char *, long)`, defined in *interpreter.h*

This function converts from a C string to an array of characters (`HArrayOfChar`).

String Methods That Copy

- `makeCString`

`char *makeCString(Hjava_lang_String *s)`, defined in *javaString.h*

This function creates a new C string and initializes it from the given Java String. This function allocates gc-able temporary storage space to contain the C string and returns a pointer to that storage space. You must store this pointer in a variable until you no longer need the C string object. Once you release all references to the C string, the temporary storage space is garbage-collected. This is a good way to create new C strings from Java strings if you are comfortable with the garbage collection paradigm.

- `allocCString`

`char *allocCString(Hjava_lang_String *s)`, defined in *javaString.h*

This function is complementary to `makeCString`. Instead of allocating gc-able storage space, this method uses the equivalent of "malloc" to allocate storage space for the returned C string. Once this C string is returned to you, the Java runtime no longer holds any references to that string. It is then your responsibility to "free" the string pointer when you're finished with the string. This is a good way to create C strings from Java Strings if you're more comfortable explicitly freeing the C string than having the runtime garbage collect it mysteriously in the background.

- `javaString2CString`

`char *javaString2CString(Hjava_lang_String* jstr, char* buf, int len)`, defined in *javaString.h*

This function copies data characters from the Java String into a waiting C string buffer. It's your job to provide an appropriately sized buffer, as this method allocates no memory. This function returns a pointer to the C string, which is the same as the buf pointer you pass in.

Methods That Create New Strings

- `Object2CString`

`extern char *Object2CString(JHandle *)`, defined in *interpreter.h*

This function can be used like the Java `java.lang.Object.toString` method to create a string that describes the given `Object`. In this case, however, you're creating a C string instead of a Java string.

- `javaStringPrint`

`void javaStringPrint(Hjava_lang_String *)`, defined in *javaString.h*

This function prints the given Java `String` object to stdout.

String Utility Functions

- `javaStringLength`

`int javaStringLength(Hjava_lang_String *)`, defined in *javaString.h*

This function returns the length of the given Java String object. Similar to the C function `strlen`.

Exception/Error Handling

- `SignalError`

`SignalError(struct execenv *, char *, char *)`, defined in *interpreter.h*

This function allows you to throw a Java exception up from the C world for a Java exception handler (`catch` statement) to catch. This is very useful for error-handling, because it allows you to wrap your native functions with Java error-handling and recovery methods, which increases the amount of platform-independent code.

At the time of this writing, some Java runtime environments still do not deal well with SignalError being called from your native code. Specifically, certain Java runtimes will sometimes exit if this function is called. If your application stops running suddenly, or your Java runtime exits, and you know you're using this function in your native code, you might try running the code under a different runtime environment or restructure your code so as to avoid using this function.

Long Integer Manipulation Routines

The 64-bit Java `long` type is currently implemented on some platforms as a struct with a "high" 32-bit value and a "low" 32-bit value. This makes manipulating a long more difficult than manipulating simple integer values in native C code.

In order to make the manipulation of these values a bit easier, the creators of the Java runtime added a set of long integer manipulation routines defined in the *typedefs_md.h* header file. These methods map between the Java `long` type and other types such as C `int`, C `long`, floating point values, and string values.

I won't be covering these methods in great detail, but we will be using at least one of these methods in the "Native Glue Example" later in this chapter. If you want an overview of these methods, see *typedefs_md.h*.

Platform-Specific Native Linking

Each platform has its own quirks to linking in native libraries. In the sections that follow we'll explore how to build and link in native code that implements the `NativeGlueExample` native methods under Win32, Solaris, and MacOS..

None of the JDK 1.0 environments seems to deal well with creating headers and stub files for Java classes that contain underscores ("_"). This is partially due to the way the various compiler environments "mangle" function names using underscores, and partially due to lack of support by the JDK tools. For instance, only the MacOS JDK version of *javah* seems to be able to correctly generate native header stubs files from a Java class whose name contains underscores. You might be wise to avoid using underscores in your class and method names, if you intend to link with native code

Linking MacOS Shared Libraries

The MacOS Java runtime uses the Shared Library Manager to load native libraries at runtime via the `System.loadLibrary` method. In order to link to MacOS native code, you need to create a Shared Library. In this section we'll look at creating a MacOS Shared Library that works with the `NativeGlueExample` class we showed earlier.

Before we get started, note that there are some restrictions on using MacOS Shared Libraries:

- You must have the basic MacOS support for Shared Libraries installed, including the Shared Library Manager extension, and at least System 7.1.

- The MacOS JDK 1.0 only supports linking to PowerPC-compatible Shared Libraries.

- You need a development environment that can produce PowerPC Shared Libraries. For our examples we'll be using Metrowerks CodeWarrior, but there are other C development environments for MacOS that can produce Shared Libraries (MPW, Symantec, and so forth).

- Depending on how your MacOS environment is configured, you may need to move your Shared Library around so that the Shared Library Manager can find it at runtime. Good places to put it are: (1) in your *Extensions* folder, (2) in the *Extensions:JavaSoft:Other Libraries* folder, (3) in the same folder as the *Java Runner* application, and (4) in the same folder as the class file you're executing. Note that you can also just place an alias to the Shared Library into one of these folders— you don't need to put the Shared Library itself there. What you might want to do is build the library once and place an alias to it into the *System:Extensions:JavaSoft* folder. Note that if you're using a Java runtime other than the Sun JDK runtime, you'll need to place the library appropriately.

In order to create a MacOS Shared Library, we need to create a CodeWarrior project file and add the following files:

- The *Java Shared Library* file. Probably the best way to add this is to create an alias to the *(Startup Disk):System Folder: Extensions: JavaSoft Folder: Java Shared Library* file and place it into the same folder as your native code project. Then, add the alias to your project.

- The native source file. We'll examine an example source file in a moment.

- The *InterfaceLib* and the *MathLib*. These are typically included in the "Mac C/C++" project templates that CodeWarrior provides.

- You need to include a C-source file that loads the native ".stubs" file and sets up some flags for building the Shared Library. We'll examine the contents of such a file in a moment.

- Under CodeWarrior's Preferences:Project , set "Project Type" to be "Shared Library." The file type should be "shlb" and "Java" should be the file creator. Set the name of the file to be exactly the same as the name of the library you load with System.loadLibrary. Unlike the other Java runtimes, the MacOS runtime doesn't add any prefixes, suffixes, or extensions to the library filename passed to System.loadLibrary.

- Under Preferences:Access Paths, add a copy of the *Java Include Files* folder to your access path. This will give your project access to MacOS-native Java include files as well as regular Java runtime include files such as *native.h*.

The Native Implementation File

The native implementation file, "NativeGlueExampleNative.c" is shown below.

Example 8-4 MacOS-Native Implementation of NativeGlueExample Methods

```
/*

NativeGlueExampleNative.c

An example implementation of native methods.

*/

/* platform-specific Headers */
/* This one is for MacOS Shared Library */
#include <CodeFragments.h>

/* ANSI C headers */
#include <stdio.h>

/* javah-generated header */
#include "NativeGlueExample.h"


/* === NativeGlueExample_dumpIntegers ====
Dump a set of signed integer values to stdout.
covers byte, short, int, long Java types
*/
void NativeGlueExample_dumpIntegers(struct HNativeGlueExample* this,
                                    /*char*/ long myByte,
                                    /*short*/ long myShort,
                                    long myInt,
                                    int64_t myLong)
{
    char dumpBuf[255];
    dumpBuf[0] = '\0';

    printf("myByte: %d myShort: %d myInt: %ld ",
           myByte, myShort, myInt);

    /*
    int64_t is a special type in MacOS native world
    (2, 32-bit values wrapped in a struct)
    so it requires some special handling
    see typedefs_md.h for more info
    */
    ll2str(myLong, dumpBuf, (char*)(dumpBuf + 128));
    printf("myLong: %s \n", dumpBuf);
```

```
} /* NativeGlueExample_dumpIntegers */

/* === NativeGlueExample_dumpFloats ===
Dump a set of floating-point numeric types to stdout.
Covers float and double Java types
*/
void NativeGlueExample_dumpFloats(struct HNativeGlueExample* this,
                                  float myFloat, double myDouble)
{
    printf("myFloat: %g myDouble: %g \n", myFloat, myDouble);
}

/* === NativeGlueExample_dumpString ===
Dump a string to stdout.
Covers String Java type.
*/
void NativeGlueExample_dumpString(struct HNativeGlueExample* this,
        struct Hjava_lang_String* myString)
{
    /* see javaString.h for info on makeCString */
    printf("myString: %s \n", makeCString(myString));
}

/* === NativeGlueExample_dumpByteArray ===
Dump a byte array to stdout.
Covers byte[] Java type
*/
void NativeGlueExample_dumpByteArray(struct HNativeGlueExample* this,
        struct HArrayOfByte* myByteArray, long count)
{
    int i;
    /* A Java byte array is simply a chunk of memory */
    char* charP = (char*) unhand(myByteArray);

    printf("myByteArray: ");
    for (i = 0; i < count; i++)
    {
        printf("%c,", charP[i]);
    }
    printf("\n");

} /* NativeGlueExample_dumpByteArray */

/* === NativeGlueExample_dumpInstanceVars ===
Dump all instance vars to stdout.
Covers accessing instance vars.
*/
void NativeGlueExample_dumpInstanceVars(struct HNativeGlueExample* this)
{
    /* see javaString.h for info on makeCString */
    printf("fInstanceInt: %ld fInstanceFloat: %f fInstanceString: %s\n",
            unhand(this)->fInstanceInt,
```

```
        unhand(this)->fInstanceFloat,
        makeCString(unhand(this)->fInstanceString));

} /* NativeGlueExample_dumpInstanceVars */


/* === NativeGlueExample_updateInstanceVars ===
Tweak the Java class instance vars from inside native code.
*/
void NativeGlueExample_updateInstanceVars(struct HNativeGlueExample* this)
{
    unhand(this)->fInstanceFloat = 43.02;
    unhand(this)->fInstanceInt = 24;
}
```

Note that this file contains a couple MacOS-specific features:

- We include the *CodeFragment.h* file. This is required for exporting these functions, with the help of the stubs file, in a Shared Library.

- In the MacOS Java runtime, the Java long type is represented by a C struct containing two 32-bit integers (the high and low 32-bits of the 64-bit long). Because of this, we need to use the functions listed in *Java Include Files:mac:typedefs_md.h* for manipulating the int64_t type to which a Java long is mapped. In this example we specifically use the ll2str function to obtain a string representation of an int64_t.

Native Stubs Wrapper File

We also create a file that loads in the stubs source file generated by *javah*. This file is responsible for loading the stubs file and setting some compile-time flags for our Shared Library. The source for this file is shown below.

Example 8-5 MacOS Native Stubs Wrapper File

```
/*
 libstubs.c

 Includes necessary system-dependent includes.
 Modifies export controls for the linker

*/

/* mandatory Java stubs include */
#include <StubPreamble.h>

/* modify CodeWarrior export controls for our Shared Library*/
#pragma export on
#pragma require_prototypes off
```

```
/* Finally, include the generated stubs file */
#include "NativeGlueExample.stubs"
```

Linking Win32 DLLs

In the Win32 world, the Java runtime can link to native code encapsulated in a DLL. The Win32 Java runtime uses the DLL loading mechanism to load native libraries at runtime..

 The Win32 Java runtime is very sensitive to the naming and location of DLLs that you load with `System.loadLibrary`. You need to adhere to the following scheme:

- Name your DLL something something similar to *MyCode.dll*. The *.dll* extension is required. This is standard for Win32 DLLs.

- Place the DLL into one of the directories you've previously defined as being a directory from which the system should load DLLs. The default search order for Win32 is:

    a. Application load directory. In this case, it would typically be the home directory for *java.exe*.

    b. Any directories listed in your LD_LIBRARY_PATH variable. You can define this variable in your *AUTOEXEC.BAT* file, or elsewhere, or you can simply use the defaults described here.

    c. The current working directory. This would typically be the directory from which you launch the Java interpreter and your main class.

    d. 32-bit Windows system directory (*C:\WINDOWS\SYSTEM32*) This allows 32-bit DLLs to be found before 16-bit DLLs.(Note: Under Windows/NT the path is *\winnt\system32*).

    e. 16-bit Windows system directory (*\WINDOWS\SYSTEM*): You should *always* build a 32-bit DLL in order to be compatible with the Win32 Java runtime, so there's really no reason to place your DLL into the 16-bit directory.

    f. The Windows main directory. This depends on your system configuration.

g. Any directories listed in your PATH variable, defined in
AUTOEXEC.BAT or elsewhere.

Building the DLL

In this section we'll look at the basics of creating a 32-bit DLL that links to the
NativeGlueExample class we showed previously. We'll be using the Borland
C++ 5.0 IDE for Win32.

First of all, we're going to rebuild the same *NativeGlueExample.class* file using the
BC5 Java tools. By checking the "generate .C and .H files" checkbox in Project
Attributes:Java, we will force BC5's *javah* tool to generate the proper header and
stubs file.

Once that's complete, let's take a look at the header and stubs files generated. It's
interesting to compare the format of these files to the files generated previously
under MacOS. The header file is shown below.

Example 8-6 BC5 *javah*-Generated Header File for Win32 NativeGlueExample

```
/* DO NOT EDIT THIS FILE - it is machine generated */
#include <native.h>
/* Header for class NativeGlueExample */

#ifndef _Included_NativeGlueExample
#define _Included_NativeGlueExample
struct Hjava_lang_String;

typedef struct ClassNativeGlueExample {
    long fInstanceInt;
    float fInstanceFloat;
    struct Hjava_lang_String *fInstanceString;
#define NativeGlueExample_MAX_FLOAT 3.17885e-314f
#define NativeGlueExample_MAX_DOUBLE 1.79769e+308D
#define NativeGlueExample_MAX_BYTE 127L
#define NativeGlueExample_MAX_SHORT 32767L
#define NativeGlueExample_MAX_INT 2147483647L
#define NativeGlueExample_MAX_LONG 9223372036854775807LL
} ClassNativeGlueExample;
HandleTo(NativeGlueExample);

#ifdef __cplusplus
extern "C" {
#endif
__declspec(dllexport) void NativeGlueExample_dumpIntegers(
    struct HNativeGlueExample *,char,short,long,int64_t);
__declspec(dllexport) void NativeGlueExample_dumpFloats(
    struct HNativeGlueExample *,float,double);
__declspec(dllexport) void NativeGlueExample_dumpString(
    struct HNativeGlueExample *,struct Hjava_lang_String *);
__declspec(dllexport) void NativeGlueExample_dumpByteArray(
    struct HNativeGlueExample *,HArrayOfByte *,long);
__declspec(dllexport) void NativeGlueExample_dumpInstanceVars(
```

```
    struct HNativeGlueExample *);
__declspec(dllexport) void NativeGlueExample_updateInstanceVars(
    struct HNativeGlueExample *);
#ifdef __cplusplus
}
#endif
#endif
```

Notice the differences between the format of this generated file and the MacOS version. While the format is similar, there are a few things that are tailored to each platform.

First of all, the declaration of the native functions is different. Each function declaration is prefixed with `__declspec(dllexport)`, which the compiler uses as a tag to indicate that these functions will be exported from a DLL. Secondly, the definition of MAX_LONG is slightly different than from the MacOS definition. Again, this is because the definition of long constants varies between platforms.

Now let's look at the native stubs file that BC5 generated, *NativeGlueExample.c*. Because this file is a bit lengthy, we'll simply look at the method declaration for the `dumpByteArray` method.

Example 8-7 BC5 *javah*-Generated Stub for **dumpByteArray** Method

```
/* SYMBOL: "NativeGlueExample/dumpByteArray([BI)V",
Java_NativeGlueExample_dumpByteArray_stub */
__declspec(dllexport) stack_item*Java_NativeGlueExample_dumpByteArray_stub(
stack_item *_P_,struct execenv *_EE_) {extern void
NativeGlueExample_dumpByteArray(void *,void *,long);(void)
NativeGlueExample_dumpByteArray(_P_[0].p,((_P_[1].p)),((_P_[2].i)));return
_P_;}
```

Notice that once again, this declaration is similar but not identical to the MacOS version. The main difference is that each function stub is prefixed with `__declspecl(dllexport)`. The second major difference is that the `extern` functions are listed as having a single `void*` parameter instead of the actual list of parameters that each function takes. This format is different because the compiler and linker on the different platforms can deal with different declaration formats.

These two machine-generated files form the core of the headers. Now we're going to write a couple more native files and use these in the project.

The first is the native implementation file itself. To create this, I simply took the function prototypes defined in the generated header file and began implementing them. The implementation file is shown below.

Example 8-8   Native Function Implementation for Win32 NativeGlueExample

```
/*

NativeGlueExampleNative.c

An example implementation of native methods.

*/
/* javah-generated header */
#include "NativeGlueExample.h"

/* platform-specific Headers */
/* these are for Win32 */
//#include <windows.h>

/* ANSI C headers */
#include "stdio.h"


/* === NativeGlueExample_dumpIntegers ==== 
Dump a set of signed integer values to stdout.
covers byte, short, int, long Java types
*/
/* notice how param types are slightly different than for MacOS */
void NativeGlueExample_dumpIntegers(struct HNativeGlueExample* this,
                              char myByte,
                   short myShort,
                        long myInt,
                        int64_t myLong)
{
    char dumpBuf[255];
    dumpBuf[0] = '\0';

    printf("myByte: %d myShort: %d myInt: %ld ",
           myByte, myShort, myInt);

    /*
    int64_t is a special type in Win32-native world
    (2, 32-bit values wrapped in a struct)
    so it requires some special handling
    see typedefs_md.h for more info
    */
    /*
    ll2str(myLong, dumpBuf, (char*)(dumpBuf + 128));
    printf("myLong: %s \n", dumpBuf);
    */
    /*
    Apparently there's a bug here that prevents us from linking in
    ll2str...doesn't seem to be accessible.
    */
```

```
} /* NativeGlueExample_dumpIntegers */

/* === NativeGlueExample_dumpFloats ===
Dump a set of floating-point numeric types to stdout.
Covers float and double Java types
*/
void NativeGlueExample_dumpFloats(struct HNativeGlueExample* this,
                                  float myFloat, double myDouble)
{
    printf("myFloat: %g myDouble: %g \n", myFloat, myDouble);
}

/* === NativeGlueExample_dumpString ===
Dump a string to stdout.
Covers String Java type.
*/
void NativeGlueExample_dumpString(struct HNativeGlueExample* this,
      struct Hjava_lang_String* myString)
{
    /* see javaString.h for info on makeCString */
    printf("myString: %s \n", makeCString(myString));
}

/* === NativeGlueExample_dumpByteArray ===
Dump a byte array to stdout.
Covers byte[] Java type
*/
void NativeGlueExample_dumpByteArray(
      struct  HNativeGlueExample* this,
      struct HArrayOfByte* myByteArray, long count)
{
    int i;
    /* A Java byte array is simply a chunk of memory */
    char* charP = (char*) unhand(myByteArray);

    printf("myByteArray: ");
    for (i = 0; i < count; i++)
    {
        printf("%c,", charP[i]);
    }
    printf("\n");

} /* NativeGlueExample_dumpByteArray */

/* === NativeGlueExample_dumpInstanceVars ===
Dump all instance vars to stdout.
Covers accessing instance vars.
*/
void  NativeGlueExample_dumpInstanceVars(
    struct HNativeGlueExample* this)
{
    /* see javaString.h for info on makeCString */
    printf("fInstanceInt: %ld fInstanceFloat: %f fInstanceString: %s\n",
```

```
    unhand(this)->fInstanceInt,
    unhand(this)->fInstanceFloat,
    makeCString(unhand(this)->fInstanceString));

} /* NativeGlueExample_dumpInstanceVars */


/* === NativeGlueExample_updateInstanceVars ===
Tweak the Java class instance vars from inside native code.
*/
void  NativeGlueExample_updateInstanceVars(
    struct HNativeGlueExample* this)
{
    unhand(this)->fInstanceFloat = 43.02;
    unhand(this)->fInstanceInt = 24;
}

/* NativeGlueExampleNative.c */
```

We should carefully examine the changes to this file from the MacOS version. First of all, you'll notice that I commented-out the 112str call. This is because there seems to be a bug in the current version of the BC5 linker or in the *bccjavai.lib* library itself such that the code which implements the 112str function cannot be found at link time. You could probably reimplement the equivalent of 112str fairly easily, though by the time you read this, the bug will likely be fixed.

You need to include the bccjavai.lib library in your BC5 project. This allows your native code to link to any native code in the Win32 Java runtime that it'll need. Normally, this file is stored in *(BC5 dir)\java\lib\bccjavai.lib.*

You also need to create a header file that modifies the way BC5 will build your native DLL and reads in the stubs file. The source of such a file is shown below.

Example 8-9 **Header File Which Modifies BC5 Build Characteristics and Loads the Native Stubs File**

```
/*
 libstubs.c

 Includes necessary system-dependent includes.
 Modifies export controls for the linker

*/

/* modify BC5 options to build DLL properly */
#pragma option -vu

/* Finally, include the generated stubs source file */
#include "NativeGlueExample.c"
```

Once you've set up these environment variables correctly, your system shouldn't have any problem finding the DLL. When you're distributing your software to the end user, probably the easiest thing to do is either to install the DLL into one of the default DLL directories listed above, or simply stuff the DLL into the same directory as the Java class file that utilizes the DLL.

Linking Solaris Dynamic Libraries

The Solaris Java runtime uses Solaris's "dynamic library" linking mechanism to load native libraries at runtime and call them from the Java interpreter. In order to use native code in the Solaris environment, you need to create a Solaris dynamic library..

The Solaris Java runtime is very sensitive to the name passed to the System.loadLibrary function. Here's a naming scheme that should work:

- Name your native library something like *libMyCode.so*. It must have the string ".so" appended and the string "lib" prepended.

- In your Java code, call System.loadLibrary("MyCode"). The Solaris Java runtime will automatically append the ".so" and prepend the "lib" to the library name, and it will attempt to load a dynamic library with the resulting name from any of the directories defined in your LD_LIBRARY_PATH environment variable. This leads to the next point.

- Make sure you place the properly-named dynamic library into the correct directory, or add the correct directory to your LD_LIBRARY_PATH environment variable. You can add the directory to your LD_LIBRARY_PATH either manually using setenv or automatically by placing "set LD_LIBRARY_PATH ..." in your *.login* or *.cshrc* file, or another configuration file your system shell loads.

  - Alternatively, you can include the entire pathname of the dynamic library in your Java code, as in: System.load("/home/todd/libMyCode.so"). This is probably a bad idea since all of your code will then only execute in a single environment (an environment that contains the path */home/todd/*). However, if you're just trying to get started with testing your dynamic library, and you're having problems setting up your LD_LIBRARY_PATH, this quick hack might help get you started.

Note that for the sake of brevity we do not include a Solaris implementation of the `NativeGlueExample` native methods in this section. However, it should be a straightforward exercise to take the Win32 code and port it to Solaris following the same basic steps we outlined previously. You simply write your Java code including native methods, compile the Java, run the class file through javah, and finally implement the native functions based on the javah-generated prototypes.

Later in this chapter we'll review a more useful Solaris native code sample that shows in detail how to implement a dynamic library and link it to Java.

Using an Abstraction Layer to Make Porting between Platforms Easier

It's very important to provide an abstraction layer between your native implementation and whatever Java code is going to use it. This allows you to move the same Java code to different platforms more easily than if you created a new interface every time you changed platforms.

Why Define an Abstraction Layer?

When you're writing Java communications code that depends on a native library, it's sometimes difficult to see why you should bother to create a platform-independent abstraction layer between your native code and your Java code. After all, if you're going to make your application platform-specific, you might as well go all the way, right?

What I'm suggesting here is the opposite approach. You want to make your code as platform-independent as possible, and only add in the platform-dependent pieces in a manner that makes those pieces replaceable later. In the future you may find yourself porting your Win32-specific Java code to Solaris or vice versa.

You can do this the stupid way or the smart way. The stupid way involves writing a bunch of custom code every time you adapt to a new platform. The smart way involves carefully picking the layer at which you separate the platform-specific code from the platform-independent code.

The ConnectionEnd Abstraction Layer

In this section we'll look at an example abstraction layer for portable Java communications code: the `ConnectionEnd` abstract class.

The ConnectionEnd class provides a generic interface to a communications tool. ConnectionEnd provides basic methods for setting up a connection, sending and receiving data, and tearing down a connection. For the most part it hides the platform-dependent details from your Java code so that you can create fairly platform-independent communicating Java code.

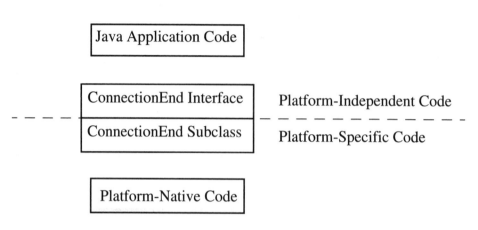

Figure 8–1 `ConnectionEnd` Lifts and Separates.

`ConnectionEnd` sits on top of platform-specific native communications tool implementations. The table below lists the core methods of `ConnectionEnd`.

Table 8-1 ConnectionEnd Class Methods

Method	Description
Instantiate	This is used to create the `ConnectionEnd` object initially. This gives your native code a chance to allocate memory, and bind other resources.
Connect	Connect actively opens a connection to a remote connection end. Examples include dialing a modem, opening a serial connection, or opening an AppleTalk connection.
Accept	Accept passively waits for someone to actively attempt a connection to this `ConnectionEnd`. Examples include setting up a modem to wait for an incoming call and waiting for an AppleTalk connection. Technically, a serial Accept is the same as a serial Connect since there's really no distinction between the connector and the connectee.
getInputStream	For clients that want a streams interface to the `ConnectionEnd`, this method provides an `InputStream` from which data can be read.

Table 8-1 ConnectionEnd Class Methods *(Continued)*

Method	Description
getOutputStream	For clients that want a streams interface to the ConnectionEnd, this method provides an OutputStream to which data can be written.
write	This method allows you to send data directly via the ConnectionEnd to the remote connection end.
read	This method allows you to directly read data from the remote side.
Disconnect	This method closes the connection immediately, or after it finishes all pending I/O requests.
Dispose	This method completely disposes of the native ConnectionEnd resources. The ConnectionEnd should not be reused after this point.
getState	Get the numeric state of the ConnectionEnd (uninitialized, instantiating, instantiated, connecting, listening, connected, disconnecting, disposing). This method allows you to query the status of the ConnectionEnd. This can be useful for determining whether a connection is open and so on.

Note that the ConnectionEnd interface is similar to the java.net.SocketImpl interface. This was intentional.

Below is the source of the ConnectionEnd class.

Example 8-10 Implementation of the ConnectionEnd Abstract Class

```java
package JNC;

import java.io.*;

public abstract class ConnectionEnd
{

public static final int
    STATE_UNINIT = 0,
    STATE_INITIALIZED = 1,
    STATE_CONNECTING = 3,
    STATE_LISTENING = 4,
    STATE_DATAXFER = 5;

//core I/O streams
protected CE_InputStream    fInputStream= null;//core input stream
protected CE_OutputStreamfOutputStream= null;//core output stream

protected int fConnState = STATE_UNINIT;
```

```
//=== Creation Methods
/**
*placeholder constructor
*/
public ConnectionEnd()
{
    //by default, does nothing!
}//ConnectionEnd

/**
* Instantiate. This is used to create the ConnectionEnd object initially.
* From this state, one can Bind or Dispose.
*
* @param parms The parameters used to instantiate a ConnectionEnd object.
Typically this includes info on the type of service requested (serial, modem,
ADSP, etc.)
*/
public abstract void Instantiate(String parms) throws IOException;


/**
* Connect actively opens a connection to a remote connection end.
* From this state, one can Disconnect.
*
* @param parms This parameter tells the ConnectionEnd how to connect or where
to connect to. This parameter could include things like ADSP NBP address.
*/
public abstract void Connect(String parms) throws IOException;

/**
* Accept.  Accept passively waits for someone to actively attempt a connection
to this ConnectionEnd. From this state, one can Disconnect.
*
* @param parms This parameter could tell the ConnectionEnd how to set up a
listening service. For instance, it could tell an ADSP server what NBP
name/type to publish on the network.
*/
public abstract void Accept(String parms) throws IOException;


/**
* getState. Get the numeric state of the ConnectionEnd.
*
* @return int The current state of the ConnectionEnd.
*/
public abstract int  getState();


//=== I/O Methods

/**
* Read some bytes from the connection
*/
```

```java
public abstract int read(byte[] buf, int offset, int count) throws
IOException;

/**
* Write out bytes on the connection
*/
public abstract void write(byte[] buf, int offset, int count) throws
IOException;


//=== Teardown Methods
/**
* Disconnect closes the connection immediately or after finishing all pending
IO requests, depending on parameters.
* From this state, one can re-Connect or UnBind.
*
* @param hardClose This parameter determines whether Disconnect closes
immediately (true) or waitings for pending IO requests to complete (false)
*/
public abstract void Disconnect(boolean hardClose) throws IOException;


/**
* Dispose completely disposes of the ConnectionEnd and associated objects.
* The object should not be reused after this method is called.
*/
public abstract void Dispose() throws IOException;


//=== Here we implement some non-abstract methods so that our subclasses
won't have to reimplement them...


/**
*    getInputStream
*    @returns The main InputStream for this ConnectionEnd
*/
public InputStream getInputStream()
{
    if (fInputStream == null) {
        //on demand, create a new input stream for our clients that want a
streams interface
        fInputStream = new CE_InputStream(this);
    }

    return (InputStream)fInputStream;
}//getInputStream


/**
*    getOutputStream
*    @returns The main OutputStream for this ConnectionEnd
*/
```

```
public OutputStream getOutputStream()
{
    if (fOutputStream == null) {
        //on demand, create a new output stream for our clientsthat want a
streams interface
        fOutputStream = new CE_OutputStream(this);
    }

    return (OutputStream)fOutputStream;
}//getOutputStream


/**
* track the numeric state of the ConnectionEnd
* @param state The new state to set.
*/
protected void setState(int state)
{
    fConnState = state;
}//setState


/**
* Get the numeric state of the ConnectionEnd.
* @return int The current state of the ConnectionEnd.
*/
public  int  getState()
{
    return fConnState;
}//getState

}/* class ConnectionEnd */
```

Note that we provide a protected method setState that allows
ConnectionEnd subclasses to track the state of their underlying native
connection ends more easily.

We also defined two support classes for ConnectionEnd: CE_InputStream
and CE_OutputStream. These classes wrap around the ConnectionEnd's
read and write methods, respectively, in order to export a streams interface to
ConnectionEnd. The implementation of these classes is shown below.

Example 8-11 Implementation of CE_InputStream

```
package JNC;
import java.io.*;


/**
* A non-abstract subclass of InputStream that provides
* a stream interface to the ConnectionEnd methods
*/
```

```
public class CE_InputStream extends InputStream
{

public ConnectionEnd fConnectionEnd;

/**
* Construct a new CE_InputStream given a target ConnectionEnd
* @param targetCE The ConnectionEnd this CE_InputStream will wrap around
*/
public CE_InputStream(ConnectionEnd targetCE)
{
    fConnectionEnd = targetCE;

}//CE_InputStream

/**
* implement the one abstract read method
* @returns int The byte read.
* @throws IOException if read fails
*/
public  int read() throws IOException
{
    byte[] tempBuf = new byte[1];
    fConnectionEnd.read(tempBuf,0,1); //read a single byte

    return tempBuf[0];
}//read

/**
* override this read method for speed
* @returns The number of bytes read.
* @throws IOException if read fails
*/
public  int read(byte[] buf, int offset, int count) throws IOException
{
    return fConnectionEnd.read(buf,offset,count);
}//read

}/* class CE_InputStream */
```

Example 8-12 Implementation of CE_OutputStream

```
package JNC;
import java.io.*;


/**
* Provide a non-abstract subclass of OutputStream
*/
public class CE_OutputStream extends OutputStream
{

public ConnectionEnd fConnectionEnd;
```

```
/**
* Construct a new CE_OutputStream given a target ConnectionEnd
* @param targetCE The ConnectionEnd this CE_OutputStream will wrap around
*/
public CE_OutputStream(ConnectionEnd targetCE)
{
    fConnectionEnd = targetCE;
}//CE_OutputStream

/**
* implement the one abstract write method
*/
public void write(int b) throws IOException
{
    byte[] tempBuf = new byte[1];
    tempBuf[0] = (byte) b;

    fConnectionEnd.write(tempBuf,0,1); //write a single byte
}//write

/**
* override this read method for speed
*/
publicvoid write(byte[] buf, int offset, int count) throws IOException
{
    fConnectionEnd.write(buf,offset,count); //write out the selected bytes
}//write

}/* class CE_OutputStream */
```

In these special subclasses of InputStream and OutputStream we implement the methods necessary for transforming a connection end into a stream: the critical methods read and write.

Dynamically Loading and Configuring ConnectionEnd

We'd really like the ability to load different kinds of ConnectionEnd subclasses on the fly, and configure them at runtime. To do this, we'll split each ConnectionEnd subclass into two files: a ConnectionEnd subclass file, and a ConnectionEnd configuration settings file. The subclass file will contain a platform-specific subclass implementation. The configuration settings file will contain configuration information applicable to the machine on which the code is running.

The format of the configuration settings file is a simple text format similar to a MacOS CommToolbox preferences configuration string:

```
Baud 9600 dataBits 8 Parity None StopBits 1 Port "Modem Port"
```

This format consists of a series of name/value pairs, where the names and values are separated by whitespace. Names or values that contain whitespace (such as "Modem Port" above) should be enclosed in quotes. This is a straightforward token format similar to HTML tag tokens.

Separating the code and configuration files in this manner allows us to do a few cool things:

- Configure the ConnectionEnd settings at runtime, before the ConnectionEnd subclass is instantiated, just by modifying the configuration settings text file.

- Save user preferences into the configuration settings file, so that we can preserve user preferences such as baud rate between invocations of this subclass.

- Allows us to load the ConnectionEnd subclass at runtime instead of having to "import" it into our other code.

Later in this chapter we'll look at loading and processing these configuration files.

Interfacing to Win32 serial communications

In this section we'll examine a ConnectionEnd subclass that interfaces to a Win32-native serial communications DLL.

First we need to create a ConnectionEnd subclass to implement the Java portion of this example.

The ConnectionEnd subclass for Win32 source is shown below.

Example 8-13 Java Implementation of CESerialWin32

```
/**
*   CESerialWin32.java
*
*   This file shows how to glue a Win32 serial connection to Java
*   code using native libraries.
*/

import java.io.*;
import java.util.*;
import JNC.*;


public class CESerialWin32 extends ConnectionEnd
{

//parity constants
public static final int
    PARITY_NONE = 0,
    PARITY_EVEN = 2,
```

```java
        PARITY_ODD  = 4;

//stop bits constants
public static final int
    STOPBITS_NONE = 0,
    STOPBITS_ONE= 1,
    STOPBITS_TWO= 2;

protected int
    fConnHandle, //this is a ref to the comms port Handle
    fBaud = 9600, //the baud rate to connect at
    fDataBits = 8,
    fParity = PARITY_NONE, //parity to use {PARITY_NONE...}
    fStopBits = STOPBITS_ONE,
    fFlowControl = 0;//{FC_NONE, FC_HW, FC_SW)

//the port to be used for the connection
//(you might want to change this default)
protected StringfPortStr = "COM4";

/**
 * Add a link to our native serial library.
 * The Win32 Java runtime library loading code will append ".dll" to the
 * library name passed to loadLibrary before attempting to
 * load the library. Thus, the actual name of our native
 * library is "CESerWin32Native.dll".
 */
static {
    System.loadLibrary("CESerWin32Native");
}


/**
 * Open a new serial connection with the given characteristics
 */
native int nativeOpen(
    int baud,//speed (for instance, 9600)
    int dataBits,//number of data bits (typically 8)
    int parity,//parity (typically PARITY_NONE)
    int stopBits, //number of stop bits (typically 1)
    int flowcontrol,//type of flow control (typically none)
    String portStr);//comm port to use (typically COM2)

/**
 * Close the serial connection referenced by fConnHandle
 */
native void nativeClose();

/**
 * placeholder constructor
 */
public CESerialWin32()
{
```

```
    //by default, does nothing
}//CESerialWin32


/*======
* processConfigStr and processAttribute have been
* removed from this listing. see "CESerialWin32.java"
* for their complete implementation.
*======== */


/**
* Used to create the ConnectionEnd object
* initially. From this state, one can Connect or Dispose.
*
* @param parms The parameters used to instantiate a ConnectionEnd
* object. Typically this includes info on the type of service
* requested (serial, modem, ADSP, etc.).
* Assumed to be a synchronous method
*(completes or fails right away)
*/
public  void Instantiate(String parms) throws IOException
{
    //process any parameters provided
    if (parms != null) processConfigStr(parms);
    //update our state
    setState(ConnectionEnd.STATE_INITIALIZED);
}//Instantiate


/**
* Connect actively opens a connection to a remote connection end.
* From this state, one can Disconnect.
*
* @param parms This parameter tells the ConnectionEnd how
* to connect or where to connect to.
* This method is assumed to be synchronous.
*/
public  void Connect(String parms) throws IOException
{
    if (parms != null) processConfigStr(parms);

    int anErr = 0;
    anErr = nativeOpen(fBaud, fDataBits, fParity, fStopBits,
                        fFlowControl, fPortStr);
    if (anErr == 0)
        setState(ConnectionEnd.STATE_DATAXFER);

}//Connect


/**
* Accept. Accept passively waits for someone to actively
```

```
* attempt a connection to this ConnectionEnd.
* From this state, one can Disconnect.
*
* @param parms This parameter could tell the ConnectionEnd
* how to set up a listening service. Assumed to be synchronous
*/
public  void Accept(String parms) throws IOException
{
    Connect(parms);
    //for a serial connection, accept is the same as connect
}//Accept


/**
*    read some data from the native connection
*/
public native int
read(byte[] buf, int offset, int count) throws IOException;

/**
*    write some data out on the native connection
*/
public native void
write(byte[] buf, int offset, int count) throws IOException;

/**
* Disconnect closes the connection immediately or after finishing all
* pending IO requests, depending on parameters.
* From this state, one can re-Connect or UnBind.
*
* @param hardClose This parameter determines whether
* Disconnect closes immediately (true) or waits
* for pending IO requests to complete (false)
*/
public  void Disconnect(boolean hardClose) throws IOException
{
    nativeClose();
    //no more connection open...set state correctly
    setState(ConnectionEnd.STATE_INITIALIZED);
}//Disconnect


/**
* Dispose completely disposes of the ConnectionEnd and
* associated objects.
* The CE should not be reused after this method is called.
*/
public  void Dispose() throws IOException
{
    fConnHandle = 0;
    //native stuff is completely uninitialized now
    setState(ConnectionEnd.STATE_UNINIT);
}//Dispose
```

```
}/* class CESerialWin32 */
```

Note that this Java source file is really just a layer of glue between ConnectionEnd clients and our native code. This layer is really only used to persistently hold variables, such as fConnHandle, which the native library cannot easily hold onto itself.

Note also that for the sake of brevity we've removed the `processConfigStr` and `processAttribute` methods from the listing above. This methods are used to process the `ConnectionEnd` configuration file mentioned previously. If you're interested in the specifics of their implementation, refer to the main source code file.

Implementing the Win32 Native Serial Communications DLL

Next we need to implement the native library with which the CESerialWin32 class will interface. We'll create a DLL which calls `CreateFile` to open a serial port. In this example we open the COM4 serial port, but you can change this parameter to meet your needs.

As in Unix, a Win32 serial port can be opened via a file-like interface. In fact, you open a serial interface in the same way that you open a file. We will show how to pass communications setup parameters between Java and the Win32 C++ world.

The native implementation of `CESerialWin32Native` is shown below.

Example 8-14 Implementation of CESerialWin32Native.c

```
/* =============================================================
   CESerialWin32Native.c
   This is an example of how to glue Win32 comms
   functions to Java code.
   =============================================================
*/

/* our include file for this CESerialWin32Native implementation */
#include "CESerialWin32Native.h"

/* ==== nativeOpen ==== 
Open a serial connection with the given parameters.
Stuff the resulting Connection Handle into the
Java struct passed in.
*/
long _export
CESerialWin32_nativeOpen(HCESerialWin32* self,
                      long baud, long dataBits,long parity,
                         long stopBits, long flowCtrl,
                         struct Hjava_lang_String* portStr)
{
    char portStrBuf[BUF_LEN];
```

```
        HANDLE connH;
        BOOL success;
        DWORD realParity, realStopBits;

         //convert port string to cstring
         javaString2CString(portStr, portStrBuf, BUF_LEN);

        // Open the comm port (COM or LPT)
         connH = CreateFile(portStrBuf, //ie "COM2"
                           GENERIC_READ|GENERIC_WRITE,
                           0, 0, OPEN_EXISTING,
                           FILE_ATTRIBUTE_NORMAL, 0);

         if (connH == INVALID_HANDLE_VALUE) ThrowOnErr("CreateFile ");

        switch (parity) {

         default:
            realParity = NOPARITY;
        }

        switch (stopBits) {

         default:
            realStopBits = ONESTOPBIT;
        }

         //set the port parameters
         success = SetupPortParms( connH, baud, dataBits,
                                  realParity, realStopBits);
         if (!success) ThrowOnErr("SetupPortParms ");

         SetPortTimeouts(connH, 1000,1,1000,1,1000 );

         // Set the Data Terminal Ready line-- we're ready for bytes!
         EscapeCommFunction(connH, SETDTR);

         /* tuck away a ref to the conn handle into the java obj */
         unhand(self)->fConnHandle = (long) connH;

        return 0;
} /* nativeOpen */

/* ===== nativeClose ====
Close the serial connection on the port
defined by the Connection Handle contained
within the Java struct passed in
*/
void _export
CESerialWin32_nativeClose(HCESerialWin32* self)
{
    /* retrieve the conn handle from the java object */
    HANDLE connH = (HANDLE) unhand(self)->fConnHandle;
```

```
     // Clear the DTR line so we can use this port in the future!
     EscapeCommFunction(connH, CLRDTR);

     CloseHandle(connH);//completely release the comm port

     unhand(self)->fConnHandle = 0;
}/* nativeClose */

/* ===== read ====
Read some bytes from the comm port
return number of bytes read
*/
long _export
CESerialWin32_read(
    HCESerialWin32* self,//ref to java object
    HArrayOfByte* buf,//buf to slurp bytes into
    long offset,//where to start stuffing bytes
    long toRead)//how many bytes to read in
{
    HANDLE connH = (HANDLE) unhand(self)->fConnHandle;

    BOOL success;
    char* inBuf = (char*) ( unhand(buf) + offset );
    int curRead;
    int totalRead = 0;

    while (totalRead < toRead) {
    success = ReadFile(connH, (void*)inBuf,
              (toRead - totalRead), &curRead, 0);
    if (!success) ThrowOnErr("ReadFile ");
    printf("read: %d \n",curRead);
      totalRead += curRead;
      inBuf = (char*) (inBuf + curRead);
    }

    printf("wanted: %d  read: %d \n",toRead,totalRead);

    return totalRead;
}/* read */

/* ===== write ====
Write out some bytes on the comm port
*/
void _export
CESerialWin32_write(
    HCESerialWin32* self,//class that called func
    HArrayOfByte* buf,//buf from which to send bytes
    long offset,//where to start pulling bytes from buf
    long toWrite)//how many bytes to write out
{
    HANDLE connH = (HANDLE) unhand(self)->fConnHandle;
    BOOL success;
```

```
     void* outBuf = (void*) ( unhand(buf) + offset );
      int numWrite = toWrite;

     //send some data!
     success = WriteFile(connH, outBuf, toWrite,&numWrite, 0);

      if (!success) ThrowOnErr("write ");


}/* CESerialWin32_write */

/* ===== SetupPortParms =======
  Initialize some settings on a communications port
*/
BOOL
SetupPortParms(
    HANDLE comHandle,//the magic win32 ref to a comm port
    int baud, int dataBits, int parity, int stopBits)
{
    BOOL success;
    DCB dcb;

    // Get the current settings of the COM port
    success = GetCommState(comHandle, &dcb);
    if (!success)  return success;

    // Modify the baud rate, etc.
    dcb.BaudRate = baud;
    dcb.ByteSize = dataBits;
    dcb.Parity = parity;
    dcb.StopBits = stopBits;

    // Apply the new comm port settings
    success = SetCommState(comHandle, &dcb);

   return success;
}//SetupPortParms

/* ======= SetPortTimeouts =======
  Setup various timeout values on the comm port
*/
void
SetPortTimeouts(HANDLE comHandle,
    int readIntTimeout,
    int readTotalTimeoutMult,
    int readTotalTimeoutConst,
    int writeTotalTimeoutMult,
    int writeTotalTimeoutConst)
{
    // Change the ReadIntervalTimeout so that
    // ReadFile will return immediately. See
    // help file
    COMMTIMEOUTS timeouts;
```

```
        timeouts.ReadIntervalTimeout = readIntTimeout;
        timeouts.ReadTotalTimeoutMultiplier = readTotalTimeoutMult;
        timeouts.ReadTotalTimeoutConstant = readTotalTimeoutConst;
        timeouts.WriteTotalTimeoutMultiplier = writeTotalTimeoutMult;
        timeouts.WriteTotalTimeoutConstant = writeTotalTimeoutConst;
        SetCommTimeouts( comHandle, &timeouts );
}/* SetPortTimeouts */


/* ==== ThrowOnErr ===
   We encountered a native error.
   Pass an exception up to the Java world.
*/
void
ThrowOnErr(char* prefixStr)
{
    char errStr[64];
    DWORD anErr = GetLastError();

    sprintf(errStr,"%s failed with native error: %d",
                prefixStr, anErr);

    /* throw an appropriate ex up to the java layer */
    SignalError(EE(), "java/lang/IOException", errStr);

}/* ThrowOnErr */
```

Notice that we use the basic CreateFile Win32 API function to create a file handle that points to a serial port. This is similar to the way in which you create a serial connection under Unix.

We use the java2CString function to convert the port string passed in to Open to a C string buffer. We can then pass this off to the CreateFile function.

In SetPortTimeouts we set up a series of default time-outs for connecting and reading/writing data. This allows us to make synchronous calls during Connect, Read, and Write, since we know that if the operations fail they will time-out within a certain fixed time.

The ThrowOnErr function is useful for throwing up an exception to the Java world when the native library encounters an error condition. This reduces the amount of the error handling code that needs to be included in the native library.

How to Tweak This Sample for Your Own Demented Purposes

This example allows you to access any interface which works via the Win32 file API. In this example we showed how you can open a serial port, but you could also open a telnet session, for instance, using this same interface. If you have code that provides some other communications solution via the File API, you can also access that.

Interfacing to Solaris Dynamic Libraries

In this section we're going to look at creating and linking to a Solaris-native serial communications dynamic library.

Creating a Solaris Serial ConnectionEnd

This example shows how to open a serial connection. Here we're going to open a POSIX-compliant serial connection using the constants provided in *termios.h*.

Here we open a serial connection using the parameters passed in via the ConnectionEnd interface.

The Java ConnectionEnd code for Solaris is slightly different because we need to keep track of the system "file descriptor" that the OS uses to reference the serial connection.

Example 8-15 Solaris Serial ConnectionEnd Java Code

```
/**
* cesersol.java
* Example for native methods under Solaris
* @author Todd Courtois
*/

import JNC.*;

import java.io.*;
import java.util.*;

/**
* cesersol.java
* Linking to a native dynamic comms library under Solaris
* @author Todd Courtois
*/
public class cesersol extends ConnectionEnd {

protected int
    fFileDescriptor, //this is a ref to the comms port
    fBaud = 9600, //the baud rate to connect at
    fParity = 0, //parity to use
    fFlowControl = 0;//hardware / (xon/xoff) / none

protected StringfPortStr = "ttya";
/**
```

```java
 * Static section lets us add our native library to the link mix.
 * Note that loadLibrary is case sensitive, and the name
 * of the library must match precisely - we use a
 * Solaris dynamic library to contain the native code.
 */
static {
    System.loadLibrary("cesersol");//load in our native code
};


/**
 * Open a new serial connection with the given characteristics
 */
native int nativeOpen(int baud,  int parity,  int flowcontrol, String
portStr);

/**
 * Close the serial connection referenced by the current file descriptor
 */
native int nativeClose();


/**
 * placeholder constructor
 */
public cesersol()
{
    //by default, does nothing
}

/*======
 * processConfigStr and processAttribute have been
 * removed from this listing. See "cesersol.java"
 * for their complete implementation.
 *======== */

/**
 * Instantiate. This is used to create the
 * ConnectionEnd object initially.
 * From this state, one can Connect or Dispose.
 * This method is assumed to be synchronous
 * (completes or fails right away)
 *
 * @param parms The parameters used to instantiate a ConnectionEnd
 * object. Typically this includes info on the type of service
 * requested (serial, modem, ADSP, etc.).
 */
public  void Instantiate(String parms) throws IOException
{
    //just process any parms provided
    if (parms != null) processConfigStr(parms);
    setState(ConnectionEnd.STATE_INITIALIZED); //update state
}// Instantiate
```

```
/**
 * Connect actively opens a connection to a remote connection end.
 * From this state, one can Disconnect.
 * This method is assumed to be synchronous
 * (completes or fails right away)
 *
 * @param parms This parameter tells the ConnectionEnd how to
 * connect or where to connect.
 */
public  void Connect(String parms) throws IOException
{
    if (parms != null) processConfigStr(parms);

    int anErr = 0;
    anErr = nativeOpen(fBaud,  fParity, fFlowControl, fPortStr);
    if (anErr == 0) {
        setState(ConnectionEnd.STATE_DATAXFER);
    }
}// Connect


/**
 * Accept. Accept passively waits for someone to actively
 * attempt a connection to this ConnectionEnd.
 * From this state, one can Disconnect.
 *
 * @param parms This parameter could tell the ConnectionEnd
 * how to set up a listening service.
 */
public  void Accept(String parms) throws IOException
{
    //for a serial connection, accept is the same as connect
    Connect(parms);
}//Accept


/**
 *read some data from the native connection
 */
public native int
read(byte[] buf, int offset, int count) throws IOException;

/**
 *write some data out on the native connection
 */
public native void
write(byte[] buf, int offset, int count) throws IOException;


/**
 * Disconnect closes the connection immediately or
```

```
* after finishing all pending IO requests, depending on
* parameters.
* From this state, one can re-Connect or Dispose
*
* @param hardClose This parameter determines whether Disconnect
* closes immediately (true) or waiting for pending IO requests
* to complete (false)
*/
public  void Disconnect(boolean hardClose) throws IOException
{
    nativeClose();
    //update state now that there's no more connection open.
    setState(ConnectionEnd.STATE_INITIALIZED);
}//Disconnect


/**
* Dispose completely disposes of the ConnectionEnd and
* associated objects.
* The CE should not be reused after this method is called.
*/
public  void Dispose() throws IOException
{
    fFileDescriptor = 0;
    //native stuff is completely uninitialized now
    setState(ConnectionEnd.STATE_UNINIT);
}// Dispose

}/* class cesersol */
```

Note that once again this Java class mainly provides some glue between the
`ConnectionEnd` interface and the underlying native code. It stores variables
such as `fFileDescriptor` persistently because the native code cannot easily do
so. It also processes the `ConnectionEnd` configuration strings as appropriate.

Implementing the Solaris Native Communications Dynamic Library

Now let's look at the Solaris native implementation. For convenience, we've split
up the Solaris native code into several files by functionality: *cesersolnative.c*
provides the basic interface methods, *serctrl.c* deals with setup and teardown of
the file descriptor, and *sersend.c* and *serrecv.c* deal with sending and receiving data,
respectively. Let's look first at the main native code.

Example 8-16 Solaris Native Serial Implementation

```
/* ======================================================
"cesersolnative.c"
This file contains implementations of the native methods of a
serial ConnectionEnd for Solaris.
======================================================*/
```

```
/* OS Headers */

/* "javah" generated Header */
#include "cesersol.h"

/* Our own useful headers */
#include "serctrl.h"

/* Java Runtime Headers */
#include "interpreter.h"
#include "javaString.h"
#include "exceptions.h"

/* a prototype used only in this file.... */
void ThrowOnError(char* , int );

/* ==== nativeOpen ====
Open a new native connection given the various setup parameters
*/
long cesersol_nativeOpen(struct Hcesersol* self,
            long baud,
            long parity,
            long flowcontrol,
            Hjava_lang_String* portStr)
{
    int fd = -1; /* bogus file descriptor */

    /* call out to our native serial port open func */
    fd = ser_open(baud,parity,flowcontrol, makeCString(portStr));

    if (fd < 0) return -1; /* couldn't open the fd for some reason */

    /* stash away the file descriptor into the java struct */
    unhand(self)->fFileDescriptor = fd;

}/* cesersol_nativeOpen */

/* ==== nativeClose ====
Close the native connection
*/
long cesersol_nativeClose(struct Hcesersol* self)
{
    int fd;
   /* get the file descriptor */
    fd = unhand(self)->fFileDescriptor;
    return ( ser_close(fd) );

}/* cesersol_nativeClose */

/* ===== read ====
Read some data in from the connection.
return number of bytes read
*/
```

```
long cesersol_read(
    struct Hcesersol* self,
    struct HArrayOfByte* buf,
    long offset, long toRead)
{
    int fd;
    int anErr = 0;
    char* inputBuf;
    long count = toRead;

    fd = unhand(self)->fFileDescriptor;
    inputBuf = (char*) unhand(buf);

    anErr = ser_recv_block( fd, inputBuf,  (int)offset,(int *) &count);

    ThrowOnError("read",anErr);

    return count; /* contains actual bytes read! */
}/* cesersol_read */

/* ==== write ====
Write out some data on the connection
*/
void cesersol_write(
    struct Hcesersol* self,
    struct HArrayOfByte* buf,
    long offset, long toSend)
{
    int fd;
    char* outputBuf;
    int count = toSend;
    int anErr = 0;

    fd = unhand(self)->fFileDescriptor;
    outputBuf = (char*) unhand(buf);

    anErr = ser_send_block( fd, outputBuf,  (int)offset, (int*)&count );

    ThrowOnError("write",anErr);
}/* cesersol_write */


/* === ThrowOnError ====
Look at the err parameter passed in:
if it's not 0, then throw!
*/
void ThrowOnError(char* prefixStr, int anErr)
{
    if (anErr != 0) {
        //throw an IOException!
        char errStr[64];
        sprintf(errStr,"native %s failed with error: %d",prefixStr,anErr);
```

```
        SignalError(EE(), "java/lang/IOException", errStr);
        //SignalError(struct execenv *, char *, char *);
    }
}/* ThrowOnError */
```

The *serctrl.c* file contains code for setting up and tearing down the connection.

Example 8-17 **Connection Setup and Teardown Code**

```
#include"serctrl.h"


/* ============= ser_open ==================
Open the serial port.
Return valid file descriptor if opened OK, -1 if error.
==========================================*/

int
ser_open(int baud,/*(in) baud rate such as 9600 */
         int par,/*(in) parity to use (PARITY_NONE, PARITY_EVEN,
PARITY_ODD) */
         int flowCtrl,/*(in) flow control to use* /
         char* portStr)/*(in) port string such as "ttyb" */
{
    int       fd;
    int       curFlags = 0;
    char      devname[64];
    int       realBaud = 0;
    struct termiosportSettings;

    /* open the port "device" first */
    strcpy(devname, "/dev/");
    strcat(devname, portStr);/* something like "ttyb" or "ttya" */
    /* open the device read/write, nonblocking */
    if ( (fd = open(devname, O_RDWR | O_NONBLOCK)) < 0) {
        printf("can't open %s: %s\n",devname, strerror(errno));
        return(-1); /* bogus fd */
    }

    /* check the port's state */
    if (tcgetattr(fd, &portSettings) < 0) {
        printf("tcgetattr error");
    }

    /* set the new parity */
    switch (par) {
        case (PARITY_NONE):
      portSettings.c_cflag = CS8;
        break
      case (PARITY_EVEN):
      portSettings.c_cflag = CS7|PARENB;
        break;
      case (PARITY_ODD):
      portSettings.c_cflag = CS7|PARENB|PARODD;
```

```
        break;
    default:
    printf("ser_open unknown parity: %d \n", &par);
        exit(2);
} /* switch */

/* set some basic flags */
portSettings.c_cflag |=
CREAD |/* enable receiver */
    HUPCL;/* lower  lines on last close */
                /* 1 stop bit (since CSTOPB unset) */

portSettings.c_cflag |= CLOCAL;/* ignore  status lines */
portSettings.c_oflag  = 0;/* turn off all output processing */

/* Could add flow control processing here... */
portSettings.c_iflag  =
IXON | IXOFF |/* Xon/Xoff flow control (default) */
    IGNBRK |/* ignore breaks */
    ISTRIP |/* strip input to 7 bits */
    IGNPAR;/* ignore input parity errors */

portSettings.c_lflag  = 0;/* everything off in local flag:
                            disables canonical mode, disables
                            signal generation, disables echo */

portSettings.c_cc[VMIN]  = 1;/* 1 byte at a time, no timer */
portSettings.c_cc[VTIME] = 0;/* (See {Fig call_read_counts}) */


/* determine the actual baud rate */
switch (baud){
    case (9600):
        realBaud = B9600;
        break;
    case (19200):
        realBaud = B19200;
        break;
    case (38400):
        realBaud = B38400;
        break;
    case (57600):
        realBaud = B57600;
        break;
    default:
        realBaud = B9600;
}

/* set both input and output baud rates the same */
cfsetispeed(&portSettings, realBaud);
cfsetospeed(&portSettings, realBaud);

/* flush the new settings */
```

```
    if (tcsetattr(fd, TCSANOW, &portSettings) < 0)
        printf("ser_open tcsetattr error\n");

    /* now, turn off nonblocking (make synchronous) */
    /* first, get the current flags settings */
    if ( (curFlags = fcntl(fd, F_GETFL, 0)) < 0) {
        printf("fcntl F_GETFL error");
    }

    /* clear (turn off) the nonblocking flag*/
    curFlags &= ~O_NONBLOCK;

    /* now set the flags as we want them */
    if (fcntl(fd, F_SETFL, curFlags) < 0) {
        printf("fcntl F_SETFL error");
    }
    return(fd);
}/* ser_open */

/* ======== ser_close =============
Shut down the serial connection and clean up.
Return 0 if OK, -1 if error.
 =============================*/
int ser_close(int fd)
{
    return ( close(fd) ); /* close the file descriptor */

}/* ser_close */
```

The *serrecv.c* file contains code for receiving data on the serial connection.

Example 8-18 Serial Read Code

```
#include"serctrl.h"

/* ======== ser_recv_block =============
Read a whole block of data from the given file.
Return 0 if recvd all OK, -1 if not.
======================================*/
int
ser_recv_block(int fd,/*(in) file from which to read bytes*/
              char *buf,/*(in/out) buffer in which to stuff read bytes */
              int offset,/*(in) where to start stuffing bytes in buf*/
              int* recvCount )/*(in/out) desired byte count/ bytes read */
{
    int curRecvd = 0;/* bytes received during most recent call to read() */
    int actualRecvd = 0; /* total bytes read from the file descriptor */
    int recvGoal = *recvCount; /*number of bytes we'd like to receive */


    /*
        loop trying to receive as many bytes as requested.
        we loop because read may return with fewer bytes than requested,
        even if there's not a serious error condition.
```

```
    */
    while (actualRecvd < recvGoal) {

        curRecvd = read(fd,(buf + offset),(recvGoal - actualRecvd));
        printf("curRecvd: %d\n",curRecvd);
        actualRecvd += curRecvd;/* track how many bytes we've received */
        offset += curRecvd;

        /* check to see whether there was a relevant error */
        if ((actualRecvd != recvGoal) &&  (errno == EINTR )) {
            printf("actualRecvd: %d\n", actualRecvd);
            *recvCount = actualRecvd;/* we recvd some bytes OK */
            return(-1);
        }
    }/* while */

    return(0);
}/* ser_recv_block */
```

The *sersend.c* file contains the code for sending data over the serial connection.

Example 8-19 Serial Write Code

```
#include"serctrl.h"

/* ======== ser_send_block =============
Send a whole block of data out on the given file descriptor.
Return 0 if sent OK, -1 if not.
===================================*/
int
ser_send_block(int fd,/* (in) file descriptor on which to send bytes */
               char* buf,/* (in) buffer from which to write bytes */
               int offset,/* (in) where to start pulling bytes from buf */
               int* sendCount ) /*(in/out) desired byte count / bytes sent */
{
    int sendGoal = *sendCount; /*num of bytes we'd like to send */

    /* try to write out sendGoal # of bytes,
    find out how many bytes were actually written */
    *sendCount = write(fd, (buf + offset), sendGoal);

    if (*sendCount != sendGoal) {
        printf("ser_send_block write error");
        return(-1);
    }
    return(0);
} /* ser_send_block */
```

Tweaking This Sample for Other Devices

In Solaris, as in the rest of the Unix world, some external device drivers are exported as files sitting under the /dev directory. In this example we tapped into a serial port, which is typically */dev/ttya*, or */dev/ttyb* (under some flavors of Unix, it might be */dev/ttyfa*, */dev/ttyfb* for serial ports with hardware flow-control enabled).

In this example we have set up some configuration parameters which are fairly specific to serial communications; however, you migtht have a device driver mounted on your system that accepts similar parameters. For instance, you might have a data collection bus card installed that exports a serial interface. You can interface with these drivers by simply changing the name of the port our sample used to the name of the device. For instance, you could interface to a device at */dev/collector* should by passing in the string "collector" as the port name (our code will prepend the "/dev") automatically.), and changing the communications parameters as appropriate.

Interfacing to the MacOS CommToolbox

In this section we'll look at creating and linking to a MacOS-native Shared Library that utilizes the Communications Toolbox.

CommToolbox Review

The MacOS CommToolbox is a standard set of interfaces for communications tools. There are three main tool types supported: File Transfer Tools, Terminals, and CommTools.

File Transfer tools sit on top of CommTools and provide a way for the user to send and receive files reliably. An example of a File Transfer Tool is the XMODEM Tool typically installed on a Mac.

Terminals are user-interface elements used for displaying incoming and outgoing data to the user. Examples of Terminals include the TTY and VT100 tools typically installed on a Mac.

For our purposes, we're most interested in CommTools. CommTools are the low-level communications drivers that communicate data over some kind of link, using some kind of protocol. Examples of commonly-used CommTools are the Serial Tool, the Apple Modem Tool, and the AppleTalk ADSP Tool. The Serial Tool provides an interface to the Mac's serial port(s). The Apple Modem Tool provides a standard interface to modems attached to the Mac. The AppleTalk ADSP Tool provides an interface to the Mac's ADSP protocol stack.

Creating an AppleTalk ADSP Connection

For our example of MacOS-native linking, I've chosen to interface to the AppleTalk ADSP Tool. ADSP is a MacOS-native reliable stream communications protocol analogous to TCP. It isn't as widely used as TCP, but in the Apple universe, at least, it's fundamental.

In this example we'll look at implementing a `ConnectionEnd` subclass which allows you to create ADSP connections, the `ceCTBMac` class.

The Java portion of the `ceCTBMac` implementation is shown below.

Example 8-20 Java Source for Class ceCTBMac

```
package JNC;

import java.io.*;

/**
 * ceCTBMac.java
 * Example for linking to mac-native communications
 */
public class ceCTBMac extends ConnectionEnd implements Runnable {

public static final String
    COMMTOOL_ID_ADSP = "AppleTalk ADSP Tool",
    COMMTOOL_ID_MODEM = "Apple Modem Tool",
    COMMTOOL_ID_SERIAL = "Serial Tool",
    COMMTOOL_NAME_LABEL = "ceCTBMacToolName";

public static final boolean fDebugOn = true;

protected String fCommToolIDStr = COMMTOOL_ID_ADSP;

protected boolean fContinueIdling = true;

protected Thread fIdlerThread = null; //drives our runnable interface
public boolean fListenComplete = false;
public int fLastAsyncErr = 0;


//this will hold a ref to a ConnHandle
public int fConnRec = 0;
//this will store the procID of the CommTool service used
public intfCTBProcID = 0;
public int fIdlerDelay = 500; //milliseconds to wait between calls to
nativeIdle

/**
 * Static section lets us add our library to the link mix.
 * Note that loadLibrary is case sensitive, and the name
```

```
 * of the code fragment must match precisely - we use the
 * Code Fragment Manager to resolve these names, as described in
 * "Inside Macintosh: PowerPC System Software"
 */
static {
    System.loadLibrary("ceCTBMacNative");//load in our native code
};


/**
 * Native instance methods
 * These are glue to the native CTB methods
 */
native void nativeInstantiate(String serviceID, String parms);
native void nativeConnect(String parms);
native void nativeListen(String parms);
native void nativeIdle(); //idle the native code
native void nativeDisconnect(boolean hardClose);
native void nativeDispose();


/**
 * a placeholder constructor
 */
public ceCTBMac()
{
}//ceCTBMac


/**
 * start idling the CTB
 */
protected void startIdler()
{
    fContinueIdling = true;
    if (fIdlerThread == null) {
        if (fDebugOn) System.out.println("startIdler...");
        fIdlerThread = new Thread(this);
        fIdlerThread.start();
    }
    else
        if (fDebugOn) System.out.println(
            "startIdler: fIdlerThread already exists?! ");

}//startIdler


/**
 * stop idling the CTB
 */
protected void stopIdler()
{
    if (fDebugOn) System.out.println("stopIdler...");
```

```
        fContinueIdling = false;
        if (fIdlerThread != null) {
            fIdlerThread.stop();
            fIdlerThread = null;
        }
}//stopIdler


/**
 * This method allows us to call the CTB idler method,
 * which gives processor time to the CTB
 */
public void run()
{
        if (fDebugOn) System.out.println("ceCTBMac:run()");

        while (fContinueIdling) {
            //give the native code a chance to idle
            if (getState() > 0) nativeIdle();
            try {fIdlerThread.sleep(fIdlerDelay);}
            catch (Exception sleepEx) {
                if (fDebugOn) System.out.println("sleepEx: " + sleepEx);
                fContinueIdling = false;
            }
        }
}//run

/**
 * Instantiate. This is used to create the ConnectionEnd
 * object initially.
 * From this state, one can Connect or Dispose.
 * @param parms The parameters used to instantiate a
 * ConnectionEnd object. Typically this includes info on the
 * type of service requested
 * (serial, modem, ADSP, etc.).  Assumed to be a synchronous
 * method (completes or fails right away)
 */
public  void Instantiate(String parms) throws IOException
{

        //we do one nasty thing here, which is to filter the incoming
        //parms string for any CommTool name info in the following format
        // ceCTBMacToolName "AppleTalk ADSP Tool"
        //This allows us to instantiate the correct commtool
        int idOffset = -1;
        if ((idOffset = parms.lastIndexOf(COMMTOOL_NAME_LABEL)) >= 0 )
            try {
                //there's a commtool name string name/value
                //pair in the string
                //go slurp it
                //note: the tool name MUST be enclosed in quotes
                int firstDblQuoteOffset =
```

```
                    parms.indexOf((int)'"', idOffset);
                int secondDblQuoteOffset =
                    parms.indexOf((int)'"',firstDblQuoteOffset + 1);
                fCommToolIDStr =
                    parms.substring(firstDblQuoteOffset +1,
                                  secondDblQuoteOffset );
                //now we gotta remove this info from the string,
                //because the commtool won't recognize it
                //start just after the last dbl quote, whitespace
                parms = parms.substring(secondDblQuoteOffset + 2);
            }
            catch (Exception parseEx) {
                    System.err.println("parsing parms threw: " + parseEx);
            }

        if (fDebugOn) System.out.println(
            "fCommToolIDStr: " + fCommToolIDStr);

        nativeInstantiate(fCommToolIDStr,parms);

        //update state
        setState(ConnectionEnd.STATE_INITIALIZED);
        startIdler();
}// Instantiate


/**
 * Connect actively opens a connection to a remote
 * connection end.
 * From this state, one can Disconnect.
 * Assumed to be a synchronous method (completes or fails
 * after some period of time)
 *
 * @param parms This tells the ConnectionEnd how to connect
 *   or where to connect to. This parameter could include things
 *   like ADSP NBP address.
 */
public  void Connect(String parms) throws IOException
{
    nativeConnect(parms);
    setState(ConnectionEnd.STATE_CONNECTING);
}// Connect


/**
 * Accept. There are two ways to open a connection.
 * Accept passively waits for someone
 * to actively attempt a connection to this ConnectionEnd.
 * From this state, one can Disconnect.
 * Assumed to be a synchronous method (completes or fails
 * after some period of time)
 * @param parms This parameter could tell the ConnectionEnd how to
 *   set up a listening service. For instance, it could tell an ADSP
```

```
*    server what NBP name/type to publish on the network.
*/
public  void Accept(String parms) throws IOException
{
    fListenComplete = false;
    nativeListen( parms);
    setState(ConnectionEnd.STATE_LISTENING);

    while (!fListenComplete) {

        try { Thread.currentThread().sleep(1000); }
        catch (Exception sleepEx) {};

    }

    if (fListenComplete && (getState() != ConnectionEnd.STATE_DATAXFER)) {
        throw new IOException("Accept failed with err: " + fLastAsyncErr);
    }
}//Accept

/**
*read some data from the native connection
*/
public native int
read(byte[] buf, int offset, int count) throws IOException;

/**
*write some data out on the native connection
*/
public native void
write(byte[] buf, int offset, int count) throws IOException;

/**
* closes the connection immediately or after finishing all
* pending IO requests, depending on parameters.
* From this state, one can re-Connect or UnBind.
*
* @param hardClose This parameter determines whether Disconnect
* closes immediately (true) or waitings for pending IO requests
* to complete (false)
*/
public  void Disconnect(boolean hardClose) throws IOException
{
    nativeDisconnect( hardClose);
    setState(ConnectionEnd.STATE_INITIALIZED);
}// Disconnect


/**
* Dispose completely disposes of the ConnectionEnd
* and associated objects.
* The object should not be reused after this method is called.
*/
```

```
public  void Dispose() throws IOException
{
    stopIdler();
    nativeDispose();
    //native stuff is completely uninitialized now
    setState(ConnectionEnd.STATE_UNINIT);
}// Dispose


} /* class ceCTBMac */
```

Notice that the ceCTBMac class creates a separate thread that calls the CommToolbox function CMIdle. This is required so that the CommToolbox will get a sufficient timeslice to operate properly. (Remember, the MacOS doesn't yet provide true preemptive multitasking, so we have to provide the CommToolbox with our forced timeslice.)

The native implementation for ceCTBMac is shown below.

Example 8-21 Native Implementation of ceCTBMac

```
/*
 * File: ceCTBMacNative.c
 *
 * Implementations of ceCTBMac_Native native communications
 * library for MacOS
 */

//Our own useful headers
#include "ceCTBMacNative.h"


/*
 Handy utility method converts Java String to Pascal string
 Needed because so many Connection Manager methods use Pascal strings...
 */
void javaStringToStr255( struct Hjava_lang_String* jStr, Str255 pStr)
{
    char* tempCString;
    int len;

    tempCString = makeCString(jStr);
    len = strlen(tempCString);
    pStr[0] = len; //slam in the length byte
    pStr[1] = '\0';
    strncpy(( (char*)pStr + 1),tempCString, len + 1);//copy the null as well

}/* javaStringToStr255 */


/*
 Modify the given tool configuration given a new parms String
 */
```

```
void modifyToolConfig(ConnHandle connRec, struct Hjava_lang_String* parms)
{
    OSErr anErr = noErr;
    char* configStr;

    configStr = makeCString(parms);

    if ( (configStr != nil) && (strlen(configStr) > 0) ) {
        anErr = CMSetConfig(connRec, configStr);
        //err code < 0 indicates something nasty happened
        //err code > 0 indicates position where parsing stopped
        if (anErr < 0) ThrowOnError("modifyToolConfig", anErr);
    }
} /* modifyToolConfig */



/* ========== nativeInstantiate ==========

This method kickstarts the CommToolbox,
creates a new CommTool with the requested type,
given the request parms,

and stuffs the results into the "parent" java object

*/
void  ceCTBMac_nativeInstantiate(struct HceCTBMac* this,
                                 struct Hjava_lang_String* serviceID,
                                 struct Hjava_lang_String* parms)
{

    OSErr           anErr = noErr;
    CMBufferSizes   sizes;//buffer sizes for this commtool

    Str255          fCommToolName;
    ConnHandle      fConnRec ;
    int             fCTBProcID;//ID of the CommTool

    //the gist of the following code is that we have to convert a
    //Java String to a Pascal string for the CM to be happy.
    javaStringToStr255(serviceID, fCommToolName);

#if FOR_CE_CTB_DEBUG
    fprintf(stdout, "instantiate: '%s' '%s'\n",
        makeCString(serviceID),makeCString(parms));
#endif

    anErr = InitCM();//init the Mac Connection Manager
    require(anErr == noErr, InitCMFailed);

    // Get the ProcID associated with the CTB tool
    fCTBProcID = CMGetProcID( fCommToolName );
```

```
    require_action(fCTBProcID != -1, NoCTBTool, anErr = cmNoTools;);


    //set up the various buffer sizes
    //let's just ask for the defaults?
    sizes[cmDataIn]  = 0;//basic input
    sizes[cmDataOut] = 0;//basic output
    sizes[cmCntlIn]  = 0;//control input
    sizes[cmCntlOut] = 0;//control output
    sizes[cmAttnIn]  = 0;//attention input
    sizes[cmAttnOut] = 0;//attention output
    sizes[cmRsrvIn]  = 0;//?? reserved input
    sizes[cmRsrvOut] = 0;//?? reserved output

    // Allocate a connection record for the CTB connection
    fConnRec = CMNew(fCTBProcID,//the CommTool's ID
                    // data only, do all config in the background
                    cmData | cmNoMenus | cmQuiet,
                    sizes,//default buffer sizes
                    0,
                    0);

    require_action(fConnRec != nil, CantAllocConnRec, anErr = memFullErr;);

    // Configure the connection with the config string passed in
    modifyToolConfig(fConnRec,parms);

    //tuck away the procID in the java object instance
    unhand(this)->fCTBProcID = (long)fCTBProcID;
    //tuck away the connection record
    unhand(this)->fConnRec = (long)fConnRec;

    //tuck away a ref to the main java struct...used by completion routines
    CMSetUserData(fConnRec, (long) this);

    return;

// ===== Clean-up =====

CantConfig:
    CMDispose(fConnRec);
    fConnRec = nil;

CantAllocConnRec:
NoCTBTool:
InitCMFailed:
    ThrowOnError("Instantiate",anErr);
}/* nativeInstantiate */

/* ===== nativeConnect =====
    form an active connection

*/
```

```
void ceCTBMac_nativeConnect(struct HceCTBMac* this,
                 struct Hjava_lang_String* parms)
{
    OSErr anErr = noErr;
    //access fConnRec in the java struct
    ConnHandle fConnRec = (ConnHandle) unhand(this)->fConnRec;
    //time in ticks to wait for open to complete; -1 for no timeout
    unsigned longtimeout = 3600;

#if FOR_CE_CTB_DEBUG
    fprintf(stdout, "Connect: '%s' \n",makeCString(parms));
#endif

    //if there are any new parms, config the tool
    modifyToolConfig(fConnRec,parms);

    // Try to start the open request
    anErr = CMOpen(fConnRec, false /*async*/, nil /*OpenCompProc*/, timeout);

    // Make sure we started the request OK
    require(anErr == noErr, CantStartRqst);

    return;

// ===== Clean-up =====

CantStartRqst:
CantAlloc:
PendingListen:
PendingOpen:
AlreadyOpen:
NoConnRec:

    ThrowOnError("Connect",anErr);

} /* nativeConnect */


/* ===== ListenCompletionProc =====

    ListenCompletionProc is the completion proc that's called when an async
listen call has completed.
    We simply find the listen request in the object array and mark it
complete.
*/
pascal void ListenCompletionProc(
    ConnHandletheConn)         // (in)Handle to the target connection record
{
    struct HceCTBMac* theVars = ( HceCTBMac*) (*theConn)->userData;


    if ( (*theConn)->errCode == 0) {
        unhand(theVars)->fConnState = ceCTBMac_STATE_DATAXFER;
```

```
            //we don't do any security checking here...
            CMAccept(theConn, true);
        }
        else {
            unhand(theVars)->fConnState = ceCTBMac_STATE_INITIALIZED;
            unhand(theVars)->fLastAsyncErr = (*theConn)->errCode;
        }

        unhand(theVars)->fListenComplete = true;

}
/* ListenCompletionProc */



/* ====== nativeListen =====
Wait for an incoming connection. In other words, be a server!
*/
void ceCTBMac_nativeListen(struct HceCTBMac* this, struct Hjava_lang_String*
parms)
{
    ConnectionCompletionUPP openCompProc;
    OSErr anErr = noErr;
    // time in ticks to wait for open to complete; -1 for no timeout
    unsigned longtimeout = 3600;
    //access fConnRec in the java object
    ConnHandle fConnRec = (ConnHandle) unhand(this)->fConnRec;

#if FOR_CE_CTB_DEBUG
    fprintf(stdout, "nativeListen: '%s' \n",makeCString(parms));
#endif
    //if there are any new parms, config the tool
    modifyToolConfig(fConnRec,parms);

    openCompProc =
        NewConnectionCompletionProc(ListenCompletionProc);

    // Try to start the listen request
    anErr = CMListen(fConnRec, true , openCompProc , timeout);
    require(anErr == noErr, CantStartRqst);

    return;

// ===== Clean-up after err =====

CantStartRqst:
CantAlloc:
PendingListen:
PendingOpen:
AlreadyOpen:
NoConnRec:

    ThrowOnError("Listen",anErr);
} /* nativeListen */
```

```
/* ===== read ====

Read some data in from the connection

return number of bytes read?

*/
long  ceCTBMac_read(struct HceCTBMac* this,
                    struct HArrayOfByte* buf,
                    long offset, long count)
{
    OSErr anErr = noErr;
    long toRead = count;
    CMFlags readFlags = 0;

#if FOR_CE_CTB_DEBUG
    fprintf(stdout, "read offset: %d count: %d \n",offset,count);
#endif

    anErr =CMRead((ConnHandle) unhand(this)->fConnRec,
                (Ptr) ( unhand(buf) + offset ), &toRead,
                cmData /*channel*/, false /*async*/,
                NULL /*RecvComProc */, -1 /*no timeout */,&readFlags);


    ThrowOnError("read",anErr);
    return toRead; //contains actual bytes read!
}//read


/* ==== write ====

Write out some data on the connection

*/
void ceCTBMac_write(struct HceCTBMac* this, struct HArrayOfByte* buf, long
offset, long count)
{
    OSErr anErr = noErr;
    long toWrite = count;
    CMFlags writeFlags = 0;

#if FOR_CE_CTB_DEBUG
    fprintf(stdout, "write offset: %d count: %d \n",offset,count);
#endif

    anErr = CMWrite((ConnHandle) unhand(this)->fConnRec, (Ptr) ( unhand(buf)
+ offset ), &toWrite,
                    cmData, false /* async */, NULL /* SendCompProc */, -1 /*
no timeout */, writeFlags);
```

```
    ThrowOnError("write",anErr);
    //if  ( (anErr != noErr) || (count != toWrite) ) {
}//write


/* ==== nativeIdle ====
    Give up some time to the CTB as often as possible
*/
void ceCTBMac_nativeIdle(struct HceCTBMac* this)
{
    //access fConnRec in the java struct
    ConnHandle fConnRec = (ConnHandle) unhand(this)->fConnRec;

    //call the Connection Manager's idle routine
    CMIdle(fConnRec);


#if FOR_CE_CTB_DEBUG
    fprintf(stdout, "nativeIdle done! \n");
#endif

}//nativeIdle



/* ======= nativeDisconnect ====
Blow away any open connection.
*/
void ceCTBMac_nativeDisconnect(struct HceCTBMac* this, /*boolean*/ long
hardClose)
{
    OSErr anErr = noErr;
    ConnHandle fConnRec = (ConnHandle) unhand(this)->fConnRec;  //access
fConnRec in the java struct
    boolean doHardClose = (hardClose != 0);

    anErr = CMClose(fConnRec, false /* async */,
                    nil /* async completor ProcPtr */,
                    -1 /* no timeout */,
                    doHardClose /* hard close */);

    ThrowOnError("Disconnect",anErr);

}

/* ==== nativeDispose =====
Dispose of any CommTool resources allocated.

After this call, our parent object is essentially useless.
*/
void ceCTBMac_nativeDispose(struct HceCTBMac* this)
{
```

```
    ConnHandle fConnRec = (ConnHandle) unhand(this)->fConnRec;   //access
fConnRec in the java struct

    CMDispose(fConnRec);
    unhand(this)->fConnRec = nil;//clear the connection record

}


/* === ThrowOnError ====

    Look at the OSErr parameter passed in
    if it's not noErr, then throw!
*/
void ThrowOnError(char* prefixStr, OSErr anErr)
{
    if (anErr != noErr) {
        //throw an IOException!
        char errStr[64];
        sprintf(errStr,"native %s failed with error: %d",prefixStr,anErr);

        SignalError(EE(), "java/lang/IOException", errStr);
        //SignalError(struct execenv *, char *, char *);
    }

}
```

How to Tweak This Sample for Other CommTools (Modem, Serial, etc.)

The MacOS CommToolbox provides a fairly consistent API to wildly diverse communications ports and drivers. Here we've shown how to interface to the Mac's built-in ADSP tool, but you could also interface easily to the two most widely available Mac CommTools: the Apple Modem Tool and the Serial Tool. There are also a number of other CommTools that third-parties provide for Mac users. Many of these are related to TCP, the interface for which Java already provides for your code. But there are others such as X.25 and ISDN, and some related to bus cards. Depending on your application, you might find it useful to be able to control these other CommTools directly from your Java code.

All you really need to do in order to tweak this code for other CommTools is to pass tool-specific configuration parameters (such as phone number for the Modem Tool), and a different service ID upon instantiation.

Putting It Together: A Cross-Platform Terminal Emulator

We now have three different native subclasses of the ConnectionEnd class. Let's take these subclasses and wrap them under a common umbrella and show how you might use these tools with your Java code.

In this section we'll examine a simple terminal emulator that sits on top of our three ConnectionEnd subclasses.

Platform-Independent Configuration

One of the first issues that pops up with any cross-platform communicating application will be configuration. How do you write your code in such a way as to make it easy to select different communications options on different platforms? On the Mac, if you're setting up an AppleTalk ADSP connection, the configuration settings are obviously going to be different than if you're setting up a Solaris serial connection.

Fortunately, we've already done a bit of the real work by rolling code into each of the `ConnectionEnd` subclasses that supports passing configuration parameters to each of the main `ConnectionEnd` methods. Note that the `Instantiate`, `Accept`, and `Connect` methods each accept a `String` parameter that can be used to pass in configuration settings. We're going to take advantage of this to create a configuration file format that is compatible with these methods.

Let's define a ConnectionEnd-subclass-independent configuration file format.

This format should include:

- The name of the `ConnectionEnd` subclass which should be instantiated

- Configuration strings for the `Instantiate`, `Accept`, and `Connect` methods

A sample configuration file which sets up `ceCTBMac` for an AppleTalk ADSP connection is shown below.

Example 8-22 **Sample Configuration File for a ConnectionEnd subclass**

```
# The format of this file is as follows:
# lines beginning with pound sign are comments
# all lines are terminated by EOL, which is \n
# the order of lines is as follows:
# 1. the name of the ConnectionEnd subclass to load (terminated by EOL)
# 2. Instantiate parameters (could be empty string terminated by EOL)
# 3. Accept parameters (could be empty string terminated by EOL)
# 4. Connect parameters (could be empty string terminated by EOL)
#
ceCTBMac
ceCTBMacToolName "AppleTalk ADSP Tool"
LocalADSPName "jADSP Server" LocalADSPType "jADSP Type"
RemoteADSPName "mobile thex" RemoteADSPType "jADSP Type"
```

Notice that the first noncomment line in this sample configuration file contains the name of the `ConnectionEnd` subclass. This will allow our terminal emulator application to determine which `ConnectionEnd` subclass to instantiate and configure with these configuration strings.

Now, in order to allow the user to pick a configuration file for use with the terminal emulator, we need to create a helper class that allows the user to pick a file. This helper class will use the `java.awt.FileDialog` and simply allow the user to pick a file with a certain filename extension (in this case, we've chosen ".cfg"). The implementation of this class is covered in detail in "Configuration File Loader" on page 309.

Once the user selects a configuration file, we can begin the real work of setting up the user interface for the terminal emulator. The user interface for this terminal emulator will be very simple: it won't resemble the sophisticated UI of common commercial terminal emulators with which you might be familiar.

The user interface needs a minimal set of elements:

- An area to view incoming data

- An area to type in outgoing data

- Buttons to Connect, Accept, and Disconnect

- A button to select or reselect the configuration file to be used.

We will implement this user interface in a class called `FunkyTerm`. The source for the main `FunkyTerm` implementation is shown below.

Example 8-23 Terminal Emulator Implementation

```
import JNC.*;
import java.io.*;
import java.awt.*;


/**
 * A cross-platform terminal emulator that
 * utilizes ConnectionEnd
 */
public class FunkyTerm extends Frame implements Runnable
{
public final static String CONFIG_FILE_EXTENSION = ".cfg";

public static int fMaxDisplayWidth = 200;
public static int fMaxDisplayHeight = 100;

protected DataInputStream fConfigFile = null;
protected ConnectionEnd fConnectionEnd = null;
protected String fCESubclassName = null;
```

```
protected  int fOutstandingRequest = 0;
public final static int REQ_CONNECT = 2;
public final static int REQ_LISTEN = 4;

protected Thread fRequestRunnerThread = null;
protected boolean fContinueRunning = true;

//UI stuff
protected BorderLayout fUberLayoutMgr;
protected StdioShell vIODisplay  = null;
protected PanelvButtonPanel = null;
protected ButtonvConnectButt = null;
protected ButtonvListenButt = null;
protected ButtonvDisconnectButt = null;

protected String fInstantiateParms = "";
protected String fAcceptParms = "";
protected String fConnectParms = "";

public boolean fDebugOn = true;


/**
* constructor
*/
public FunkyTerm()
{
    //get the connection mode from the user...
    pickConnectionMode();
    setConfigParms();
    initConnectionEnd();

    //init the ui
    fUberLayoutMgr = new BorderLayout(0,0);
    this.setLayout(fUberLayoutMgr);

    vButtonPanel = new Panel();
    add("North",vButtonPanel);

    vConnectButt = new Button("Connect");
    vButtonPanel.add(vConnectButt);

    vListenButt = new Button("Listen");
    vButtonPanel.add(vListenButt);

    vDisconnectButt = new Button("Disconnect");
    vButtonPanel.add(vDisconnectButt);

    this.setTitle("Controls");//give the button panel a title

  vIODisplay = new StdioShell("FunkyTerm", null,//no initial stream
                  320,240);
  vIODisplay.resize(320,240);
```

```
    vIODisplay.show();

    fRequestRunnerThread = new Thread(this);
    fRequestRunnerThread.start();

}//FunkyTerm

/**
 * Handle various UI events
 */
public boolean handleEvent(Event evt)
{

    boolean wasHandled = false;
    switch(evt.id) {
        case (Event.ACTION_EVENT):
        {
            //check to see whether arg is a string
            if ( ((String)evt.arg).equals("Connect") ) {
                fOutstandingRequest = REQ_CONNECT;
                wasHandled = true;
            }
            else if ( ((String)evt.arg).equals("Listen")) {
                fOutstandingRequest =  REQ_LISTEN;
                wasHandled = true;
            }
            else if ( ((String)evt.arg).equals("Disconnect")) {
                shutdownConnectionEnd();
                wasHandled = true;
            }
            break;
        }

        case (Event.WINDOW_DESTROY):
        {
            if (fDebugOn) System.out.println(
                "FunkyTerm got WINDOW_DESTROY evt!");
            fContinueRunning = false;
            shutdownConnectionEnd();
            wasHandled = true;
            System.exit(0);
            break;
        }

    }

    if (!wasHandled) return super.handleEvent(evt);
    else return true;

}//handleEvent

/**
 * start the CE actively attempting to connect
```

```
*/
protected void startCEConnect()
{
    if (fDebugOn) System.out.println("startCEConnect....");

    //make sure the CE exists
    if (fConnectionEnd == null) initConnectionEnd();

    //make sure we're in an OK state to attempt this operation
    if (fConnectionEnd.getState() == ConnectionEnd.STATE_INITIALIZED) {
        try { fConnectionEnd.Connect(fConnectParms); }
        catch(IOException ex) {
            System.err.println("Connect ex: " + ex);
            return;
        }

vIODisplay.setDisplaySourceStream(fConnectionEnd.getInputStream());
    }
}//startCEConnect

/**
 * start the CE passively listening for a connection
 */
protected void startCEListen()
{
    if (fDebugOn) System.out.println("startCEListen....");

    //make sure the CE exists
    if (fConnectionEnd == null) initConnectionEnd();

    //make sure we're in an OK state to attempt this operation
    if (fConnectionEnd.getState() == ConnectionEnd.STATE_INITIALIZED) {
        try { fConnectionEnd.Accept(fAcceptParms); }
        catch(IOException ex) {
            System.err.println("Accept ex: " + ex);
            shutdownConnectionEnd();
            return;
        }
        vIODisplay.setDisplaySourceStream(fConnectionEnd.getInputStream());
    }

    if (fDebugOn) System.out.println("startCEListen done");

}//startCEListen

/**
 * create a new ConnectionEnd instance and
 * call CE.Instantiate
 */
protected void initConnectionEnd()
{
```

```
    if (fDebugOn) System.out.println("initConnectionEnd start....");

    Class loadClass;
    try { loadClass = Class.forName(fCESubclassName);}
    catch (ClassNotFoundException cnfEx) {
        System.err.println("couldn't load class file: " + cnfEx);
        return;
    }

    try { fConnectionEnd = (ConnectionEnd)loadClass.newInstance();}
    catch (InstantiationException instEx) {
        System.err.println("couldn't create new " +
            fCESubclassName + ": " + instEx);
        return;
    }
    catch (IllegalAccessException accEx) {
        System.err.println("couldn't create new " +
            fCESubclassName + ": " + accEx);
        return;
    }

    try { fConnectionEnd.Instantiate(fInstantiateParms); }
    catch (IOException ioEx) {
        System.err.println("Instantiate ex: " + ioEx);
        return;
    }

    if (fDebugOn) System.out.println("initConnectionEnd done....");

}//initConnectionEnd


/**
* shutdown and cleanup the connection end
*/
protected void shutdownConnectionEnd()
{
    if (fDebugOn) System.out.println("shutdownConnectionEnd start....");

    if (fConnectionEnd != null) {

        int curState = fConnectionEnd.getState();

        switch (curState) {

            case (ConnectionEnd.STATE_DATAXFER):
                try {fConnectionEnd.Disconnect(true);}
                catch (IOException discoEx) {};

            case (ConnectionEnd.STATE_CONNECTING):
            case (ConnectionEnd.STATE_LISTENING):
            case (ConnectionEnd.STATE_INITIALIZED):
                try {fConnectionEnd.Dispose();}
```

```
                    catch (IOException dispoEx) {};

              default:
                  fConnectionEnd = null;
            }

        vIODisplay.setDisplaySourceStream(null);

    }

    if (fDebugOn) System.out.println("shutdownConnectionEnd done....");


}//shutdownConnectionEnd

/**
 * Open a file chooser and pick the appropriate
 * configuration file to use.
 */
protected void pickConnectionMode()
{

    FileSelector fs;
    fs = new FileSelector(CONFIG_FILE_EXTENSION);

    String fileName = fs.getSelectedFilename();

    if (fileName != null) {
        if (fDebugOn) System.out.println(
            "selected filename: " +fileName);

        try {
                fConfigFile =
                    new DataInputStream(new FileInputStream(fileName));
        }//read mode
        catch (IOException ioEx) {
            System.err.println(
                "couldn't open " + fileName + " error: " + ioEx);
        }
    }

    //get rid of awt junk when we're done with it...
    fs.dispose();

}//pickConnectionMode

/**
 * get the next line that doesn't begin with #
 */
public  String getNextValidLine(DataInputStream srcFile)
{
    String curLine = "#";
```

```
    try {
        while ((curLine != null) && curLine.startsWith("#")) {
            curLine = srcFile.readLine();
        }
    }
    catch (IOException ioEx) {
        System.err.println("readLine failed: " + ioEx);
    }
    catch (Exception genEx) {
        System.err.println("readLine failed: " + genEx);
    }

    if ((curLine != null) && curLine.startsWith("#")) curLine = null;

    return curLine;
}// getNextValidLine


/**
* load configuration settings from the config file
*/
protected void setConfigParms()
{
    String curLine = null;

    if (fConfigFile != null) {

        curLine = getNextValidLine(fConfigFile);
        if (curLine != null) fCESubclassName = curLine;
        else return;
        if (fDebugOn) System.out.println(
            "fCESubclassName: '" + fCESubclassName + "'");


        curLine = getNextValidLine(fConfigFile);
        if (curLine != null) fInstantiateParms = curLine;
        else return;
        if (fDebugOn) System.out.println(
            "fInstantiateParms: '" + fInstantiateParms + "'");

        curLine = getNextValidLine(fConfigFile);
        if (curLine != null) fAcceptParms = curLine;
        else return;
        if (fDebugOn) System.out.println(
            "fAcceptParms: '" + fAcceptParms + "'");

        curLine = getNextValidLine(fConfigFile);
        if (curLine != null) fConnectParms = curLine;
        else return;
        if (fDebugOn) System.out.println(
            "fConnectParms: '" + fConnectParms + "'");

    }
```

```
    }/* setConfigParms */


    /**
     * this is where we carry out asynchronous operations
     */
    public void run()
    {
        while(fContinueRunning) {

            try {fRequestRunnerThread.sleep(1000);}
            catch (Exception intEx) {
                if (fDebugOn) System.out.println(
                    "sleep ex: '" + intEx + "'");
            };

            if (fOutstandingRequest != 0) {

                switch (fOutstandingRequest) {

                    case (REQ_CONNECT):
                        startCEConnect();
                        fOutstandingRequest =0;
                        break;

                    case (REQ_LISTEN):
                        startCEListen();
                        fOutstandingRequest = 0;
                        break;
                }

            }
        }
    }//run

    /**
     * static method used to launch the FunkyTerm class
     */
    public static void main(String[] args)
    {

        FunkyTerm theFunkyTerm = new FunkyTerm();

        theFunkyTerm.resize(fMaxDisplayWidth,fMaxDisplayHeight);
        theFunkyTerm.show();

    }

}/* class FunkyTerm */
```

Let's review quickly what a few of the `FunkyTerm` methods do:

- `initConnectionEnd` and `shutdownConnectionEnd` are used to create and tear down a connection end, respectively.

- The `setConfigParms` method simply reads in a series of lines from the configuration file. If a line is blank, it simply skips to the next line (and pulls the line's attributes into the next configuration option.

- Many of the time-consuming tasks for this class are launched from a separate thread in the `run` method. This prevents `FunkyTerm` from locking up the user interface while it does its work.

- The `pickConnectionMode` method allows the user to pick the particular connection configuration file to use. The `getNextValidLine` and setConfigParms methods are used to parse that configuration file and set up the connection end appropriately.

New in JDK 1.1: The Java Native Interface (JNI)

In JDK 1.1, Sun has attempted to develop a more robust native code interface called the JNI.

Although the JNI is significantly more robust than the JDK 1.0 native linking interface we've reviewed previously in this chapter, it is also significantly more complicated. In this chapter we'll briefly review the important changes in the JNI; however, if you see yourself interfacing to a great deal of native code under JDK 1.1, you might be wise to obtain a book specifically focused on the JNI, such as the forthcoming JNI book from Prentice-Hall PTR written by Rob Gordon.

In general, using the JNI from Java code is very similar to using the JDK 1.0 native interface. For instance, native libraries are still Loaded with the `System.loadLibrary` method. However, there are some changes to how you build a native library. Also, at the time of this writing, the JDK 1.1 JNI is really only supported under the Win32 and Solaris platforms.

New Way to Use javah

In order to build native headers for use with JNI, you must execute *javah* in a new way:

```
javah -jni classfile
```

The -jni flag tells *javah* to produce the newer JNI header file format and not the older JDK 1.0 format.

New Native Method Naming Scheme

JNI uses a new naming scheme for implementations of native methods. A brief explanation of this naming scheme might help you to be able to read and understand native header files and stubs generated by javah.

- Every native method name begins with the prefix "Java_".

- A fully-qualified class name in a "mangled" format follows. For instance, native methods of a class named "MyClass" in the package "MyPackage" would begin with "Java_MyPackage_MyClass".

- An underscore ("_") separates the classname from method names. (Thus "Java_MyPackage_MyClass_methodName".)

- The method name is mangled as well. The mangling scheme is straightforward:

  - Unicode characters are escaped as "_0XXXX"

  - The underscore character itself is escaped as "_1".

  - The semicolon character (";") is escaped as "_2".

  - The left bracket character ("[") is escaped as "_3".

  - In fully qualified class names, the underscore character is used to substitute for the slash character ("/"). Thus "java/lang/String" becomes "java_lang_String".

  - For clarity's sake, it's probably a good idea to avoid using underscores in the names of your Java native method declarations.

- Overloaded native methods (two or more native methods with the same name but different parameters) will have two underscores ("__") and a mangled "argument signature" appended to the method name, in order to uniquely identify each method. The arguments are mangled as follows:

  - All of the arguments are concatenated together as special type codes. There are no underscores between arguments.

- All the immediate types are given as single uppercase characters:

Table 8-2 Immediate Argument Types versus Type Code

Immediate Type	Mangled Type Code
boolean	Z
byte	B
char	C
double	D
float	F
int	I
long	J
short	S

- Reference types (such as java.lang.String) begin with the type code "L", follow with the fully-qualified class name, and end with a semicolon. Thus, an argument of the type `java.lang.String` becomes "Ljava/lang/String;". However, once this name is run through the classname mangler previously mentioned, it becomes "Ljava_lang_String_2".

Putting this all together, a method declared in `MyPackage.MyClass` as follows:

```
native double myMethod(boolean, String);
```

Would map to a long mangled name of:

```
Java_MyPackage_MyClass_myMethod__ZLjava_lang_String_2
```

As you can see, the JNI naming scheme is more detailed than JDK 1.0 native library naming scheme, and thus it generally results in longer native method names.

New Native Type Mapping

The JNI has created several new native types that correspond to Java types.

Table 8-3 Java Immediate Types versus JNI Native Types

Java Immediate Type	Native Type	Description
boolean	jboolean	8 bits, unsigned
byte	jbyte	8 bits, signed
char	jchar	16 bits, signed
double	jdouble	64 bits, floating point
float	jfloat	32 bits, floating point
int	jint	32 bits, signed
long	jlong	64 bits, signed
short	jshort	16 bits, signed
void	void	The void type

The JNI also defines a few standard reference types.

Table 8-4 Java Reference Types versus JNI Native Types

Java Reference Type	Native Type	Description
Object	jobject	All Java objects not otherwise typed.
java.lang.Class	jclass	Class objects
java.lang.Array	jarray	Array objects
Object[]	jobjectArray	An array of Object references
boolean[]	jbooleanArray	An array of boolean values

New Parameters to Native Methods

The JNI defines a new way of calling native methods. The first two parameters passed to every native method have been changed.

The first parameter to each native method is a pointer to the JNI environment interface. This is similar to the "Execution Environment" passed to native methods under JDK 1.0. The type is JNIEnv*. This pointer is only valid for the duration of the method call and should not be stored away and used at a later time. This is referred to as a "local reference."

The second parameter is a pointer to the object which contains the native method being called. This is similar to the object handle provided under JDK 1.0 in that it allows your native code to access the Java object instance. This pointer is only valid for the duration of the method call.

New Java Native Utility Methods

The JNI also exports a vastly expanded set of native utility functions that can be called from within native code. Many of these utility functions are focused around allowing native code to safely access data stored in Java objects.

Under the JNI it is no longer acceptable to have native code directly read from or write to fields in Java objects. Instead, native code must go through a set of accessor functions to interface with Java objects. The following pseudocode demonstrates how you might get, modify, then set an integer field value in a Java object from native code:

```
ID = GetFieldID()
jint val = GetIntField(ID)
val++;//modify the field value
SetObjectField(ID, val)
```

Also, it is now possible to safely access strings and arrays of Java values from native code. You generally do this as in the following pseudocode example:

```
char* chars;
chars = GetStringUTFChars(jstring);//get the array of characters
newJstring = NewStringFromUTFChars(chars);//build an independent jstring
chars[0] = 'K';//set one of the characters
ReleaseStringUTFChars(chars, jstring);//causes jstring to be updated
```

Notice that you need to explicitly release pointers to arrays of Java values when you are finished with them. Note also that the various GetFooChars/GetFooArray methods allow you to make either an independent copy of the values stored in the Java array or simply access and update the values directly. This can save memory depending on your application.

We will not cover these accessor functions in depth, but the table below gives a brief introduction.

Table 8-5 New JNI Native Utility Functions

Function	Description
GetFieldID	Gets the unique field ID of a Java class field.
GetStaticFieldID	Get the unique field ID of a static Java class field.
GetObjectField	Given a field ID, get the field value.
GetStaticIntField	Given a static field ID, get field value.
SetObjectField	Given a field ID, set the field value.
GetStringUTFChars	Get the array of UTF-8 characters from a String.
GetObjectClass	Get the class of an object.
ReleaseStringUTFChars	Release memory allocated to hold UTF characters
NewStringUTF	Creates a new String object from an array of UTF-8 characters.
GetStringChars	Takes the Java string and returns a pointer to an array of Unicode characters that comprise the string.
ReleaseStringChars	Releases the pointer to the array of Unicode characters.
NewString	Constructs a new java.lang.String object from an array of Unicode characters.
GetStringLength	returns the length of a string that is comprised of an array of Unicode characters.
GetStringUTFLength	Returns the length of a string if it is represented in the UTF-8 format.
GetArrayLength	Get the length of an array.
ReleaseIntArrayElements	Free the memory allocated for Int array elements.
GetBooleanArrayElements	Returns a pointer to the block of elements in a Java boolean array.
GetByteArrayElements	Returns a pointer to the block of elements in a Java byte array.
GetCharArrayElements	Returns a pointer to the block of elements in a char array.

Table 8-5 New JNI Native Utility Functions *(Continued)*

Function	Description
GetShortArrayElements	Returns a pointer to the block of elements in a short array.
GetIntArrayElements	Returns a pointer to the block of elements in an int array.
GetLongArrayElements	Returns a pointer to the block of elements in a long array.
GetFloatArrayElements	Returns a pointer to the block of elements in a float array.
GetDoubleArrayElements	Returns a pointer to the block of elements in a double array.
GetObjectArrayElement	Returns the object element at a given index.
SetObjectArrayElement	Modifies the object element at a given index.

In addition to the accessor functions there is also a complete set of functions for calling Java methods safely from within native methods. We will not review these methods in detail, but basically the JNI provides a way to safely call any Java method from inside a native function.

Summary

The JDK 1.0 native interface can be used to quickly link native code to Java code. In this chapter we've looked at several different examples of native code libraries for several different platforms.

The new JNI in JDK 1.1 can be used to more safely link native code to Java code. Although the JNI is a bit more complicated than the JDK 1.0 interface, it is also more thorough and robust.

Depending on your application, you might choose to use the JDK 1.0 native interface because it is simpler or because it is available on your target platform. You might choose the JNI because it is more robust and safe, and will be more maintainable as newer versions of the Java API evolve.

APPENDIX

- An HTTP Transaction Handler

- A Configuration File Loader

- A StdioShell

- A ScheduledEvent Class

Utility Classes Used in the Examples

T his appendix provides implementation details and explanations for various utility classes used in the main examples which are not strictly communications-centric.

An HTTP Transaction Handler

Let's encapsulate the basics of handling an HTTP transaction into a single class. This class is used by the various HTTP server examples in the book.

An HTTP server needs to deal with the following during a transaction:

- The client sends a request that includes the name of the file. The server needs to read in this request and parse various attributes of the request.

- The server needs to return the requested file (if it exists), along with type and length information. It needs to return an error if it can't find the file.

Below is the implementation of the `HttpTransactionHandler` class which deals with these issues.

Example Appendix-1 **Implementation of an HTTP Transaction Handler**

```
package JNC;

import java.io.*;
import java.net.*;
import java.util.*;
```

```
/**
* A handler for http transactions
*/
public class HttpTransactionHandler
{
//response status constants
public final static int
    REPLY_ERROR_NO_ERROR = 200,
    REPLY_ERROR_NO_SUCH_FILE = 404;

public final static String
    REPLY_EXPLANATION_OK = " OK ",//no problem
    REPLY_EXPLANATION_ERROR = " ERROR ";//error of some sort

//debug
public static boolean fDebugOn = true;

//hooks connecting us to the client
DataInputStream fClientInputStream;
DataOutputStreamfClientOutputStream;

//info about the content file
DataInputStreamfContentInputStream;
long            fContentLength = 0;
String          fContentPath;
String          fContentFilename;
long            fContentLastModified = 0;
int                 fReplyErrorCode =
                        REPLY_ERROR_NO_ERROR; //no error by default
String          fReplyErrorExplanation = REPLY_EXPLANATION_OK;


/**
* Instantiate a new transaction handler.
* @param clientInputStream The stream where the client sends us
*    its request
* @param clientOutputStream The stream where we return content to
*    the client
*/
public HttpTransactionHandler(
    DataInputStream clientInputStream,
    DataOutputStream clientOutputStream)
{
    setIOStreams(clientInputStream, clientOutputStream);
}//HttpTransactionHandler

/**
* Set the input and output streams for the transaction.
* @param clientInputStream The stream where the
*    client sends us its request
* @param clientOutputStream The stream where we return
*    content to the client
```

```
*/
public void setIOStreams(
    DataInputStream clientInputStream,
    DataOutputStream clientOutputStream)
{
    fClientInputStream = clientInputStream;
    fClientOutputStream = clientOutputStream;
}//setIOStreams

/**
 * Handle the current requested transaction.
 */
public void handleTransaction() throws Exception
{
    fContentPath = this.getRequestedFilename(fClientInputStream);

    try {

        if (fContentPath.startsWith("/")) {
            //prepend a "current directory" dot
            fContentPath = "." + fContentPath;
        }

        if (fContentPath.endsWith("/")) {
            //append the default doc name...
            fContentPath += "index.html";
        }

        //try to find this file...will throw if not found
        File contentFile = new File(fContentPath);

        //get the length of the file
        fContentLength = contentFile.length();
        //get the mod date of the file
        fContentLastModified = contentFile.lastModified();
        //strips directory stuff from the filename
        fContentFilename = contentFile.getName();
        fContentInputStream =
            new DataInputStream(new FileInputStream(fContentPath));

    }
    catch (Exception couldNotOpenFileEx) {
        if (fDebugOn) System.err.println(
            "threw opening file " + fContentPath +
            " (" + couldNotOpenFileEx + ")");
        buildErrorReplyInfo();
    }

    if (fDebugOn) System.out.println("starting reply...");

    /*
     * We build a StringBufferInputStream here because
     * the more obvious implementation:
```

```
    *   fClientOutputStream.writeBytes(getReplyHeader());
    *
    *   ...is EXTREMELY slow. Basically, it sends a series of TCP
    *   packets out containing single-byte data.   The
    *   DataOutputStream.writeChars method is so slow because it
    *   writes out data on the output stream a single byte at a time
    *   instead of sending the data in the big blocks that TCP loves.
    *
    *   Using our "block move" copySrcToSink method, in combination
    *   with the StringBufferInputStream, improves the efficiency
    *   tremendously.
    */
    StringBufferInputStream headerStream =
        new StringBufferInputStream(getReplyHeader());
    copySrcToSink(   (InputStream)headerStream,
                     (OutputStream)fClientOutputStream);
    headerStream = null;

    if (fDebugOn)
        System.out.println("done with reply header...");

    //save the content file....
    copySrcToSink(   (InputStream)fContentInputStream,
                     (OutputStream)fClientOutputStream);
    if (fDebugOn)
        System.out.println("done copying content data...");

}/* handleTransaction */

/**
 * Take a source data input stream and a sink data ouput stream
 * copy input to output
 */
public static void copySrcToSink(InputStream src, OutputStream sink)
{
    byte[] tempBuf = new byte[1024];
    int bytesRead = 1;

    try {
        do {
            bytesRead = src.read(tempBuf,0,1024);

            if (bytesRead > 0) {
                if (fDebugOn)
                    System.out.println("bytesRead: " + bytesRead);
                sink.write(tempBuf,0,bytesRead);
                sink.flush();
            }
        } while (bytesRead >= 0);
    }
    catch (IOException ioEx) {
        System.err.println("copySrcToSink failed with: " + ioEx);
    }
```

```
} /* copySrcToSink */


/**
 * Given an HTTP 1.0 request on the srcStream,
 * find the requested filename and return it as a string
 */
protected String getRequestedFilename(DataInputStream srcStream)
{
    boolean foundFilename = false;
    String retVal = "/"; //default document?

    try {

        //gets first line, should contain
        //"GET foo.html HTTP/1.0"
        String firstLineStr = srcStream.readLine();
        StringTokenizer tokSource =
            new StringTokenizer(firstLineStr);

        while (!foundFilename) {
            //should return a string for the next token
            String curTok = tokSource.nextToken();
            if (fDebugOn)
                System.out.println("curTok: " + curTok);

            if (curTok.equals("GET")) {
                curTok = tokSource.nextToken();
                retVal = curTok;
                foundFilename = true;
            }
        }
    }
    catch (Exception ex) {
        if (fDebugOn) System.err.println(
                        "getRequestedFilename threw: " + ex);
    }

    if (fDebugOn) System.out.println("retVal: " + retVal);
    return retVal;
}//getRequestedFilename


/**
 * Build the HTTP reply header
 * This includes things like the MIME content type,
 * length, mod date, and so on.
 */
protected String getReplyHeader()
{

    if (fDebugOn) System.out.println("getting content type...");
```

```
        String contentTypeStr =
            URLConnection_Wrapper.guessContentTypeFromName(
                                        fContentFilename);

        if (fDebugOn)
            System.out.println("building header str...");

        String headerStr =

        "HTTP/1.0 " + fReplyErrorCode + fReplyErrorExplanation + "\n" +
        "Date: " + (new Date()).toGMTString() + "\n" +
        "Server: Todd's_Skanky_Web_Server/1.0\n" +
        "MIME-version: 1.0\n" +
        "Content-type: " + contentTypeStr + "\n" +
        "Last-modified: " +
            (new Date(fContentLastModified)).toGMTString() + "\n" +
        "Content-length: " + fContentLength +
        "\n\n"; //this last seq terminates the header

        if (fDebugOn) System.out.println("reply header: " + headerStr);

        return headerStr;

}//getReplyHeader

/**
* We couldn't find the content file the client requested
* Return a proper error message to the client.
*/
protected void buildErrorReplyInfo()
{
    String errorContentStr =
        "Could not find the requested file: " + fContentPath + "\n";
    StringBufferInputStream localStream =
        new StringBufferInputStream(errorContentStr);

    //get the length of the content
    fContentLength = localStream.available();
    //get the modification date of the file (or at least fake it)
    fContentLastModified = (new Date()).getTime();
    fContentFilename = "error.html";
    fContentInputStream = new DataInputStream(localStream);

    fReplyErrorCode = REPLY_ERROR_NO_SUCH_FILE;
    fReplyErrorExplanation = REPLY_EXPLANATION_ERROR;

}//buildErrorReplyInfo

}//class HttpTransactionHandler
```

Notice that this example takes advantage of another utility class that we've provided: the URLConnection_Wrapper class. This class simply provides some public static methods that export some handy protected static java.net.URLConnection methods. The most useful of these is the guessContentTypeFromName method. This method simply guesses the MIME type of a file based on its filename extension (e.g., ".gif", ".jpeg", etc.)

Notice also that we use a StringBufferInputStream here to copy the HTTP reply header info to the output stream. This is because the more obvious implementation (simply writing the header string to the output stream using DataOutputStream.writeChars or PrintStream.print) is extremely slow. See the note in the source code for a more detailed explanation.

Displaying Text and Obtaining User Input Quickly

One of the most common problems in communicating and networking applications is: How can you display lots of text quickly in a scrolling text view, and simultaneously obtain user input? In this section we'll look at creating a StdioShell class that addresses this problem, using techniques we've already learned.

Let's start by splitting the problem into its two component parts— displaying scrolling text quickly and obtaining user input. To display scrolling text, we're going to develop a subclass of java.awt.TextArea. This class has a few basic requirements:

- It must be able to display data from an incoming InputStream.

- It must run asynchronously— that is, after we hand it an InputStream, it must be able to update the screen display independent of our other code.

- It must provide for a scrollback buffer. This allows the user to scroll back to see data that was already displayed but scrolled offscreen. It must also deal with cleaning up the scrollback buffer as more and more text is displayed.

- It must deal with wrapping text to the width of the display.

The implementation of the QuickTerm class is shown below.

Example Appendix-2 Implementation of the QuickTerm class

```
package JNC;

import java.awt.*;
import java.io.*;
```

```
/**
 * A class that displays text input in a scrolling view.
 */
public class QuickTerm extends TextArea implements Runnable
{

public boolean fDebugOn = false;

//the maximum number of screens of characters to buffer
public int fMaxNumScreens = 10;
//the size of the scrollback buffer
public int fMaxCharCount;
//the number of characters currently buffered
protected int fTotalCharCount = 0;
//the number of columns of characters to display
protected int fNumCols = 80;

//the stream from which to read input data to be displayed
protected DataInputStream fInputStream;
//the thread that drives our Runnable interface
protected Thread fTicklerThread;
//flag that tells us to stop displaying
protected boolean fContinueDisplay = true;


/*
 * @param rows The number of rows to display
 * @param cols The number of columns to display
 * @param srcStream The InputStream from which to read
 *    the text data to be displayed.
 */
public QuickTerm(int rows, int cols, InputStream srcStream)
{
    super("Welcome!\n",rows,cols);
    fNumCols = cols;
    //set up a monospace font
    super.setFont(new Font("Courier", Font.PLAIN, 6));

    //calculate the size of our character buffer
    fMaxCharCount = rows * (cols * fMaxNumScreens);

    setInputStream(srcStream);

    //turn off editing so the user can't type over the display
    this.setEditable(false);

    //kickstart our thread
    fTicklerThread = new Thread(this);
    fTicklerThread.start();
}//QuickTerm

/**
 * set the input stream for the terminal to read from
```

```
*/
public void setInputStream(InputStream srcStream)
{
    if (srcStream != null) {
        try {
            fInputStream = new DataInputStream(srcStream);
        }
        catch (Exception constructEx) {
            System.err.println("constructEx: " + constructEx);
            return;
        }
    }
    else fInputStream = null;

}//setInputStream

/*
 * Take a string and blast it onto the display
 * @param str The String to append to the display.
 */
public void appendText(String str)
{
    if (fDebugOn) System.out.println("appendText: " + str);

    String newStr = "";
    int newStrLen = str.length();

    //are we appending more than one line?
    int numLines = (newStrLen / fNumCols) +
        (((newStrLen % fNumCols) > 0) ? 1 : 0);
    if (numLines > 1) {
        //perform necessary wrapping
        int offset = 0;
        String tempStr;
        for (int idx = 0; idx < numLines; idx++) {
            int newOffset = fNumCols*(idx + 1) - 1;
            if (newOffset > (newStrLen -1)) newOffset = (newStrLen -1);
            tempStr = str.substring(offset,newOffset);
            newStr += "\n" + tempStr;
            offset = newOffset;
        }
        newStrLen = newStr.length();
    }
    else {
        //if just one line, then prepend "\n" and display
        newStr = "\n" + str;
        newStrLen += 1;
    }

    //if we've exceeded our scrollback buffer size...
    if ((newStrLen + fTotalCharCount) > fMaxCharCount) {
        //remove as many characters from the top as
        //we're about to append to the bottom
```

```
        super.replaceText("",0,newStrLen);
        fTotalCharCount -= newStrLen;
    }
    //now use TextArea's method to place text in the display
    super.appendText(newStr);
    fTotalCharCount += newStrLen;

} //append text


/**
 * Method that continuously updates the screen display
 */
public void run()
{
    while (fContinueDisplay) {

        try {
            if (fInputStream != null) {
                String tmpStr = null;
                //read all available lines
                while (
                    //this blocks waiting for a whole line
                    (tmpStr = fInputStream.readLine()) != null) {
                    this.appendText(tmpStr);
                }
            }
            //after reading all we can, give up time to other tasks
            try {fTicklerThread.sleep(50);}
            catch (InterruptedException iEx) {};
        }
        catch (Exception runEx) {
            System.err.println("runEx: " + runEx);
            fContinueDisplay = false;
        }
    }
}//run

} /* class QuickTerm */
```

As you can see, we've met our requirements as follows:

- We use `TextArea.appendText` as our main method for displaying text. This takes advantage of TextArea's built-in scrolling features.

- We set up a driver thread and a run method that polls an incoming `InputStream` for new data and displays received lines of text.

- The `QuickTerm.appendText` method deals with wrapping text to the specified number of columns, and with cleaning up the scrollback buffer.

Now that we have a way to display text, let's create a `CmdTextArea` class that reads command-line text from the user. This class has the following requirements:

- Need to be able to filter for and act on specific command keys. For instance, when the user types control-U, we'd like to be able to erase all of the current input.

- Need to terminate input on a carriage-return and forward the command input to the appropriate receiver.

Let's first define an interface for the target of a `CmdTextArea`: the `UserTypingTarget` interface:

Example Appendix-3 The UserTypingTarget Interface

```
package JNC;

/**
* An interface used to pass back user input
*/
public interface UserTypingTarget
{
     public void acceptUserCommand(String cmdString);

}
```

As you can see, classes that implement the `UserTypingTarget` interface need only implement one method— the `acceptUserCommand` method, which will receive the text the user typed.

The implementation of the `CmdTextArea` class is shown below.

Example Appendix-4 Implementation of the CmdTextArea class

```
package JNC;

import java.awt.*;

/**
* A class that allows multiline input with carriage-return termination

* as well as some convenient command keys.
*/
public class CmdTextArea extends TextArea
{
//the receiver for all the user's typing
protected UserTypingTarget fTargetShell;

/*
* @param targetShell The parent user interface.
```

```
* @param rows The number of text rows to provide
* @param cols The number of text columns to provide
*/
public CmdTextArea( UserTypingTarget targetShell,
                    int rows, int cols)
{
    super(rows, cols);//tell TextArea our size
    fTargetShell = targetShell;
}//CmdTextArea

/*
* This is where we do all of the interesting cmd-key filtering
* Currently we support CR to terminate and clear the current input,
* Ctrl-U to erase the entire current input
*/
public boolean handleEvent(Event evt)
{
    //if the evt is a key press, filter it
    if (evt.id == Event.KEY_PRESS) {

        switch (evt.key) {

            case (10):  //user hit return/enter
                //hand input to our target
                fTargetShell.acceptUserCommand(this.getText());
                //clear out the input field...
                this.setText("");
                break;

            case (21): //user hit ctrl-U
                //clear out the input field...
                this.setText("");
                break;

            default: //we don't handle this particular key
                return super.handleEvent(evt);
        }
        return true;

    }
    else return super.handleEvent(evt);
}//handleEvent

}/* class CmdTextArea */
```

As you can see, we met the requirements for CmdTextArea as follows:

- The CmdTextArea.handleEvent method filters events of type Event.KEY_PRESS and acts on the ctrl-U (21) and return/enter (10) keys.

- When the user types a ctrl-U we clear the input field text.

- When the user types return/enter, we forward the input field text to the `CmdTextArea`'s `UserTypingTarget` and clear the input field.

Now that we have both a way to display text data in a terminal window, and a way to grab command line input from the user, let's put these two classes together in a `StdioShell` class.

The `StdioShell` class needs to do the following:

- It needs to be displayable as a top-level window, because it may be the only user interface that a given application has.

- Allow automatic "echo" of the user input to the text display area.

- It needs to export an InputStream on which is written out all of the user's typing. This is so that an interested `StdioShell` client can receive the user's input.

The implementation of the `StdioShell` class is shown below.

Example Appendix-5 **Implementation of the StdioShell class**

```
package JNC;

import java.io.*;
import java.awt.*;


/**
* A class for displaying a stdin and stdout.
* Useful when your platform doesn't have stdin/stdout,
* or you want to launch multiple i/o windows
*/
public class StdioShell extends Frame implements UserTypingTarget
{
public boolean fDebugOn = true; //toggles debugging
public boolean fEchoOn = true; //toggles local echo of user input

protected QuickTerm fDisplayArea;
protected CmdTextArea fInputField;
protected BorderLayout fUberLayoutMgr;

protected PrintStream fOutputStream;
protected PipedInputStream fResultStream;

/**
* Constructor
* @param title The title to be displayed on the window
* @param srcStream An input stream from which we can pull data to display
* @param maxWidth The maximum width of the window
* @param maxHeight max height of the window
```

```
    */
    public StdioShell(String title, InputStream srcStream,
                      int maxWidth, int maxHeight)
    {

        try {
            PipedOutputStream tempOutStream = new PipedOutputStream();
            fOutputStream = new PrintStream(tempOutStream);
            fResultStream = new PipedInputStream(tempOutStream);
        }
        catch (IOException ioEx) {
            System.err.println(
                "StdioShell stream allocation failed: " + ioEx);
            return;
        }

        setTitle(title);

        fUberLayoutMgr = new BorderLayout(0,0);
        this.setLayout(fUberLayoutMgr);

        fDisplayArea = new QuickTerm(24,80, srcStream);
        add("North",fDisplayArea);

        fInputField = new CmdTextArea(this, 2, 80);
        add("South",fInputField);

    }//StdioShell

    /**
     * @param srcStream The input stream to use for display
     */
    public void setDisplaySourceStream(InputStream srcStream)
    {
        fDisplayArea.setInputStream(srcStream);

    }//setDisplaySourceStream

    /**
     * Provide an InputStream that contains the user input...
     */
    public InputStream getInputStream()
    {
        return (InputStream)fResultStream;
    }//getInputStream

    /**
     * This accepts a string from the user input field
     * @param cmdStr The user input string.
     */
    public void acceptUserCommand(String cmdStr)
    {
```

```
    if (fDebugOn) System.out.println(cmdStr);

    if (fOutputStream != null) {
        fOutputStream.println(cmdStr);
        if (fEchoOn) fDisplayArea.appendText("--->" + cmdStr);
    }
}//acceptUserCommand


/**
 * Handle the WINDOW_DESTROY event as an app closure.
 */
public boolean handleEvent(Event evt)
{
    if (evt.id == Event.WINDOW_DESTROY) System.exit(0);
    return super.handleEvent(evt);
}//handleEvent

}//class StdioShell
```

The StdioShell class meets its requirements as follows:

- It is subclassed from java.awt.Frame so that it can be displayed as a top-level window on a given platform. Thus it can be used as the sole user interface for an application.

- By setting its public fEchoOn variable, a StdioShell client can toggle local user input echoing. The acceptUserCommand method checks this flag to see whether it should both forward the user input *and* echo it to the display area.

- Its constructor allows the StdioShell client to specify an InputStream.

- It needs to be displayable as a top-level window, because it may be the only user interface that a given application has.

- It needs to export an OutputStream on which is written out all of the user's typing. This is so that an interested StdioShell client can receive the user's input.

The ScheduledEvent Class

The ScheduledEvent class encapsulates all of the information necessary to schedule an event to occur on a given date and time.

The source for the ScheduledEvent class is shown below.

Example Appendix-6 ScheduledEvent Implementation

```
package JNC;

import java.io.*;
import java.util.*;

/**
 * Class that allows events to be scheduled
 */

public class ScheduledEvent
{

public boolean fDebugOn = true;

//all times listed are in milliseconds
public static long
    TIME_INTERVAL_MINUTE = 60*1000,
    TIME_INTERVAL_HALF_HOUR= 30*TIME_INTERVAL_MINUTE,
    TIME_INTERVAL_HOUR= 60*TIME_INTERVAL_MINUTE,
    TIME_INTERVAL_DAY = 24*TIME_INTERVAL_HOUR,
    TIME_INTERVAL_WEEK =  7*TIME_INTERVAL_DAY;

protected long fStartTime;//when does this event first occur?
protected long fEndTime;//when does this event last occur?
protected long fTimeIncrement;//event interval (how often)


/**
 * Create a new ScheduledEvent based on a
 * starting and ending date, and a time increment
 */
public ScheduledEvent(Date startTime, Date endTime,
                        long timeIncrement)
{
    fStartTime = startTime.getTime();
    fEndTime = endTime.getTime();
    fTimeIncrement = timeIncrement;

    if (fTimeIncrement <= 0)
        fTimeIncrement = TIME_INTERVAL_DAY; //one day default
}//ScheduledEvent


/**
 * Read in the flattened info and inflate self based on it.
 * @param srcStr String containing a "flattened" scheduled event,
 *    in ASCII EOL-delimited format.
 */
public ScheduledEvent(String srcStr)
{
```

```
    try {
        StringTokenizer theTokenizer =
            new StringTokenizer(srcStr,"|\n");

        String tokStr = theTokenizer.nextToken();
        fStartTime = Date.parse(tokStr);

        tokStr = theTokenizer.nextToken();
        fEndTime = Date.parse(tokStr);

        tokStr = theTokenizer.nextToken();
        fTimeIncrement = Long.parseLong(tokStr);
    }
    catch (Exception instEx) {
        System.err.println("parsing srcStr threw: " + instEx);
    }

}//ScheduledEvent

/**
 * Dump a String representation of this object
 */
public String toString() //Overrides Object.toString()
{
    String startDateStr = (new Date(fStartTime)).toString() + "|";
    String endDateStr = (new Date(fEndTime)).toString() + "|";
    String timeIntervalStr = Long.toString(fTimeIncrement) + "\n";
    String retVal = startDateStr + endDateStr + timeIntervalStr;

    return retVal;
}//toString


/**
 * Get the next occurrence of this event, in
 * raw (long) date format
 */
public long getNextOccurrenceRaw()
{
    Date currentTime = new Date(); //slurps in the system clock time
    return getNextOccurrenceAfterRaw(currentTime.getTime());
}//getNextOccurrenceRaw


/**
 * Get the next occurrence of this event,
 * after the given date,
 * in raw (long) date format
 */
public long getNextOccurrenceAfterRaw(long afterTime)
{
    //we know that the max delay is fTimeIncrement, min is zero
```

```
      long testTime = fStartTime;

      //starting at fStartTime,
      //keep adding the interval time until
      //we find an event that occurs at or after afterTime
      while (testTime < afterTime) {
          testTime += fTimeIncrement;
      }

      if (fDebugOn) System.out.println("testTime: " + testTime);
      return testTime;
}//getNextOccurrenceAfterRaw


/**
* Get the next occurrence of this event,
* after the current time, in Date format
*/
public Date getNextOccurrence()
{
    return (new Date(getNextOccurrenceRaw()) );
}//getNextOccurrence


/**
* Get the next occurrence of this event.
* after the given date, in Date format
*/
public Date getNextOccurrenceAfter(Date givenTime)
{
    long  rawGivenTime = givenTime.getTime();
    if (fDebugOn)
        System.out.println("rawGivenTime: " + rawGivenTime);

    return (new Date( getNextOccurrenceAfterRaw(rawGivenTime ) ) );
}//getNextOccurrenceAfter


}//class ScheduledEvent
```

Notice that the ScheduledEvent class provides a method for generating a String representation of the event. This is handy for debugging, and it also allows you to store a ScheduledEvent in a text file. ScheduledEvent includes a complementary constructor that constructs a ScheduledEvent from the same String format as generated by ScheduledEvent.toString. So you can imagine storing ScheduledEvents in a text file and reading them from the file at runtime.

Configuration File Loader

One of the first issues that pops up with any cross-platform communicating application will be configuration. How do you write your code in such a way as to make easy to select different communications options on different platforms? Under MacOS, if you're setting up an AppleTalk ADSP connection, the configuration settings are obviously going to be different than if you're setting up a Solaris serial connection. Thus, in order to use our `ConnectionEnd` subclasses on various platforms, we need some way to configure them.

Fortunately, we've placed code into each of the `ConnectionEnd` subclasses that supports passing configuration parameters to each of the main `ConnectionEnd` methods. Note that the `Instantiate`, `Accept`, and `Connect` methods each accept a `String` parameter that can be used to pass in configuration settings. We're going to take advantage of this to create a configuration file format that is friendly to these methods.

Let's define a `ConnectionEnd`-subclass-independent configuration file format.

This format should include:

* The name of the `ConnectionEnd` subclass that should be instantiated.

* Configuration strings for the `Instantiate`, `Accept`, and `Connect` methods.

A sample configuration file that sets up the `ceCTBMac` for an AppleTalk ADSP connection is shown below.

Example Appendix-7 Sample Configuration File for a ConnectionEnd subclass

```
# The format of this file is as follows:
# lines beginning with pound sign are comments
# all lines are terminated by EOL, which is \n
# the order of lines is as follows:
# 1. the name of the ConnectionEnd subclass to load (terminated by EOL)
# 2. Instantiate parameters (could be empty string terminated by EOL)
# 3. Accept parameters (could be empty string terminated by EOL)
# 4. Connect parameters (could be empty string terminated by EOL)
#
ceCTBMac
ceCTBMacToolName "AppleTalk ADSP Tool"
LocalADSPName "jADSP Server" LocalADSPType "jADSP Type"
RemoteADSPName "mobile thex" RemoteADSPType "jADSP Type"
```

Notice that the first noncomment line in this sample configuration file contains the name of the `ConnectionEnd` subclass. This will allow our terminal emulator application to determine which `ConnectionEnd` subclass to instantiate and configure these configuration strings.

Now, in order to allow the user to pick a configuration file for use with the terminal emulator, we need to create a helper class that allows the user to pick a file.

This helper class will use the `java.awt.FileDialog` and simply allow the user to pick a file with a certain filename extension (in this case, we've chosen ".cfg").

The source for the `FileSelector` class is shown below.

Example Appendix-8 **Class Which allows the User to Pick a Configuration File**

```
package JNC;

import java.io.*;
import java.awt.*;

/**
 * FileSelector.java
 * Class useful for selecting a file based on its
 * extension (".txt",".html", ".class", etc.);
 */
public class FileSelector  extends Frame implements FilenameFilter
{
String fFilenameExtension = ".cfg";
String fSelectedFilename = null;
FileDialog fChildFileDialog;

public boolean fDebugOn = true;

/**
 * @param fileExtension The filename extension on which to
 * filter (".java",".txt",etc.)
 */
public FileSelector(String fileExtension)
{
    super("FileSelector");
    this.show();
    fFilenameExtension = fileExtension;


    fChildFileDialog =
        new FileDialog(this, "Select a File", FileDialog.LOAD);
    this.hide();

    if (fChildFileDialog != null) {
        fChildFileDialog.setFilenameFilter(this);
        //set filename & extension to be more robust under Win32
      fChildFileDialog.setFile("*"+ fFilenameExtension);
      //this is a modal dialog: when show() returns, the user
      //will have picked a file or canceled the operation
        fChildFileDialog.show();
```

```
        fSelectedFilename = fChildFileDialog.getDirectory() +
                        "/" + fChildFileDialog.getFile();

        if (fDebugOn) System.out.println(
            "fSelectedFilename: " + fSelectedFilename);
    }
}//FileSelector

/**
* @return String The filename the user selected, if any.
*/
public String getSelectedFilename()
{
    return fSelectedFilename;
}//getSelectedFilename

/**
* required FilenameFilter method
* @return true if the given file should be listed to the user
* We return true for files with the proper extension,
* and for directories (to allow the user to navigate
* through directories)
*/
public boolean accept(File directory, String filename)
{
    boolean retVal = false;
    retVal = filename.endsWith(fFilenameExtension);

    if (fDebugOn) System.out.println(
        "accept: " + filename + " ? " + (retVal ? "yes!" : "NO!"));
    return retVal;
} //acceptFile


}/* class FileSelector */
```

Notice that this class first builds a new `Frame` instance and makes that `Frame` the parent of the main `FileDialog`. It might seem strange that we initially show, then hide, this parent `Frame`. This is because the `FileDialog` class requires a valid, has-been-shown `Frame` as the parent. On some platforms, such as MacOS, you can get away with passing a null or not-yet-shown `Frame` in for the parent argument; however, our solution should work on all platforms.

Notice, also, that we both create a `FilenameFilter` to filter filenames that end with ".cfg", as well as pass the string "*.cfg" as the "filename" parameter. This works around a problem with the JDK 1.0 Win32 Java runtime where the `FilenameFilter` seems to be ignored and only the default filename parameter is used by the `FileDialog` class.

Index

Java™ Development Kit
Version 1.1.x
Binary Code License

This binary code license ("License") contains rights and restrictions associated with use of the accompanying software and documentation ("Software"). Read the License carefully before installing the Software. By installing the Software you agree to the terms and conditions of this License.

1. Limited License Grant. Sun grants to you ("Licensee") a non-exclusive, non-transferable limited license to use the Software without fee for evaluation of the Software and for development of Java™ compatible applets and applications. Licensee may make one archival copy of the Software. Licensee may not re-distribute the Software in whole or in part, either separately or included with a product. Refer to the Java Runtime Environment Version 1.1 binary code license (http://www.javasoft.com/products/JDK/1.1/index.html) for the availability of runtime code which may be distributed with Java compatible applets and applications.

2. Java Platform Interface. Licensee may not modify the Java Platform Interface ("JPI", identified as classes contained within the "java" package or any subpackages of the "java" package), by creating additional classes within the JPI or otherwise causing the addition to or modification of the classes in the JPI. In the event that Licensee creates any Java-related API and distributes such API to others for applet or application development, Licensee must promptly publish an accurate specification for such API for free use by all developers of Java-based software.

3. Restrictions. Software is confidential copyrighted information of Sun and title to all copies is retained by Sun and/or its licensors. Licensee shall not modify, decompile, disassemble, decrypt, extract, or otherwise reverse engineer Software. Software may not be leased, assigned, or sublicensed, in whole or in part. **Software is not designed or intended for use in on-line control of aircraft, air traffic, aircraft navigation or aircraft communications; or in the design, construction, operation or maintenance of any nuclear facility. Licensee warrants that it will not use or redistribute the Software for such purposes.**

4. Trademarks and Logos. This License does not authorize Licensee to use any Sun name, trademark or logo. Licensee acknowledges that Sun owns the Java trademark and all Java-related trademarks, logos and icons including the Coffee Cup and Duke ("Java Marks") and agrees to: (i) to comply with the Java Trademark Guidelines at http://java.com/trademarks.html; (ii) not do anything harmful to or inconsistent with Sun's rights in the Java Marks; and (iii) assist Sun in protecting those rights, including assigning to Sun any rights acquired by Licensee in any Java Mark.

5. Disclaimer of Warranty. Software is provided "AS IS," without a warranty of any kind. ALL EXPRESS OR IMPLIED REPRESENTATIONS AND WARRANTIES,

INCLUDING ANY IMPLIED WARRANTY OF MERCHANTABILITY, FITNESS FOR A PARTICULAR PURPOSE OR NON-INFRINGEMENT, ARE HEREBY EXCLUDED.

6. Limitation of Liability. SUN AND ITS LICENSORS SHALL NOT BE LIABLE FOR ANY DAMAGES SUFFERED BY LICENSEE OR ANY THIRD PARTY AS A RESULT OF USING OR DISTRIBUTING SOFTWARE. IN NO EVENT WILL SUN OR ITS LICENSORS BE LIABLE FOR ANY LOST REVENUE, PROFIT OR DATA, OR FOR DIRECT, INDIRECT, SPECIAL, CONSEQUENTIAL, INCIDENTAL OR PUNITIVE DAMAGES, HOWEVER CAUSED AND REGARDLESS OF THE THEORY OF LIABILITY, ARISING OUT OF THE USE OF OR INABILITY TO USE SOFTWARE, EVEN IF SUN HAS BEEN ADVISED OF THE POSSIBILITY OF SUCH DAMAGES.

7. Termination. Licensee may terminate this License at any time by destroying all copies of Software. This License will terminate immediately without notice from Sun if Licensee fails to comply with any provision of this License. Upon such termination, Licensee must destroy all copies of Software.

8. Export Regulations. Software, including technical data, is subject to U.S. export control laws, including the U.S. Export Administration Act and its associated regulations, and may be subject to export or import regulations in other countries. Licensee agrees to comply strictly with all such regulations and acknowledges that it has the responsibility to obtain licenses to export, re-export, or import Software. Software may not be downloaded, or otherwise exported or re-exported (i) into, or to a national or resident of, Cuba, Iraq, Iran, North Korea, Libya, Sudan, Syria or any country to which the U.S. has embargoed goods; or (ii) to anyone on the U.S. Treasury Department's list of Specially Designated Nations or the U.S. Commerce Department's Table of Denial Orders.

9. Restricted Rights. Use, duplication or disclosure by the United States government is subject to the restrictions as set forth in the Rights in Technical Data and Computer Software Clauses in DFARS 252.227-7013(c) (1) (ii) and FAR 52.227-19(c) (2) as applicable.

10. Governing Law. Any action related to this License will be governed by California law and controlling U.S. federal law. No choice of law rules of any jurisdiction will apply.

11. Severability. If any of the above provisions are held to be in violation of applicable law, void, or unenforceable in any jurisdiction, then such provisions are herewith waived to the extent necessary for the License to be otherwise enforceable in such jurisdiction. However, if in Sun's opinion deletion of any provisions of the License by operation of this paragraph unreasonably compromises the rights or increase the liabilities of Sun or its licensors, Sun reserves the right to terminate the License and refund the fee paid by Licensee, if any, as Licensee's sole and exclusive remedy.

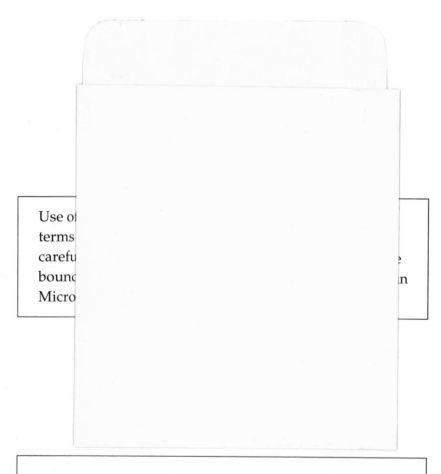

The Graphic Java 1.1 CD-ROM is a standard ISO-9660 disc. Software on this CD-ROM requires Windows 95, Windows NT, Solaris 2, or Macintosh (System 7.5).

Windows 3.1 IS NOT SUPPORTED